Modern Enlightenment

Johannes Rohbeck

Modern Enlightenment

Insights for the Crises of the Present

Johannes Rohbeck
Institut für Philosophie
TU Dresden
Dresden, Germany

ISBN 978-3-662-71639-7   ISBN 978-3-662-71637-3 (eBook)
https://doi.org/10.1007/978-3-662-71637-3

Translation from the German language edition: "Moderne Aufklärung" by Johannes Rohbeck, © Der/die Herausgeber bzw. der/die Autor(en), exklusiv lizenziert an Springer-Verlag GmbH, DE, ein Teil von Springer Nature 2023. Published by Springer Berlin Heidelberg. All Rights Reserved.

This book is a translation of the original German edition "Moderne Aufklärung" by Johannes Rohbeck, published by Springer-Verlag GmbH, DE in 2023. The translation was done with the help of an artificial intelligence machine translation tool. A subsequent human revision was done primarily in terms of content, so that the book will read stylistically differently from a conventional translation. Springer Nature works continuously to further the development of tools for the production of books and on the related technologies to support the authors.

© The Editor(s) (if applicable) and The Author(s), under exclusive license to Springer-Verlag GmbH, DE, part of Springer Nature 2025

This work is subject to copyright. All rights are solely and exclusively licensed by the Publisher, whether the whole or part of the material is concerned, specifically the rights of translation, reprinting, reuse of illustrations, recitation, broadcasting, reproduction on microfilms or in any other physical way, and transmission or information storage and retrieval, electronic adaptation, computer software, or by similar or dissimilar methodology now known or hereafter developed.
The use of general descriptive names, registered names, trademarks, service marks, etc. in this publication does not imply, even in the absence of a specific statement, that such names are exempt from the relevant protective laws and regulations and therefore free for general use.
The publisher, the authors and the editors are safe to assume that the advice and information in this book are believed to be true and accurate at the date of publication. Neither the publisher nor the authors or the editors give a warranty, expressed or implied, with respect to the material contained herein or for any errors or omissions that may have been made. The publisher remains neutral with regard to jurisdictional claims in published maps and institutional affiliations.

This Palgrave Macmillan imprint is published by the registered company Springer-Verlag GmbH, DE, part of Springer Nature.
The registered company address is: Heidelberger Platz 3, 14197 Berlin, Germany

If disposing of this product, please recycle the paper.

Preface

I have been engaged with the era of Enlightenment for as long as I have been active in academia. My dissertation was already dedicated to the Scottish Enlightenment thinker David Hume (1978). This was followed by a habilitation thesis on the *theory of progress in the Enlightenment* (1987). However, with regard to a university career, this was not a wise choice. To begin with, it is inadvisable to work on topics from the same period twice. Moreover, the European Enlightenment was not exactly in high demand.

So it was not surprising that I had to give up the academic career I had expected as a research assistant at the Free University of Berlin and initially became a secondary school teacher. In the context of teacher training for the subject of philosophy, which I directed in Berlin, I discovered philosophy didactics as an interesting and educationally significant field. In combination with a book on the philosophy of technology (1993), I was appointed, so to speak by a roundabout route, to the professorship for practical philosophy and its didactics at the Technical University of Dresden in 1993.

This reopened for me the possibility to conduct research on the philosophy of the Enlightenment. I thank Helmut Holzhey (Zurich) for inviting me in 1994 to co-edit the *Grundriss der Geschichte der Philosophie (Outline of the History of Philosophy)*, which had been founded by Friedrich Ueberweg and was now to be completely revised. In the series on the 18th century, I took on the Romance countries, that is, the two volumes on France (2008) as well as the volumes on Italy (2011), Spain and Portugal including Latin America (2015). While French philosophy had already been largely explored, it was above all the volume on Spain that required new research.

Through this twenty-year editorial activity, I was able to expand the basis for this monograph *Modern Enlightenment*.

I received support for the *Grundriss* from my wife Lieselotte Steinbrügge, a Romance studies scholar and specialist in the eighteenth century, who was Professor of French Literature and its Didactics at Ruhr University Bochum. Together with her, I edited a volume on Rousseau. For the present work, I owe her essential suggestions. I was able to draw on her contributions to gender studies in the section "The Nature of Woman." Finally, I thank her for numerous corrections and suggestions during the editing of the entire manuscript.

Earlier investigations were followed by publications on the history of technology and culture (2000), as well as specifically on the philosophy of history of the Enlightenment (2010). These were supplemented by texts on Hegel and Marx (2006), which can, with some generosity, be counted as part of the tradition of the Enlightenment. Finally, I have written systematic studies on the ethics of the future (2013) as well as on the philosophy of globalization and history (2017, 2020). With these works, I hope to be able to fulfill further prerequisites for my new project.

For on the *one* hand, I may say that I am fairly familiar with the historiography of eighteenth-century philosophy. For some time, I belonged to the inner circle of the *dix-huitiémistes*, as I experienced in numerous author conferences and international symposia. Therefore, I am by no means limiting myself here to the German Enlightenment, but am including the other European countries as well, which is by no means a matter of course for Italy and Spain. In this way, I represent Enlightenment studies, which have developed since the 1960s in independent institutions and publications.

On the *other* hand, I am pursuing the project of an *updating of Enlightenment*. The relevant topics are the ongoing secularization and the current role of scientific knowledge. Other areas include state authority, democracy, and gender politics. Particularly pressing issues are climate change, resource scarcity, and the pandemic. Globalization involves dealing with colonial history, concern for lasting peace, and the social question. All these problems are linked to certain expectations for the future. In these attempts, I proceed from the following personal observations.

At first, my nearly five decades of engagement with the *Age of Enlightenment* was met with a skeptical to dismissive attitude by academic philosophy in Germany. This was also due to the fact that, since my doctorate and habilitation, I have primarily focused on the English and French Enlightenment. While numerous French women philosophers and literary scholars, as well as German-speaking Romance studies scholars, contributed to the France volume of the *Grundriss*, the German philosophical establishment turned up its nose. The French Enlightenment was regarded by them as lacking in originality, overall as both too superficial and too radical. This seemed to confirm the fact that, at that time, the study of the Enlightenment was a domain of the Academy of Sciences in East Berlin.

Even with regard to the *current significance of Enlightenment*, I encountered a rather critical to hostile atmosphere. The objections came from a *conservative* direction, which suspected in the Enlightenment a loss of religion and tradition. Here, the aversion to the student movement was still virulent, as it had understood itself as a critique of the status quo and thus as radically Enlightenment. However, I also encountered headwind from the politically opposite side. This time it was *Critical Theory*, according to which the Enlightenment was, in tendency, totalitarian and self-destructive. The representatives of *Postmodernism*, who since the mid-twentieth century have sought to discredit modern civilization as a whole, could align themselves with this verdict.

But then came the surprise. It is not an exaggeration to say that, for a few years now, the idea of Enlightenment has become relevant again. There had already been isolated attempts to hold on to the "project of modernity." But recently, there has been an increasing number of proposals in which the Enlightenment is being rehabilitated. For the first time in my career, I have the feeling that I am no longer alone in my sympathy for this idea. This now concerns, above all, the rehabilitation of the Enlightenment within the discipline of philosophy and in the broader intellectual landscape.

The reasons for this almost unexpected elevation can only be speculated upon. My impression is that the current *crises* and *catastrophes* such as environmental destruction, global poverty, new wars, and anti-democratic populism have contributed to a renewed reflection on classical Enlightenment. During the so-called *postmodern* era, things were still quite comfortable; it was considered uneventful and boring, yet nevertheless proved to be rather stable and successful. Especially after the collapse of the socialist states, it could seem as if Western capitalism had an unlimited and carefree future ahead of it.

In the meantime, the *capitalist economic system* has entered a profound crisis. In the course of globalization, the possibilities for national corporations to expand into foreign markets have become limited, while conversely, competition from foreign goods is driving down prices and profits. Not only in Germany has the dynamism of economic growth declined since the 1970s, resulting in a deterioration of the living and working conditions of many people. With the bankruptcy of the banks in 2008, an international *financial crisis* emerged, which led to increased national debt. Another negative consequence is the *ecological crisis*, which manifests itself in the overexploitation of natural resources, the destruction of natural species, the pollution of the earth, and last but not least, in climate change.

While I was writing these lines, two acute catastrophes occurred. At the beginning, I was accompanied by the *COVID-19 pandemic*. It should be borne in mind that this virus did not strike us out of the blue, but is rather an expression of ecological, social, and economic misdevelopments. When I had almost finished the manuscript, the brutal *attack by Russia on Ukraine* was added. Many observers see this as a turning point since the Second World War. This rupture affects the entire previous world order, in which Europe must find its new role. The urgent tasks consist in establishing peace

For me, the problem arises as to whether a *new Enlightenment* can be helpful in overcoming the current crises. For the endless presence of the postmodern era has been replaced by current threats, whose mitigation in the present and future requires courageous thinking and action. With regard to the pandemic, one is compelled to acknowledge scientific knowledge and democratic decision-making. Instead of *fakes*, the investigation of facts is more necessary than ever, in this case in the fields of biology, medicine, and mathematical statistics. And in view of the unequally distributed social consequences of the pandemic and contradictory political responses, the Enlightenment ideas of truth, freedom, and human rights are more important than ever. In light of the new wars, it is necessary to recall the utopias of peace from that time.

In Germany, these guiding ideals of the Enlightenment are associated above all with the name *Immanuel Kant*. It is fitting, then, that in 2024 his three-hundredth birthday will be celebrated. Kant was born on April 22, 1724, in Königsberg, which is also where my mother came from, as she describes in detail in her autobiography. Although the occasion for my investigation is not the anniversary, Kant repeatedly comes to the fore from a thematic perspective. Yet I see the advantage of my account in placing his philosophy within the *context of the European Enlightenment*. I believe that such an embedding is appropriate for a worthy commemoration today. In this way, readers of the following pages will also come to know a *different Enlightenment*.

Johannes Rohbeck

Contents

1	**Introduction**	1
	Enlightenment and Critique of Enlightenment	4
	Science and Philosophy	10
	Modern Era, Enlightenment, and Modernity	13
	On the Contemporaneity of the Enlightenment	15
2	**Enlightenment in Europe**	21
	Where to with Europe?	23
	Diversity and Unity of the Enlightenment	26
	Europe in Self-Critical Discourse	36
	The Project of the European Union	44
3	**Critique of Religion**	51
	Postsecular Society?	54
	The Social Function of Religion	59
	Enlightenment and Counter-Enlightenment	69
	Religious and Secular Tolerance	72
4	**Human and Nature**	79
	Era of Posthumanism?	81
	Anthropology as Leading Science	83
	The Nature of Woman	91
	Gender, Identity, Anthropocene	97

Contents

5 Nature and Civilization — 105
Learning from Catastrophes? — 106
The Lisbon Earthquake — 110
Ecological Consequences — 112
Dealing with Climate and Pandemic — 118

6 Knowledge and Ability — 123
Post-factual Age? — 124
Sensual Knowledge — 130
Language Signs — 134
Value of Truth — 139

7 Morality and Politics — 145
Post-democratic Turn? — 149
Emotional and Social Intelligence — 154
Conditions of Political Rule — 160
Democracy in Transition — 163

8 Crisis of Capitalism — 169
Neoliberalism at an End — 171
Foundations of Political Economy — 175
Contingency of Social Systems — 182
Social and Ecological Upheavals — 185

9 World History and Globalization — 193
Posthistoire and Postcolonialism — 197
Historical Contingency — 206
Global Justice — 211
Responsibility for Future Generations — 216

10 Transformations — 223
Positions on the Enlightenment — 225
Contingency as Wound — 231
Limits and Potentials — 236
Enlightenment Today — 241

Literatur — 249

1

Introduction

What is Enlightenment? This question can be answered in two ways. First, Enlightenment refers to a specific historical epoch, which, as is well known, belongs to the 18th century. Second, Enlightenment is regarded as a timeless guiding idea, with which reason and critique are connected. Thus, the concept of Enlightenment oscillates between history and systematics. Yet this distinction is by no means as unproblematic as it may appear.

If one devotes oneself exclusively to the *historical epoch* of the Enlightenment, there is the danger of a merely antiquarian interest. In doing so, the potentials that can be actualized are misunderstood, if not outright denied. With a temporal distance of around 250 years, the Enlightenment seems to lie so far in the past that it is no longer able to contribute to the solution of current problems. In the worst case, the negative flip sides of modern civilization, up to and including the crises of the 20th and early 21st centuries, are blamed on the prehistory of modernity.

If, on the other hand, one focuses on the *systematic aspect* of the Enlightenment, the well-intentioned aim of asserting general principles such as the autonomy of the subject or the claim to truth certainly becomes apparent. But here the problem arises that the Enlightenment is detached from its historical context and stylized into an eternally valid doctrine. Then all that remains of the Enlightenment is the formal and abstract principle of thinking for oneself. However commendable this principle may be, without concrete content it can degenerate into a helpless cliché. Indeed, it can even become dangerous, as recently demonstrated by the so-called "lateral thinkers," who claim to make use of their own understanding.

To escape this dilemma, I attempt in this book to link the historical and systematic dimensions of the Enlightenment. For this, I use the concept of *transformation*. By this I mean the transfer and reshaping of certain theorems from the science and philosophy of the Enlightenment into other contexts, whereby certain changes are usually to be noted. If one considers the Enlightenment as an overarching development, three transformations emerge for me: *First*, an important change took place during the epoch of the Enlightenment; *second*, I understand transformation as a process in cultural history that leads beyond the 18th century into the 21st century; and *third*, I consider it necessary to continue such a process of transformation in our own time.

Already in the *epoch of the Enlightenment*, a fundamental paradigm shift took place. This concerns not only the well-known transition from rationalism to *empiricism* and *sensualism*, according to which truth means not only logical evidence but above all correspondence with empirically knowable reality. Even more important to me is the fact that, around the middle of the century, entirely *new kinds of sciences* emerged. Philosophy of language showed the extent to which human cognition is mediated by signs. With anthropology, the bodily, emotional, and social dimensions of human existence also came into view. By speaking of dark "passions," a sense for unconscious motives of action arose. Some Enlightenment thinkers even questioned reason as a spiritual substance and introduced the idea of "thinking matter." On the eve of industrialization, *political economy* arose, in which society was discovered as an independent sphere. Added to this was the entirely new discovery of *history*, so that the entire world of nature and humanity was regarded as a historical development. In this way, it became apparent for the first time that individuals are subject to social and historical *contingencies*, which, following Sigmund Freud, can be described as *wounds* to humanity.[1] My corresponding *thesis* is: Within the Enlightenment, phenomena emerged that were later attributed to m*odernity*. For this reason, my study bears the title *Modern Enlightenment*.

Furthermore, transformation here means building a *bridge from the 18th to the 21st century*. *Modern Enlightenment* therefore also means transferring the insights of the Enlightenment thinkers into the *modernity of the present day*. Despite various periods of restoration and cultural ruptures, it is unmistakable that the present-day lives of very many people, at least in Western

---

[1] For Freud and the various wounds to humanity during the Enlightenment, see the summary in Chap. 10.

countries, are decisively shaped by the achievements of the Enlightenment. These include medical advances, legal security, and political participation, as well as the shared values of freedom, equality and tolerance. When conservative politicians refer exclusively to the "Christian image of humanity," it should be remembered that human rights, democracy and science had to be established against the bitter resistance of the Catholic Church. And when European observers of the new war see "Western values" in danger, they are implicitly referring to the Enlightenment in Europe. Although the Enlightenment as a historical constellation was not permanent, it nevertheless continues to exert a lasting influence. It is therefore sensible to become aware of this long-term tradition and to recognize it as a cultural heritage.

Transformation of Enlightenment ultimately means continuing this process in the *current situation*. In doing so, a striking parallel emerges between the historical epoch of the Enlightenment and the present phase of late modernity. Around the middle of the 18th century, a profound upheaval took place, which has been referred to as the "Sattelzeit" and, more recently, as the beginning of the *Anthropocene*.[2] This refers to the beginnings of industrialization in the transition from feudalism to capitalism. The Enlighteners had an inkling of this, but were unable to fully anticipate the economic, social, and cultural consequences. In the third decade of the 21st century, we find ourselves at a similar epochal threshold, the outcome of which is again difficult to foresee. Modernity is not followed by postmodernity, but rather by a late modern capitalism, the continuation of which requires enormous social and ecological upheavals. The task is to transform the experiences of contingency from the Enlightenment into attempts to cope with technical, economic, and historical contingencies. Enlightenment today means coping with contingency.

If I now advocate updating the theoretical models of the Enlightenment, it goes without saying that such a project only makes sense in a *critical* manner. Therefore, I see my task as working out the *ambivalences* of the Enlightenment as precisely as possible by reflecting on its *limits* and *potentials*. In doing so, the usual sweeping judgments must be rejected, such as that the Enlightenment is overly intellectual and instrumentalist, male anthropocentric, Eurocentric, or even colonialist. At the same time, however, an apology for the Enlightenment is to be strictly avoided by not concealing the deficits of Enlightenment discourses.

---

[2] Koselleck 1967, p. 91; cf. Kittsteiner 1998, p. 114; Jörn Rüsen: *Historik*. Cologne 2013, p. 116; Horn, Bergthaller 2019, pp. 9, 19; for a critical view see Fulda 2022, pp. 85 f.

Exemplary cases include: European culture does serve as a guiding standard, but at the same time foreign cultures are explored and valued, and colonial slavery is also criticized. Human beings are indeed at the center of science and philosophy, but there are also approaches that seek to relativize the position of humans and reconcile them with nature. Some Enlighteners did develop a special anthropology of the female sex, in which the role of women is restricted, but at the same time the tradition of gender equality continued up to the French Revolution. The proponents of political economy praised the emerging capitalism, but demands for social justice were also voiced. Admittedly, the Enlighteners were not consistent democrats, yet they advocated constitutional monarchy, the separation of powers, and human rights.

In such cases, it is important to carry forward and further develop the aspects that are viable for the future. This applies to the position of Europe in the world and to the continuation of the European Union, as well as to the coming to terms with colonial history. The anthropology of the Enlightenment must be modified so that it is compatible with the ecological crisis and the management of natural disasters. The approaches to the emancipation of women in education and society must be recovered so that current debates about feminism are conducted within a historical framework. Last but not least, Enlightenment social criticism must be renewed in order to make today's economy and society more just. While the illusion of an enlightened prince must be abandoned and replaced by representative democracy, the idea of universal human rights must be further developed and adapted to the global situation. The same applies to the Enlightenment utopia of lasting world peace. At the same time, however, we must learn from the Enlightenment how to relate the two opposing sides to one another and thus deal with them prudently and tolerantly.

Enlightenment and Critique of Enlightenment

The concept of Enlightenment gave the epoch its name. The German word *Aufklärung* corresponds to the English *enlightenment*, the French *les lumières*, as well as the Spanish *illustración* and the Italian *illuminismo*.[3] Denis Diderot also uses the term "enlightened" (éclairé). Kant poses the question in his

---

[3] For the history of the concept, see for example: Thoma 2015, pp. 67–85; specifically on the German Enlightenment with consideration of metaphorics, Fulda 2022, pp. 28–65.

essay *What is Enlightenment?* whether his own epoch could be considered an "enlightened age" or an "age of Enlightenment."[4] These terms, which can already be traced back to the 18th century, attest to a self-understanding that was widespread throughout Europe. The light metaphor that runs through all languages expresses the common goal of letting the "light of reason" shine after the supposedly dark Middle Ages.

The Enlightenment marks a double intention: On the one hand, it was characterized by *critique of a tradition* that was perceived as dogmatic and unfree. On the other hand, the Enlighteners by no means limited themselves to a critical attitude, but undertook the attempt to construct an *independent system of thought*. In doing so, they claimed to assert reason in all areas of human life. While this kind of Enlightenment initially referred to theoretical knowledge, especially in the natural sciences, it was increasingly transferred to the fields of social practice. The aforementioned disciplines such as anthropology, philosophy of language, political economy, sociology, and philosophy of history emerged. Philosophy remained at the center, but fulfilled a more integrative function. It should be borne in mind that the concept of philosophy at that time was very broad and included the individual sciences.

In France, a supporter of the Enlightenment was called a "philosophe"— not in the sense of a specialized philosopher, but in the general meaning of a secular scholar.[5] Not least, a practical orientation was expected from the Enlightenment. Symptomatic of this program was the French *Encyclopédie* (1751–1780), in which, alongside philosophy and science, the technical achievements of craft, manufacture, and engineering were documented in texts and illustrated plates. In this context, a *philosophe* was understood as a scholar who served society and produced useful knowledge. To achieve this goal, the knowledge acquired was disseminated so that as many people as possible could benefit from it. This was accomplished through education and instruction, increasingly provided in private schools, and through new forms of communication such as salons, often hosted by learned women. A new public sphere emerged through a rapidly expanding book market, popular reference works, and journals. The Enlightenment also included the popularization of philosophy, which knew how to present itself in an accessible and entertaining manner.

---

[4] Enzyklopädie 1972, p. 320; Kant 1965, vol. XI, p. 59.
[5] Article "Philosoph," in: Encyclopedia 1972, pp. 841–848; cf. Möller 1986, pp. 212 f.; Im Hof 1993, p. 95; Porter, Teich 2000, p. 12; Stollberg-Rilinger 2000, pp. 86 f.; Müller 2002, p. 15; Schmidt, G. 2009, p. 400; Andreas Gipper in: Thoma 2015, pp. 56 f.; Andries, Bernier 2019, pp. 29–46.

Yet hardly any historical epoch and the guiding ideas that emerged from it have been and continue to be subjected to such relentless and enduring criticism as the Enlightenment. It should be recalled, often overlooked, that the Enlightenment was controversial from its very inception. The most prominent representative of this may be Jean Jacques Rousseau, who, in his *Discourse on Inequality* (1755), questioned modern civilization.[6] While Rousseau still saw himself as an Enlightener and was perceived as such throughout Europe, a much more fundamental critique of the Enlightenment arose from absolutist and Catholic quarters, which explicitly referred to itself as Counter-Enlightenment (anti-lumières).[7] In the 19th and 20th centuries, critique of the Enlightenment intensified. With Nietzsche, Marx and Freud, the unconscious driving forces of human action came to the fore. This critique remains relevant to the present day.

Conservative authors accuse the Enlightenment of having broken with established traditions such as religion, without providing an alternative orientation.[8] Others criticize the assessment that modern societies are becoming increasingly secularized, and instead claim a "post-secular society" or a "postsecularism."[9] Critical thinkers posit a *Dialectic of Enlightenment*, according to which the catastrophes of the twentieth century were already inherent in Enlightenment reason.[10] Proponents of *Postmodernism* intensify this line of argument by claiming that modern civilization destroys the ideas of the Enlightenment such as rationality, emancipation and humanism.[11] *Posthistoire* not only propagates the demise of these ideals, but even the "end" of history itself. With *Postcolonialism*, this critique is taken even further, by attributing to the entire Enlightenment a Eurocentric attitude and thus the justification of subjugation and enslavement.[12] In contrast, there are more recent attempts to update the Enlightenment in such a way that a "future of the Enlightenment," a "new," "second," or even "radical" Enlightenment appears conceivable.[13]

---

[6] Rousseau 1978, pp. 191, 213; in a more moderate way Kant 1965, vol. XI, p. 44; see Chap. 8.

[7] Schmidt, J. 1989, p. 14; Albertan-Coppola, McKenna 2003, p. 15; Sánchez-Blanco 2002, p. 125; see Chap. 3.

[8] Oelmüller 1969, pp. 9, 23; Lübbe 1986, p. 207; Bubner 1989, pp. 416 f.; cf. Goulemot 2001, p. 7; Thoma 2018, pp. 145 f.

[9] Habermas 2005, p. 120; cf. Lutz-Bachmann 2016, p. 81; Renner 2017, pp. 107 f.

[10] Horkheimer, Adorno 1987, vol. 5, pp. 25–66; cf. Strasser 1986, p. 7; Israel 2009, p. IX.

[11] Lyotard 1986, p. 96; Bartlett 2001, p. IX.

[12] Chakrabarty 2010, p. 28; Sala-Molins 2008, p. 37; cf. Lilti 2019, pp. 41–87.

[13] First *The Philosophy of the Enlightenment* (1932) by Ernst Cassirer.—Schnädelbach 1988; Rüsen, Lämmert, Glotz 1988; Mittelstraß 1989; Postman 2000; Todorow 2009; Pagden 2013; Reinalter 2016; Hampe 2018; Pinker 2018; Garcés 2019; Andries, Bernier 2019; Lilti 2019; Frick 2020.

Both in such critiques and in attempts at rehabilitation, a fundamental problem becomes apparent. On the *one* hand, these judgments are so sweeping that they do not do justice to the historical epoch of the Enlightenment. Here, contemporary commonplaces are often projected back onto the past. On the *other* hand, there are the historians of philosophy, who, although they possess detailed knowledge of the eighteenth century, for the most part do not actively participate in this fundamental debate. Even if they show a certain sympathy for the ideas of the Enlightenment, they fail to systematically elaborate on their possible updating. Thus, Enlightenment research and critique of the Enlightenment diverge, so that some controversies about the Enlightenment resemble shadowboxing.

It is precisely at this point that my own research begins. My aim is to close the original gap between historical and systematic analysis. Starting from the fundamental discussions about the Enlightenment, I will bring the concrete and diverse phenomena of this epoch into play. Thus, I do not consider *the* Enlightenment in toto as either a successful or a failed formation. Rather, I assess its concrete advantages and disadvantages with an eye to the present. Such a reconstruction involves both holding on to the achievements of the Enlightenment and naming its errors and omissions. My goal is a salvaging critique. To accomplish such a transformation, it is necessary to determine the epoch of the Enlightenment more precisely in terms of space and time.

The geographical *space* of the Enlightenment concerns Europe, so that one can speak of a *European Enlightenment*.[14] In this sense, I endeavor to address the diversity of Enlightenment*s* in the various countries (Chap. 2). While the Enlightenment in France was particularly "radical" in the sense of a tendency towards materialism and atheism, it took a rather moderate position in Reformed England and Protestant Germany. In Catholic-dominated countries such as Italy and Spain, it could only assert itself against massive resistance and rather in secret. Thus, it seems plausible to regard France, if not as a "model," then at least as the core country of the Enlightenment in Europe.[15] Nevertheless, there are sufficient commonalities to maintain the

---

[14] In doing so, I am disregarding the fact that there have also been intellectual movements outside Europe that can be described as Enlightenment. These include the Chinese Enlightenment with Confucius in the 4th century BCE and the Arab Enlightenment with Abelar in the 11th century.

[15] I focus on the countries England, France, Germany, Switzerland, Italy, Spain, and Portugal. For the other countries such as Austria, Holland, Denmark, Sweden, Poland, Russia, Hungary, and America, see Thoma 2015, pp. 107–122; cf. Mortier 1978, pp. 39–51; Jüttner, Schlobach 1992; Im Hof 1993, p. 11; Delon 1997, p. 27; Schneiders 1997, pp. 14–16; Butterwick et al. 2008, pp. 1–16.

idea of a pan-European Enlightenment. This concerns not only general principles such as reason and human rights, but also very concrete advances in science and philosophy as well as political, social, and cultural reform projects.

The question of the *time* in which the epoch of the Enlightenment began and ended, however, is more difficult to answer. Frequently, Greek and Roman antiquity are invoked, which for good reasons can be described as the early Enlightenment of Europe. In such a sequence, the 18th century then constitutes the *second Enlightenment*. This is justified insofar as quite a few Enlighteners—just as the representatives of the *Renaissance*—actually referred to ancient models.[16] What is decisive, however, is that the Enlightenment of the modern era and modernity by no means exhausts itself in such epigonism, but has produced something essentially new.

If one focuses on this "new" Enlightenment, the question of its *beginning* arises in a completely different way. Here it becomes apparent that the various answers depend on *what* is understood by Enlightenment at all and which countries are to play the decisive role. The choice of content and the periodization thus condition each other. For me, what is decisive is which new subject areas and scientific disciplines are assigned to the epoch of the Enlightenment.

Here I start from a simple observation: The more generally the historical phenomenon of the Enlightenment is defined, the broader the corresponding period is measured. This is demonstrated by the definition of the Enlightenment period from the Reformation or Renaissance of the 15th and 16th centuries to the French Revolution at the end of the 18th century. Or one attempts to draw a parallel from the Arab Enlightenment of the 9th to 12th centuries to the European modern era of the 17th century. With such an extremely broad scope, it is not surprising that the characteristics turn out to be very unspecific: such as tolerant handling of religion, liberation of humanity, and use of reason. Yet the fact that a profound transformation took place in this period must not lead to the mistaken judgment that the Enlightenment was "unclear" or even "contradictory" at its core.[17]

---

[16] There are some Enlighteners who refer to antiquity as "Enlightenment," e.g., Condorcet 1976, p. 102.—On the reception of antiquity see: Veit Elm, Günther Lottes, Vanessa de Senarclens (eds.): *Die Antike der Moderne. Vom Umgang mit der Antike im Europa des 18. Jahrhunderts*. Saarbrücken 2009; Mittelstraß distinguishes between a "first" Enlightenment of antiquity (pp. 15–86) and a "second" Enlightenment in the 17th and 18th centuries; 1970, pp. 87–132.—Those who propose a renewal for the present day arrive at a "third Enlightenment"; Hampe 2018, pp. 8 f., 82 f.

[17] Thus Frick 2020, pp. 9, 11–13.

Even if one limits the period of the Enlightenment to the 17th and 18th centuries, the specificity of science and philosophy of the 18th century is often misunderstood. Thus, it is claimed that its only merit consisted in prolonging, radicalizing, and popularizing the old problems and solutions. Then the rationalism of Descartes, Spinoza or Leibniz is regarded as the primary achievement, in comparison to which the later empiricism appears only as an intellectual decline.[18] In the field of political philosophy, the theories of natural law and the social contract of Grotius, Hobbes and Locke were repeated. Because the Enlightenment was said to lack intellectual depth, it is considered poor and desolate, so that one can only speak of the "misery of the Enlightenment."

By contrast, there is broad consensus regarding the dating of the beginning of the Enlightenment to the end of the 17th century, most often around 1680 or even somewhat earlier, in the 1650s. Politically, this date is associated with the Glorious Revolution in England and the American Declaration of Independence; scientifically, with the physics of Newton; and philosophically, with the metaphysics of Gottfried Wilhelm Leibniz as well as the epistemology of John Locke. If the end of the Enlightenment is again dated to the French Revolution or somewhat later, one can speak of a "long" 18th century.[19] In this case, it is not uncommon to claim that Enlightenment philosophy exhausted itself over the course of this century and was only capable of politicization and trivialization.

The opposite, however, is the case. For it was precisely in the second half of the 18th century that the Enlightenment opened up entirely new fields of problems and proposed new solutions. It is the novel sciences that suggest dating the period of the European Enlightenment to the time after 1750. Put differently: because these subjects and disciplines are so important, I consider such a dating to be factually justified and necessary.

---

[18] Kondylis 1981, pp. 287 ff.; Binder 1985, vol. 1, pp. 7 f.; Schmidt, J. 1989, p. 2; Möller 1986, p. 34; Haag, Wild 2019, p. 110.—For the following see Darnton 1996, p. 5; cf. Schneiders 1997, p. 18; Kopper 1996, p. IX; see in more detail Chap. 10.

[19] D'Aprile and Siebers divide the epoch of the Enlightenment into the following phases: 1. theoretically-rationalist Early Enlightenment 1680–1740; politically-practical High Enlightenment 1740–1770; literary-public Late Enlightenment 1770–1800; 2008, pp. 12–14.—Cf. Mittelstraß 1970, p. 104 f.; Alt 1996, p. 7 f.; Stollberg-Rilinger 2000, p. 14; Borgstedt 2004, p. 6 f.; Reinalter 2006, p. 11 f.; Wagner, Asmuth, Roldán, 2017, pp. 1–5; Diner 2017, p. 7 f.; Fulda 2022, p. 9 f.

Science and Philosophy

Paradigmatic for the epoch of the Enlightenment was the physics of Isaac Newton as well as the theory of the state of John Locke, both of which, however, originated in the late 17th century. But beyond that, a whole series of new scientific disciplines emerged, each with their own subject areas. Newtonian mechanics was increasingly supplemented by the science of life, and political theory by the new social sciences. I would like to highlight here anthropology and philosophy of language, as well as political economy, sociology, and historiography.

The *science of the human being* became the leading science of the 18th century, so that one can speak of an "anthropological turn" (Chap. 4). In the context of the new sciences of biology and medicine, the natural properties of the human being came to the fore. Accordingly, the human being consists not only of something spiritual, but essentially of flesh and blood. Whereas Descartes and Hobbes had still conceived of the human being as a mechanical apparatus, he was now regarded as an organism, differing from animals only by degree. This even raised the heretical question of whether the human being descends from the ape. This *biological wound* does not date only from Darwin, as Freud claimed, but belongs to the birth certificate of Enlightenment anthropology. In this natural-historical framework, the Enlighteners considered human actions to be primarily governed by physical needs, which are expanded through human labor, especially through the use of tools and machines. In the context of the Lisbon earthquake, an ecological consciousness began to emerge (Chap. 5). In addition, the function of linguistic signs was discovered, which made entirely new knowledge possible.

In the new *medicine*, particular attention was paid to the female body, in order to address the high mortality rate in childbirth. For the first time, the bodily difference between the sexes thus became a topic. Here, the position of the Enlightenment on the *gender question* was indeed ambivalent. On the one hand, the principle that all human beings are equal was a tenet of the Enlightenment, and this explicitly included women. In this respect, one can speak of a "feminist Enlightenment." On the other hand, from the mid-18th century onward, there was a tendency to exclude women from the public sphere and restrict them to the private household. To retrospectively legitimize this, certain intellectual abilities were even denied to women, in order to reduce them to a morally grounded feeling based on the family. This kind of division of labor between the sexes was not a relic of feudal times, but a new phenomenon of the onset of industrialization.

In the second half of the 18th century, an entirely new object of inquiry was explored: "society". Whereas previously the state had been regarded as the only form of community, a sphere now gained particular significance, which later in Hegel was called "civil society." What is meant here is the national economy as the sphere of social division of labor and circulation of goods. This discovery was owed to the new science of *political economy* (Chap. 8). With modern economics, economic liberalism began, which already at that time exhibited problematic features. But if one looks more closely at the relevant writings, one will find that economists such as Quesnay and Adam Smith proposed massive state interventions to improve the general welfare, including that of the socially disadvantaged. Thus, it is not yet possible to speak of a liberalist ideology, which was only later derived from this. At the same time, among philosophers, the first approaches to a more or less radical critique of modern civilization emerged, especially of the social inequality produced by capitalism. This was represented not only by the aforementioned Rousseau, but also by other, lesser-known authors. The central concept of reproduction contained both social and ecological potentials.

The new economic theory revealed that a distinct dynamic unfolds within the economic sphere. The insight into the self-regulation of social systems, or *systemic contingency*, has effects on human self-understanding that can hardly be overestimated. If it is proven that people can no longer steer their society as they once seemed able to do in the realm of politics, then human agency is significantly curtailed. Here, too, the limits of Enlightenment anthropology become apparent—an anthropology that claims to derive all cultural achievements from human nature—while the Enlighteners now, for the first time, recognize that human actions can also produce effects that were not planned by reason. In this case, I call this the *economic wounding* of humanity. Again, I would like to point out that the relativization of the human subject did not begin only with Nietzsche and Freud, but rather had its beginnings in the context of social philosophy during the course of the European Enlightenment.

Under these conditions, the *state* was no longer a rational construction according to the contract model, but rather the result of external and contingent factors, not least of all power, violence, and conquest. Law, too, was no longer interpreted according to the old model of natural law, but tended to be reinterpreted as a historically developed "positive" law of particular nation-states. This included the recognition of legal conceptions of other peoples and cultures. Although the universal human rights still applied, they were no longer understood in a universalist sense. Likewise, morality acquired a new legitimacy; it, too, was no longer interpreted in a rationalist and universalist manner, and there was now greater interest in the actual "customs and practices" in different regions and parts of the world (Chap. 7). By describing the conditions of emergence of state, law, and morality in an empirical way, the outlines of modern sociology began to take shape.

Moreover, since the mid-18th century, writings emerged that made *history* into a subject in its own right (Chap. 9). In this process, the philosophy of history gradually separated itself from historiography. Whereas philosophical reflections had previously been scattered throughout historiographical works or limited to their introductions, for the first time texts were published that provided an overview of history as a whole or addressed general themes. For explanation, results from anthropology and political economy were again drawn upon. This type of thinking is marked by a peculiar contradiction. At first, the authors understood their new science as *explanatory historiography*, oriented toward the contemporary natural sciences. Then, philosophy of history included the teleology of history, which is to be understood as an attempt to cope with *historical contingency*.

A key feature of the philosophy of history was the *secularization*. The secular approach also led to new content. In place of divine kingdoms, stages in the process of civilization appeared in the fields of science, technology, economy, and morality. With certain expectations for the future, the idea of progress emerged, which was already controversial in the 18th century. In this way, historical thought freed itself from mere chronology and developed the concept of a distinct *historical time*,[20] oriented toward the cultural achievements "made" by humans. By also investigating the origins and development of science and philosophy, the Enlightenment made itself its own subject. This constitutes its essential form of *self-reflection*.

The process of secularization is closely linked to the concept of *world history*. In the course of colonial discoveries and conquests, non-European countries such as China, India, and America came into view. The new idea of world history now explicitly presupposed the plurality of cultures, which were compared and especially valued. In particular, Persian, Chinese, and Peruvian cultures were specifically studied and appreciated. Against the usual criticism of Eurocentrism in the Enlightenment, it should not be overlooked that this school of thought made a genuine effort to take note of the many cultures of the entire globe and to integrate them into a comprehensive

---

[20] Koselleck 1979, pp. 130–143; idem 2003, pp. 317–335.

concept. Not only were previously unknown cultures described from a European perspective; there are even examples of Europe being viewed, so to speak, from the outside, from a foreign perspective. In these discourses, Europe itself was thematized and indeed critically questioned (Chap. 2). This also included the not infrequent criticism of colonial history with its conquest, exploitation, and enslavement, which seemed incompatible with the anthropological principle of equality of all human beings (Chap. 9). Although individual instances of discrimination, especially against the inhabitants of Africa, are not to be overlooked, numerous condemnations of slavery can be regarded as the first manifestations of postcolonialism.

With the emergence of novel sciences, *critique of religion* was also associated (Chap. 3). However, one should not imagine the Enlighteners' critique of religion as too radical. Only a few Enlighteners in France and England openly professed atheism and materialism; some even fought against the atheists and defended the then widespread position of deism, according to which the world may have been created by a God who, however, no longer intervenes in his work. Other Enlighteners developed the very widespread theory of "natural religion," in which church dogma was no longer central, but rather the religious need of human beings. In particular, belief in divine providence was shaken by the Lisbon earthquake of 1755 (Chap. 5). After humanity had lost its central position in the cosmos with Copernicus, it now missed its original foundation in the divine order.

More important here is the fact that criticism of religion in the 18th century underwent a fundamental shift. In this area as well, the new sciences such as anthropology, philosophy of language, social theory, and philosophy of history are applied. While the question of the truth claim of religious belief was answered more or less evasively, the social *function of religion* moved to the foreground. Thus, the emphasis shifted from the question of validity to social and political pragmatics. For the radical critics, religion served as an instrument of domination for the powerful and the wealthy. In the moderate version, most Enlightenment thinkers did not want to dispense with religion, because they saw in it a moral and thus stabilizing institution.

Modern Era, Enlightenment, and Modernity

Following my account of the new sciences in the 18th century, I repeat my initial *thesis*: Since 1750, certain features of bourgeois society have become visible that, from today's perspective, can be regarded as specifically *modern*. The *Enlightenment* thus encompasses the components *Modern Era and Modernity* (Neuzeit und Moderne). With this distinction, I make the ambitious claim of drawing a new picture of the historical epoch of the Enlightenment.

First of all, in the Enlightenment the modern *ideas of the 17th century* are continued, such as the emancipation of the individual, reason of the subject, as well as freedom of action and thought for human beings. This is well known and is not to be disputed here. On this basis, it may also be legitimate to view the Enlightenment as an overarching movement that had already begun during the Early Modern Era. Some interpreters refer to this entire complex as "Modern," from which they then attempt to distinguish the Postmodern of the 20th century. Still other authors draw a line from the Modern Era to the so-called Late Modernity of the 21st century. But such a comprehensive view has the disadvantage of overlooking the specificity of philosophy and science in the second half of the 18th century.

Beyond that, I consider the *transformation from the Early Modern Era to the Enlightenment* to be essential. Now, the constitution of the human subject changes. Already, the technical and linguistic means make possible achievements that mere understanding would not have attained. In political economy, the systemic character of the economic sphere is recognized, thereby bringing to light the *contingency* of bourgeois society. And in the philosophy of history, it is almost a topos that history as a whole is a contingent process. Such experiences of contingency, as mentioned, can be interpreted as *wounds* to human beings. Hardly has the modern human attained a previously unimaginable autonomy, than their self-empowerment in the Enlightenment suffers some significant setbacks. In order to save the concept of autonomy, I would like to speak of a *conditional autonomy*, which still leaves room for action. In this way, the hubristic notions of the Modern Era are relativized and give way to realistic expectations of Modernity. This does not constitute the "Other" of the Enlightenment,[21] but rather a specifically *other Enlightenment*.

With the distinction between Early Modern Era, Enlightenment, and Modernity, I connect the hope that criteria for the debate about the *contemporaneity of the Enlightenment* can be gained from it. For this differentiation can help to protect the Enlightenment from unjustified reproaches. Some critics identify the Enlightenment with the Early Modern Era and raise the charge of absolutized reason and an excessive mania for feasibility. When, in addition, the proponents of the so-called Postmodern equate the Modern

---

[21] Alluding to Gernot and Hartmut Böhme: *The Other of Reason*. Frankfurt a. M. 1983.

they discredit with the Cartesian subject and modern rationalism, they believe they have an easy case.[22]

But many adherents also view the Enlightenment as a mirror image of postmodern criticism, by once again invoking the modern ideal of an autonomous individual against the dominance of modern civilization. Here it is overlooked that the Enlightenment itself already prepared the particular character of Modernity. It thus seems more plausible to view Modernity as an overarching process from the Enlightenment to Late Modernity.[23] In the course of this book, it will become apparent that the *modern Enlightenment* I favor in the second half of the 18th century provides the points of reference for a transformation into the 21st century. Because I do not limit myself to a single abstract principle such as reason, the broad spectrum of the various topics mentioned will be addressed concretely. The common thread is the problem of experiencing and coping with cognitive, technical, and social contingencies.

On the Contemporaneity of the Enlightenment

In the present day, we must consider how to relate to the experience of the Enlightenment with *systemic* and *historical contingency* in the face of. Those who foreground the experience of powerlessness and measure it against an unbroken, absolute subject of action will interpret this experience as a "failed Modernity." But those who even partially acknowledge the contingent character of society and history will see in the experience of contingency a specifically modern insight of the later Enlightenment. For, soberly considered, it is not a matter of the accidents of everyday life, which have always existed, but of the relative autonomy of social systems and the process of modern civilization. Today, the task is to deal reasonably with this specifically modern insight. This in turn presupposes abandoning the false alternative between unavailability and creation myth, in order to understand coping with contingency as a task. Concretely, this means exploring and making use of the horizon of possibilities for intervention that still remains.

This conflict between the experience of contingency and the capacity for action is initially evident in the *economic sphere*. To begin with, the

---

[22] From this perspective, one might already call the modernity I have characterized postmodernity—in the sense of a "crisis of the absolute"; see Zorn 2022, p. 25.

[23] Reckwitz, Rosa 2021, pp. 69, 100–109, 119; cf. Blühdorn 2013, pp. 51 f.; for a detailed discussion see Chap. 10.

experience of political economy in the eighteenth century is to be acknowledged insofar as it recognizes that there are independent economic laws that must be respected by both entrepreneurs and politicians. This has the positive effect of curbing the planning rationality postulated by earlier rationalism. However, after economic liberalism has radicalized over the past two decades, we come to the conclusion that an apology for the economy is to be avoided. At present, we are confronted with the overwhelming power of capitalism, the social and ecological consequences of which can no longer be ignored. What is needed instead is the recovery of the political.

The excesses of economic exploitation, however, were not foreseeable at the beginning of industrialization. The authors of the then still young *political economy* explicitly cherished the hope that as many people as possible would benefit from the technical and economic advances of a country. Yet even during the Enlightenment, there already existed the aforementioned social criticism by Rousseau and other authors, to which reference can still be made today. Currently under debate are a basic income and compensation for price increases for the socially disadvantaged, further raising the minimum wage, as well as expanding protection against dismissal. In addition, transnational corporations are to be taxed equally and at higher rates, for which there are new approaches in the European Union. Finally, employees are to be more strongly involved in the management of companies, which would amount to a restructuring of joint-stock companies.

A similarly ambivalent picture emerges in the attempt to update the *political philosophy* of the later Enlightenment. Even though authors such as Montesquieu replaced the theory of the social contract with a historical analysis of the climatic and cultural conditions under which different political systems can arise, this does not exclude the possibility that normatively justified preferences for certain forms of government also come into play. Thus Rousseau proposed a new social contract with grassroots democratic elements to achieve social equality. However, despite all their criticism of existing political conditions, most Enlightenment thinkers ultimately preferred constitutional monarchy. Innovative and of lasting relevance is Montesquieu's theory of the separation of powers, as well as the defense of human rights. The current task is to recognize the democratic approaches of the Enlightenment and at the same time to further develop the present-day democracy and protect it against populism and racism. The Enlightenment provides an opportunity to study how democracy should not be treated as an abstract principle, but as a concrete form of life that must be adapted to social and cultural circumstances.

In this context, it is especially important to strengthen the *position of women* in working life as well as in politics and science, which presupposes the compatibility of family and career. In doing so, the egalitarian side of the Enlightenment should be continued, according to which men and women fundamentally have the same abilities and rights. The other side, in which women were reduced to childbirth and child-rearing, could still be defended as a population policy concession of the eighteenth century. For this kind of reduction was only ideologically exaggerated in the nineteenth and twentieth centuries and must be opposed today. In economic life, it is still necessary to pay working women the same wages as men. In addition, more women are needed in leadership positions in companies. The same applies to politics, both in political parties and in government offices. Even though there were no precedents for this in the historical era of the Enlightenment, such reforms would be in accordance with Enlightenment principles.

The philosophy of history of the Enlightenment, with its program of a "world history," represented the first *theory of globalization*. The concept of "humanity" no longer meant an abstract unity, but the beginning of global cooperation in the fields of science, politics, and economics. Some Enlightenment thinkers even hoped for more *peace* from the "spirit of commerce," which often proved to be an illusion, but has certainly been successful in the "common market" of Europe. In addition, there were several proposals for the establishment and preservation of peace among nations: first for Europe, then even for the whole world. Even in these writings on peace, the already realized cultural connections are taken as a basis in order to appeal to the corresponding interests. These Enlightenment approaches *Toward Perpetual Peace* (Kant) are still stimulating and in need of realization today. What has recently been added is the brutal war waged by Russia in Eastern Europe. Yet the prognosis that the principle of "change through trade" has thereby definitively failed seems to me premature. For these reasons, the Enlightenment hope for peace should not be abandoned.

A key feature of the philosophy of history is its orientation toward the *future*. The very idea of progress expresses the expectation that future generations may fare better, just as "progress" can already be discerned in past history. The space of historical experience and the horizon of expectation are mutually dependent.[24] Since the mid-twentieth century, the idea of progress has fallen into disrepute and has been replaced by the label *Posthistoire*. But at the latest since the beginning of the twenty-first century, it has become

---

[24] Koselleck 1979, p. 349 f.

clear that history has by no means reached its supposed end, but continues with sometimes terrible events. Current problems such as the present wars in the world, the impoverishment of poor countries, as well as the ecological crisis, demand active intervention in world history.

With an anxious gaze toward the future, the threatening *climate catastrophe* takes center stage. Without doubt, the warming of the Earth is a product of human activity, which began with the onset of industrialization. For two decades now, this period has been interpreted as the beginning of the *Anthropocene*, meaning the era in which humans are transforming the Earth so profoundly that they are putting their own conditions of existence at risk.[25] It is no coincidence that this era coincides with the emergence of anthropology, which is often branded as *anthropocentric*. Yet, upon closer inspection, it becomes clear that within it, the human being has lost the traditional special status that was still held in Christianity and early modern rationalism. Since then, humans have understood themselves as natural beings who have developed out of physical nature. Even if only traces of an ecological consciousness can be identified, humans have nevertheless moved significantly closer to their inner and outer nature, upon which they knew themselves to be dependent.

The issue of climate change ultimately concerns *scientific truth*. When, in recent times, conspiracy myths become socially acceptable, there is a danger of loss of reality and inability to act. Not least, postmodern critics have also contributed to discrediting the sciences by reinterpreting scientific facts as constructions and fictions. In response to *post-truth* and *fake news*, a new *realistic turn* is required, which, in view of the problems to be addressed, becomes an ethical imperative. In this case as well, one can orient oneself by the legacy of the Enlightenment, which accorded the sciences the highest priority. Moreover, in their critique of religion, the Enlighteners provided the theoretical means for a critique of prejudices by analyzing, above all, their social functions. This is especially true in the context of the current *Covid-19 pandemic*, in which the validity of science is under extreme pressure to justify itself.

To provide an initial overview, I will begin with a comparative account of the Enlightenment in the various countries of Europe. In these contexts, it will become apparent how the authors of the eighteenth century reflected on and practiced the Enlightenment as a genuinely European project. Following this, I will pose the question of the extent to which the memory

---

[25] Horn, Bergthaller 2019, pp. 9, 19; Rohland 2020, p. 49; Chakrabarty 2022, p. 127.

of this shared culture is capable of contributing to the legitimacy of the European Union as it exists today.

* * *

The guiding principle of this book is the *systematic interest* in transforming certain theorems of the Enlightenment into the present age. The intended systematic approach is reflected in the thematically organized chapters. These correspond neither to a chronological sequence nor to a philological order in the history of the European Enlightenment, but are devoted solely to current areas of concern. Each individual chapter follows a common structure.

The *first* section of each chapter begins with an *outline of a contemporary problem*. Here, opposing positions are sometimes presented, in which the Enlightenment and modernity are declared to be surpassed, as is expressed in several "postist" terms such as postmodernity, posthistory, posthumanism, postdemocracy, etc. When I append a question mark to these diagnoses of the times, I am expressing my doubts about such apocalyptic scenarios.

The subsequent *second* and *third* sections are devoted to various theories that emerged during the *historical epoch of the Enlightenment*. The aim here is to sharpen the profile of the European Enlightenment by highlighting what was new and specific in science and philosophy in the second half of the eighteenth century. Some things I can only present in broad strokes, but I claim originality in my selection and synthesis. Not infrequently, I also pursue my own paths in detail.

I explicitly do *not write a history of concepts* in these two sections, because I am of the opinion that individual concepts only incompletely reflect particular theories.[26] Frequently, an idea is developed before the corresponding word is available. If I were to limit myself to the history of the concept of Enlightenment, many substantive problems and insights could not even be addressed. Conversely, some discourses that are usually subsumed under the concept of Enlightenment are excluded here. This became particularly evident in the question of the periodization of the Enlightenment. Nor do I wish to embrace the label *history of ideas*, because this approach seems too immanent to me, as if philosophy had generated and transmitted its "ideas" from within itself and in isolation.

---

[26] I have demonstrated this by way of example in: "*Progress* and *History* in the Conceptual History of Reinhart Koselleck," Rohbeck 2020, pp. 159–169; see on these concepts Chap. 9.

Instead, I favor the approach of *history of science*, within whose discourse I also place the history of philosophy. This corresponds to my guiding thesis that the European Enlightenment created entirely new sciences, without knowledge of which the philosophy of this period would not be plausible at all. My concern, then, is essentially with an *interdisciplinary* approach. In the background, *social history* also plays a role; even if the beginnings of industrialization, the emerging bourgeois society, and the corresponding cultural transformation are only hinted at, these historical conditions are essential to me in order to make the new approaches in social philosophy comprehensible.

In the respective *fourth* section, the *updating* of certain ideas, concepts, and theories of the Enlightenment is finally to be undertaken. In order to ensure the current state of research is brought to bear on the present, the theories of the most recent publications are especially taken into account. The focus is on the individual disciplines of sociology, political science, economics, and history. In philosophy, the emphasis is on epistemology, ethics, political philosophy, and social philosophy. Overall, I again proceed in an interdisciplinary manner, with an emphasis on practical philosophy.

With this division of the individual chapters, I believe I am presenting a distinctive format. The aim is a synthesis of critique of the Enlightenment, Enlightenment research, and the updating of the Enlightenment. Transformation here means bridging the two epochs of the Enlightenment and late modernity as well as salvaging and further developing the achievements of the Enlightenment that are worth preserving.

2

Enlightenment in Europe

If one draws a comparison between the 18th and 21st centuries, both epochs reveal a remarkable similarity. Around the middle of the 18th century, the nation-states in Europe were only partially established. Only England and France constituted fully developed nations. Spain was still struggling for its national identity. Italy and Germany consisted merely of fragmented small states, kingdoms, and principalities. It was only in the 19th century that these nation-states developed, which then, in the 20th century, were perverted into pernicious nationalisms. Yet in the course of globalization, the nation-states are losing their former function. In their place, transnational corporations and organizations are increasingly dominant. Thus, while in the 18th century many nation-states were *not yet* developed, in the 21st century the nation-states *no longer* have their former significance.

Certain consequences can be drawn from this parallel. If today state governments are losing influence, this can also be understood as an opportunity to advance the integration of Europe not only economically, but also politically. This holds all the more in view of recent tendencies to call the European Union into question and to reactivate the national. Not least after the invasion of Ukraine as a result of Russian nationalism, a united and strong Europe is needed. Here, recalling the Age of Enlightenment may be helpful.

But first, it must be clarified how unified European culture actually was. In the relevant research, it is pointed out that there was not *the*

Enlightenment in the singular, but rather a plurality that unfolded according to countries and regions. Behind the focus on differences stand contemporary cultural studies, which are more interested in the diversity of cultures. This can be seen as a reaction to globalization, which shifts the perspective from the global back to the local and regional. National particularities are also added, for example when the Spanish only rediscovered their own Enlightenment tradition after the Franco dictatorship.

I would like to take this tendency into account, at least cursorily, in what follows, by sketching the respective Enlightenment in the most important European countries. Here, the already mentioned problem arises as to whether there was a center of the Enlightenment, such as France, which is considered particularly radical, in contrast to which the Enlightenment in other countries was largely suppressed or only half-heartedly pursued. This leads to the controversial question of the "true" Enlightenment, which is said to have been located in moderate Germany. Here it becomes apparent how a "conservative" or "progressive" attitude toward the Enlightenment can lead to the favoring of certain countries. Finally, the question arises as to how the so-called Counter-Enlightenment relates to the Enlightenment, or what of it can still be considered Enlightenment can.

For all the diversity that must be acknowledged, I nevertheless consider it mistaken to lose sight of the *unity of the Enlightenment*. For it cannot be overlooked that the representatives of the Enlightenment shared fundamental convictions, which were based on the new sciences of anthropology, political economy, and the philosophy of history. There are even convergent approaches to a critique of civilization and the insight into social and historical contingency. This specifically *modern conception of Enlightenment* in the second half of the 18th century underlies the following discussion. In doing so, I focus on the comparative aspect and refer to the more detailed accounts in the individual chapters.

In this context, it should be added that the philosophers of the Enlightenment already possessed a *consciousness of Europe*. They practically lived this interconnectedness through their correspondences, translations, mutual discursive references, through a European book market, and not least through travel, personal acquaintances, and friendships. Many scientific academies and universities were founded after the models of other European cities. Some scholars were invited from neighboring countries, even to leading positions. Frenchmen such as Montesquieu and Voltaire made pilgrimages to England and found inspiration there, just as Voltaire, Diderot, Maupertuis and La Mettrie were invited to the German courts. It can even be demonstrated that the scientists and philosophers themselves understood themselves as representatives of a European intellectual movement, by making Europe their own subject.

For this reason, it is important to me to emphatically reject the sweeping accusation of *Eurocentrism* against the Enlightenment.[1] At most, a precise relativization is up for discussion. It is true that some Enlighteners chose European civilization as the standard of the civilizational process. Especially in historiography and the philosophy of history, Greek antiquity forms the starting point and French absolutism the new high point. But it will also become apparent to what extent the Enlighteners also took into account the peoples foreign to them, whom they came to know through numerous travel accounts. In these, non-European cultures were appreciated and revalued. Particularly revealing is the reversal of perspective, when fictional persons from distant countries visit Europe and critically comment on its way of life.

The features of the European Enlightenment mentioned are significant for its transformation into the present day. Since the representatives of the Enlightenment were aware of their European context, this could serve as a model for its updating. For the *legitimation* of the European Union, it is therefore sensible to recall the common cultural roots.[2] Behind this lies the conviction that Europe owes essential achievements to its Enlightenment such as tolerance, human rights and democracy. This also applies to respectful engagement with other cultures. In view of the new war, the numerous drafts for a lasting peace in Europe and the world are especially relevant today.

Where to with Europe?

Recently, Europe has experienced a radical turning point. Putin's aggression has forced the European Union to close ranks and act together. This primarily concerned military protection, for which a new defense policy was

---

[1] I will address the Enlightenment critique of *postcolonialism* at the beginning of the ninth chapter.

[2] In the relevant literature on the European Union, a distinction is made between an "input" or "basic" legitimation, which consists in cultural commonality, and an "output-oriented" legitimation, which results from the political, legal, and social interaction and cooperation of the nation-states. There is consensus that basic legitimation is not sufficient, but forms an important complement, just as, conversely, the integration achieved is able to contribute something to cultural identity. See Scharpf 1999, pp. 18–22; cf. Cheneval 2006, pp. 6–8, 19 f.; Kohler 2006, pp. 29 f., 35; Utzinger 2006, pp. 237 f.— Specifically on the reference to Europe: Vierhaus 1988, p. 7; Faye 1992, p. 14; Negt 2010, pp. 126 f., 145, 171; Grießer 2015, pp. 7 f.

developed virtually overnight. Likewise, the energy supply with coal, oil, and gas was affected, which had to break away from dependence on Russia. Finally, it was a matter of agreeing on how to distribute the many refugees as fairly as possible among the European countries. These new tasks have led to better coordination among European governments and faster joint decision-making. If Putin intended to divide Europe, it was now welded together by his pressure.

To understand this turnaround, it is worth taking a look back. For just a few years ago, it did not seem opportune to talk about Europe at all. Unforgettable is the miserable management of the European Union in procuring vaccines to combat the Covid-19 pandemic. Even afterwards, there was no coordination whatsoever for the protection of the population, the medical care of the seriously ill, or long-term planning after the overcome catastrophe. The originally intended concerted action turned into national and regional solo efforts. This is not about centralist decision-making powers, but about coordinated political action.

How did it come to this? Immediately after the Second World War, British Prime Minister Winston Churchill proclaimed the "United States of Europe."[3] As is well known, nothing has come of this to this day. Not even peace treaties were concluded at the time, let alone provisions made for a European League of Nations. Instead, the *European Economic Community* was established with the Treaty of Rome in 1957. The extent to which economic integration was at the forefront was already evident in the fact that only the "Common Market" of Europe was spoken of. The primary goal was apparently the creation of a European capitalism, which at the time was quite successful and generally accepted.

After about twenty years, the primacy of the economy generated a certain unease. The merely "negative integration," which consisted in the removal of customs barriers, was to be supplemented by a "positive integration" aimed at political shaping.[4] A political union was to accompany the common market. As early as 1979, the *European Parliament* was established in Strasbourg, in whose elections all citizens of the European Union can participate. In Maastricht, the general right to vote for Union citizens in local elections was

---

[3] Quoted in Kreis 2006, p. 67.—For what follows see Goodman 1998, p. 334; Freiburghaus 2000, pp. 25–29; Streeck 2013, p. 237; Nida-Rümelin 2020, p. 45.
[4] Scharpf 1999, p. 27; Freiburghaus 2000, pp. 91–100; Cheneval 2006, p. 80; Lavenex 2006; pp. 97 f.; Streeck 2013, p. 240.

added. In addition, a common foreign and security policy and cooperation in the areas of justice and home affairs were decided there, which were deepened in 2007 in Lisbon with the founding of the *European Union*.

Nevertheless, the accusation has not fallen silent that the European Union suffers from a *democratic deficit*.[5] For the agreements of the heads of government lack democratic legitimacy. The executive in Brussels is also neither directly nor indirectly electable by the citizens. It constantly issues laws and regulations that cannot be understood by those affected. The bureaucracy there disregards the principle of subsidiarity, which grants countries and regions a higher degree of self-responsibility and freedom. And the European Parliament in Strasbourg, so the further complaint, lacks its own legislative competence. Put pointedly, the European Union could not join itself, because it does not meet the democratic criteria it sets for its member states.

Yet for all the criticism, it should be remembered that the European Union was originally a success story. It brought lasting peace, of which the representatives of the European Enlightenment could only dream.

A continent that for centuries was plagued by wars and civil wars has, at its core, lived for three generations in freedom and democracy. And while in the 20th century many people still had to emigrate from Europe because of poverty, general prosperity has emerged. This should not be forgotten, and Europe should be credited with holding its own in a globalized world. The current task is to seek greater political influence in the face of the rule of global capital. In view of new wars, the task has been added to protect against military threats.

Added to this is the question of what science and philosophy can contribute to the recognition of present-day Europe. In our context, it is about the culture of the European Enlightenment, which is treated as an essential prerequisite. It will also be shown that the Enlighteners of the 18th century already had formulated ideas of a cultivated and peaceful Europe, which can be updated today.

---

[5] Goodman 1998, p. 331; Scharpf 1999, p. 20; Habermas 2008, p. 123.—For criticism see Cheneval 2003, pp. 5, 13 f.; Crouch 2008, pp. 137 f.; Streeck 2013, pp. 237, 240; Nida-Rümelin 2020, p. 22.— In his new book, Wolfgang Streeck considers Europe a "doomed empire" and proposes a return to nation-states: 2021, p. 338; cf. pp. 46, 125–139, 331–386.

Diversity and Unity of the Enlightenment

The Enlightenment was anything but homogeneous. Even if one limits this epoch to the second half of the 18th century with the repeatedly mentioned characteristics, it is clear that in every country a distinct variant developed.[6] For this reason, the European Enlightenment will be characterized below, in the order of its historical emergence, in the countries of Great Britain, France, Germany, Italy, and Spain.

Great Britain.—In England, since the end of the religious wars and absolutism, a parliamentary system had been established that was able to guarantee liberal conditions and religious tolerance. Although an Anglican state church had been established, there was no longer any fundamental opposition to state and church, so that political and theological disputes lost their sharpness and produced consensual positions.[7] In philosophical discourses, this national consensus was reflected in the fact that political theory lost its original significance. And the critique of religion gave way to the compromise of a confessionally neutral philosophy of religion, as for example David Hume presented in his *Dialogues Concerning Natural Religion* (1779).

However, the decisive transformation consisted in *industrialization*, which began in England around the middle of the 18th century and then shifted to the north, giving rise to the *Scottish Enlightenment*. In this respect, Adam Smith, with his book on the *Wealth of Nations* (1776), founded classical political economy. In his *Lectures on Jurisprudence* (1759), he gave the economic system a *historical dimension* by placing civil society at the end of a long genesis.[8] The Scot Adam Ferguson also stood in this tradition; in his *Essay on the History of Civil Society* (1767), he depicted the development of all humanity from its earliest beginnings to contemporary civilization.[9] While he praised scientific, technical, and cultural achievements, he also lamented the moral decline brought about by luxury and corruption. In the British manner, this is both progress-oriented and critical of civilization.

In this way, Ferguson indirectly answered the question of why, in addition to economic and historical theory, an independent moral philosophy was able to establish itself in Great Britain at all. Apparently, in addition to the

---

[6] Mortier 1978, pp. 39–51; Jüttner, Schlobach 1992, p. 12; Alt 1996, p. 7; Schneiders 1997, pp. 16 f.; Reinalter 2006, p. 12; idem 2016, p. 36; Thoma 2015, p. 61; Andries, Bernier 2019, p. 3; Stollberg-Rilinger 2000, p. 169.

[7] Schneiders 1997, pp. 21–51; Porter 2000, p. 98; Jacob 2006, pp. 65 f.; Diner 2017, p. 45 f.

[8] Smith 1923, Book I, pp. 220 f.; Smith 1928, pp. 10–16.

[9] Ferguson 1986, pp. 337, 369, 415; see also Millar 1985, pp. 47–57.

supposedly harmonious market, an additional compensation was required. As Smith had already done, Hume also attempted to resolve this contradiction: On the one hand, in his economic essays, he too recognized the self-regulating balance of private interests. On the other hand, however, he still considered a limitation of egoisms by a *moral sentiment* to be indispensable for the existence of the commonwealth.[10] In this case, too, affirmation and skepticism were combined.

France.—In France, the *Ancien Régime* prevailed, i.e., the absolute monarchy, which was neither willing nor able to undertake comprehensive reforms. Therefore, the intellectual life of the *philosophes* did not take place at the universities, but in the bourgeois public sphere of academies, salons, and publishers. Although Paris formed the center, critical voices also made themselves heard, for example from Bordeaux. The Catholic Church and the powerful monarchy formed a solid alliance, which saw Protestantism as a religious and political threat and persecuted its adherents with bloodshed.[11] By generating a corresponding counterpressure, this clerical and absolutist system gave rise to radical positions in theory and practice, which then erupted in the French Revolution. An extreme critique of civilization also contributed to this, splitting the Enlightenment camp. Against this bloc, the Catholic apologists of the Counter-Enlightenment (anti-lumières) turned. This multiple opposition of extremes is typical of the French Enlightenment.

The *critique of religion* was particularly radical, even if those involved were not always in agreement. In *Christianity Unveiled* (1766), Paul Thiry d'Holbach subjected Catholic dogmas, especially belief in miracles, to the test of reason. But he did not dwell on theological objections; rather, he condemned above all the social function, which consisted in supporting the rule of priests and oppressing the people.[12] It is not an exaggeration to describe this position as *atheism*, which was rather rare in Europe at the time.

A similar scenario played out in the context of the theme of *materialism in anthropology*. The starting point was the physician Julien Offray de La Mettrie in his provocative work *Man a Machine* (1748), in which he denied the immateriality of the soul and leveled the distinction between mind and

---

[10] Smith 1977; Hume 1962; previously Francis Hutcheson 1986; see Chap. 7.
[11] Cassirer 1932, pp. 7 f.; Schröder et al. 1997, p. 25; Porter 1991, pp. 17 f.; Schneiders 1997, pp. 52–82; Günther Mensching in: Rohbeck, Holzhey 2008, pp. 469–475.
[12] D'Holbach n.d., pp. 55, 68, 70; for the following, pp. 79, 84, 89, 99; cf. Schröder 1998, p. 255; Mulsow 2006, pp. 56–72.—Such a radical position is otherwise found only in the clandestine writings; see Chap. 3.

body.[13] However, the restriction to physiology led to the result that the human being ultimately appeared as an egoistic hedonist. Although other French Enlighteners such as Diderot, Helvétius and d'Holbach could very well imagine sentient and thinking matter, they distanced themselves from La Mettrie's machine-man. In contrast, they set the image of a social, political, and moral human being who could be improved through education.[14]

Equally innovative was the *historicizationof anthropology*. Already Louis Leclerc de Buffon had described in his *Natural History* (1749–1767) the genesis of humanity as a natural development.[15] Étienne Bonnot Condillac was the first to investigate the constitutive significance of language in the acquisition of knowledge.[16] Montesquieu addressed in *The Spirit of Law* (1748) the natural conditions such as climate and soil for the emergence of society, state, and law.[17] Following the political economy of the physiocrat François Quesnay, Turgot devised a *Universal History* (1750/51), in which he divided the history of all humanity into civilizational stages, emphasizing above all scientific, technical, economic, and cultural progress.[18] And it is also typical for France that such theories of progress—which were not as euphoric as is often claimed—were followed by Rousseau's critique of modern civilization, who in his *Discourse on the Origin of Inequality* (1755) denounced the moral decline of modern civilization. Here, the aforementioned polarization *within* French thinkers is confirmed.

The Encyclopédie edited by Diderot and d'Alembert (1751–1780) can be regarded as a veritable symbol of cooperation, in which almost all Enlightenment thinkers from Voltaire to Rousseau participated. The organizational form was already revolutionary: with its 142 contributors, 35 volumes, more than 70,000 articles, and almost 3000 copperplate engravings, the work represented a cooperative, division-of-labor, and interdisciplinary project. As the editors announced, the aim was to assemble all the knowledge of the time: not as a metaphysical "system," but in a "systematic order" that resulted from the alphabetical arrangement and numerous cross-references. In the article "Eclecticism," Diderot even defended the *philosophe* who "tramples on previous authority and therefore dares to think

---

[13] La Mettrie 2015, pp. 27, 39, 41.
[14] In Helvétius's work *On Man* (1772), this type of anthropology became manifest: Helvétius 1976, pp. 21–52; cf. idem 1973, pp. 81, 506–514; d'Holbach 1960, pp. 67 f.
[15] Buffon 2008, pp. 15–37; see Chap. 4 and 9.
[16] Condillac 2006, pp. 171–191; see Chap. 6.
[17] Montesquieu 1951, vol. I, p. 16.
[18] Turgot 1990, pp. 168–175.

independently."[19] The aim of this extensive lexicon was to provide "useful" knowledge instead of speculation and contemplation, knowledge that came not only from the sciences but also from the workshops of the manufactories.[20] This also included medical articles in which the human being was depicted as a natural being and, for the first time, the female body was also represented.[21] The work spread throughout Europe and thus marked the transition to the Enlightenment of the second half of the eighteenth century.

Germany.—Unlike in Great Britain and France, there was up to this point in Germany no unified and centrally governed nation-state. The wars of religion divided the country and prevented profound social, political, and religious change. Yet the Protestantism that emerged from this was able to defuse religious criticism to such an extent that most authors of the German Enlightenment strove for a reconciliation between Christian faith and philosophical reason. For this reason, eighteenth-century German philosophy was established at universities such as Halle and Göttingen, although there were regional differences. Due to this academic connection, the relevant treatises were thorough, but also somewhat cumbersome, pedantic, and dry, especially since they were partly still written in Latin and only quite late in the vernacular.[22] The natural sciences were less important. While economic theory remained confined to cameralistics, interest focused on legal and political theory.

The historical root of philosophy in Germany was metaphysics of Gottfried Wilhelm Leibniz, who in his *Theodicy* (1710) advocated the doctrine of the "best of all possible worlds" and divine providence. In parallel, Christian Thomasius developed his teachings, in which he attempted to ground morality, law, and the state in a purely rational manner.[23] Upon this foundation, Christian Wolff finally built his comprehensive philosophical system, which consisted of *logic, metaphysics*, ethics, and *politics*

---

[19] Encyclopédie 1972, p. 321; see also the article "Encyclopédie," p. 449.—Similarly, the "Introduction" to the *Encyclopédie*: d'Alembert 1989, p. 87; cf. Stenger 2013, pp. 130, 299; for a critical view see Adler, Godel 2010, pp. 11 f.; Gumbrecht 2020, pp. 11, 35, 48, 350.

[20] D'Alembert 1989, pp. 12, 20, 41 f.—See also the articles "Artisan," "Craft," and "Manufacture"; Encyclopédie 1972, pp. 104, 787, 805.—See also the twelve volumes with illustrations from workshops and manufactories; Encyclopédie 1715–1780.

[21] Article "Man (homme)," in: Encyclopédie 1972, pp. 674–676; article "Woman (femme)," in: Encyclopédie 1756, vol. 6, p. 468.

[22] Schneiders 1974; ibid. 1997, pp. 83–115; Merker 1982; Möller 1986; Pütz 1991; Reed 2009; Schmidt, G. 2009; Martus 2015.

[23] Thomasius: *Doctrine of Reason* (1690/91), *Doctrine of Morals* (1692/96), and *Doctrine of Natural Law* (1705).—See also *Short Concept of All Sciences* (1754) by Johann Georg Sulzer 2014.

(1713–1721), and by 1740 had been expanded to more than twenty volumes in Latin. In some histories of philosophy, this type of rationalism is treated as the high point of the German Enlightenment. According to such a reading, the Enlightenment, since 1750, had reached its end "weakened" and "exhausted."[24] Since it was no longer capable of theoretical innovation, it produced only the *popular philosophy* of Joachim Heinrich Campe.

Yet in the context of the present book, it should be clear that these philosophical systems, including their adaptations, do not fit the formation of an Enlightenment that emerged in the second half of the eighteenth century in Britain and France. They will therefore not be further considered in what follows. This raises the question of whether a modified form of the Enlightenment, oriented toward European standards, also arose in Germany thereafter. This is precisely the case. If one leaves the orbit of the Wolffian school, new approaches can be found in the fields of criticism of religion, anthropology, and philosophy of history.

There was also in Germany a *critique of religion*, which focused on the analysis of the New Testament. In his work *The Principal Truths of Natural Religion* (1754), Hermann Samuel Reimarus criticized the biblical miracles, for example by portraying the resurrection of Christ as a deception by the disciples,[25] which provoked vehement protest from theologians. Moses Mendelssohn, son of a Jewish Torah scribe, in particular, attempted to conceive a religion common to both Jews and Christians.[26] Such attempts came quite close to the idea of a "natural religion" of Hume and Rousseau. This was not an atheistic position, but rather amounted to English and French deism.

A turn toward *anthropology* can also be observed in the German Enlightenment. It was physicians, now hardly known, who did not merely speculate about an *animal rationale*, but investigated the human being as a physical-psychological natural being with the help of the experimental method. Finally, in the German-speaking world as well, anthropology was *historicized*, so that an independent *philosophy of history* emerged, which has received less attention. The influences from France are documented, for example, when Johann Gottfried Herder explicitly praised the cultural history of Antoine-Yves Goguet, published in Paris in 1758 and soon

---

[24] Schneiders 1974, pp. 14 f.; idem 1997, pp. 8, 128; Kondylis 1981, p. 42; Müller 2002, pp. 1 f.; Martus 2015, p. 687; Reinalter 2016, p. 18.

[25] Reimarus 1985, p. 27.

[26] Mendelssohn 2009, vol. II, pp. 133 f.; see Chap. 3.

after translated into German, as a model for his own historical studies.[27] This is also the sense in which Herder's title is to be understood: *This too a Philosophy of History for the Formation of Humanity* (1774). Other authors, such as the Germans Johann Christoph Gatterer and August Ludwig Schlözer as well as the Swiss Isaak Iselin, devised *universal histories*, in which progress in science, technology, and economics formed the guiding thread.

Immanuel Kant is a point of contention. Some interpreters stylize him as the "true" Enlightenment and thereby devalue the preceding German Enlightenment as well as the European Enlightenment as a whole.[28] Other commentators even claim that Kant no longer belonged to the Enlightenment and already ushered in German Idealism.[29] This is justified insofar as Kant no longer followed English and French sensualism and based human cognition and moral judgment solely on reason. But at the same time, he criticized the metaphysics of Christian Wolff and considered the empirical basis according to Hume to be indispensable. This is especially evident in Kant's later *Anthropology from a Pragmatic Point of View* (1798), in which the "sensibility" of representations, the "feeling of pleasure and displeasure," as well as the "faculty of desire" with "affects" and "passions" are discussed in detail. Kant also continued the philosophy of history, in which he received Buffon's natural history, Montesquieu's climate theory, and even the theory of cultural stages. In the field of religion, he adopted the idea of a "natural religion" from Hume and Rousseau. There is therefore no reason to absolutize Kant's philosophy as the Enlightenment par excellence or to banish it from the European context.

Italy.—In Italy, a philosophy of Enlightenment developed within small spaces of freedom, which managed to avoid direct confrontation with the Catholic Church.[30] The influences came primarily from France, whose authors many Italian Enlighteners visited and knew personally. Thus, in Italy too, there existed the type of the *philosopho illuminato*, who, though cautiously critical of religion, was pragmatic enough to focus on concrete reforms. The emblem of this was the Milanese editorial circle of the journal *Il Caffè*, whose title symbolically expressed its program: coffee as the

---

[27] Goguet 1758; Herder 1984, vol. I, p. 86; see Chap. 9.
[28] Schneiders 1974, p. 21; Habermas 1981, pp. 444–464; Schnädelbach 1988, pp. 15–19; Mittelstraß 1989, pp. 341–360; Kopper 1996, pp. 7 f.; Godel 2007, p. 384; Garcés 2019, pp. 7, 58; see 1. Introduction.
[29] Schneiders 1997, pp. 99 f.; contra Geier 2012, p. 231.
[30] Schneiders 1997, pp. 119 f.; Rother 2005, pp. 27–62; idem in: Rohbeck, Rother 2011, pp. XV–XXXV.

"drug of Enlightenment," which rouses people from the "sleep of errors" and awakens them to new life. Since national unity in Italy was still pending, regionally distinct movements emerged. Here, a rough distinction can be made between the Enlightenment in southern Naples and that in northern Lombardy.

In the first half of the 18th century, *Naples* was the undisputed center of the Enlightenment. The outstanding figure was Giovanni Battista Vico, who, with his *New Science Concerning the Common Nature of Nations* (1725), founded an independent philosophy of history.[31] However, this work was ignored by the European Enlightenment and was only received in the historicism of the 19th century. The reasons lay, on the one hand, in its theological foundation and, on the other, in its disregard for modern civilization. It therefore fits neither chronologically nor thematically into our context. This is more true of his successor Antonio Genovesi, who devised a *Political Economy* in which he—against the doctrine of the physiocrats— declared general human labor to be the source of the value of a commodity.[32] He was later followed by the Neapolitan Gaetano Filangieri with an extensive reform program for the state, economy, and society.

In the second half of the century, the center of the Enlightenment shifted to *Milan*. Among the most influential authors was Pietro Verri, who, in his *Meditations on Happiness* (1763), developed a hedonistic anthropology that was intended to encompass the happiness of both the individual and the community.[33] He defined individual happiness rather negatively as the avoidance of pain, and "public happiness" in a thoroughly utilitarian sense as the increase and as balanced a distribution as possible of social wealth. To justify this, he used a *Political Economy* written somewhat later (1771). This theory of society was complemented by a moral philosophy that was oriented toward the Scottish Enlighteners and preferred sensibility to reason. Verri criticized the Catholic Church with its instruments of power— Inquisition, prison, and torture—and joined the European consensus of a "natural religion."

Of the later Italian philosophers, probably Cesare Beccaria was the best known. In his treatise *On Crimes and Punishments* (1764), which was circulated throughout Europe, he condemned torture and the death penalty

---

[31] Vico 1990; see also Rohbeck 2004, pp. 80–85.

[32] Antonio Genovesi: *De jure et officiis in usum tironum libri* (1767); Gaetano Fillangieri: *Scienza della legislazione* (1783); quoted in Rother 2005, pp. 271 f.; see Chap. 8.

[33] Verri 1972 and 1996; Rother 2005, pp. 54, 66; idem in: Rohbeck, Rother 2011, pp. XXVI, 273–295.

and advocated, overall, for humane punishment so as not to harden people psychologically.[34] Philosophically interesting is his justification: Beccaria replaced atonement for personal guilt with the pragmatic aim of prevention. Underlying this was a theory of globally valid human rights. In this way, Italy made a contribution to the European Enlightenment that should not be underestimated.

Spain.—How does the case stand with Spain? Was there any Enlightenment there at all? In a country where throne and altar had allied for the purpose of maintaining their power, was every striving of reason for autonomy and every impulse toward political freedom nipped in the bud by censorship and the Inquisition?

Already in the 18th century, Spain was subject to the accusation of general backwardness.[35] The article "Spain" in the French *Encyclopédie* arrived at a devastating judgment,[36] against which the Spanish ambassador in Paris had already protested, assuring that Spain had indeed embarked on the path of reforms and thereby contributed to the European Enlightenment. And this essentially included the reception of the French Enlightenment. The relevant works were often smuggled across the border. At times, clandestine writings circulated, copied and distributed by hand. Finally, Enlightenment ideas reached the Iberian Peninsula via the detour of the French Counter-Enlightenment. The irony of this history of reception consisted in the fact that, in their "refutation" of the supposed errors of Voltaire, Rousseau and other authors, the Catholic clerics presented their theories in detail and thus made them known in Spain in the first place. In this way, interested Spaniards could form a fairly accurate picture and just as well develop sympathies for them. The modern reader is left wondering whether this unintended side effect was not even consciously accepted. The anti-Enlightenment apologetics were, as it were, the message in a bottle of the European Enlightenment.

The academic philosophy of eighteenth-century Spain was almost seamlessly connected to medieval scholasticism. It was the Jesuit order that introduced the new philosophical currents. But in 1767, the Jesuits were

---

[34] Beccaria 1966, pp. 74, 107; cf. Rother 2005, pp. 74–88; idem in: Rohbeck, Rother 2011, pp. XXVII, 296–317; Frick 2020, p. 107 f.

[35] José Luis Villacañas in: Rohbeck, Rother 2016, pp. 3–26; see in the same volume also the editors' preface, pp. XI–XIV.

[36] Jaucourt 1755, p. 953.—The Spanish ambassador responded to a similar article in the *Encyclopédie méthodique* (1782) and to the travelogue *Voyage de figaro en Espagne* (1785) by Jean Marie Jérôme Fleuriot de Langle.

expelled from Spain. While the scholastic heritage continued to be cultivated at Spanish universities, learned societies, discussion circles, and academies—modeled after French and Italian examples—also emerged in Spain, and women were admitted to these as well. Especially in the field of *medicine*, the experimental method based on observation and experience prevailed over Cartesian rationalism. In the political and economic spheres, the Spanish focused on reforms in the economy and administration. Also noteworthy are the numerous travel reports and utopias in which colonial experiences from America were processed.

Against this background, the question arises once again: Was there a Spanish Enlightenment? Even though much was limited to the reception of English and French authors, Spanish philosophy of the Enlightenment did develop its own character. Three specific features can be identified: First, the Enlightenment in Spain was characterized by its aim for moderate *reforms*. Second, the authors there strove for a *reconciliation* between reason and faith. Third, this resulted in an *eclecticism* that shaped Spanish philosophy of the eighteenth century. This made it possible to apply the results and methods of the natural sciences without drawing the corresponding theological and metaphysical consequences and thus coming into conflict with the Catholic Church. An early exemplar was the philosopher Benito Martínez Feijoo, who did not produce a systematic work but rather a multitude of essays on various topics from different perspectives. The same applies to Gaspar Melchor de Jovellanos, who, at the end of the century, received the entire European Enlightenment and drafted the utopia of an enlightened age.[37] Both projects do not fundamentally differ from the eclectic method of the French *Encyclopédie*.

Synopsis.—The final topic is now the significance of each Enlightenment in the individual countries of Europe and the unity of the European Enlightenment. At first glance, it seems obvious to declare the Enlightenment in *France* as the center or even the prototype.[38] What is usually meant by this is the *radicalism* of French philosophy, which tended toward atheistic and materialistic tendencies. No less radical was Rousseau's critique of social inequality in bourgeois society and thus, overall, of modern civilization. Indirectly, these positions were reflected in the reaction of Catholic apologetics, which treated the opposing approaches of the

---

[37] Francisco Sánchez-Blanco in: Rohbeck, Rother 2016, pp. 72–79; Hans-Joachim Lope ibid., pp. 250 f.
[38] Thoma 2015, pp. 68, 71, 95; cf. Geier 2012, p. 93; on Germany see Schmidt, G. 2009, p. 398.

Enlightenment in toto as an anti-church attack. As mentioned, this threefold contrast is part of the specificity of the French Enlightenment.

This kind of radicalism is also confirmed in the receptions of neighboring countries, a process facilitated by the fact that French was the *lingua franca* for European intellectuals. When Catholic counter-Enlightenment thinkers in Italy and Spain condemned the philosophy of the Enlightenment, they primarily had the religious criticism from France in mind. French influence was particularly suspect to Spanish apologists—they denounced their compatriots who embraced the ideas of the French Enlighteners as "Frenchlings" (afrancesados). Even in Great Britain, the term *enlightenment* was rarely used, as it was identified with the French Enlightenment. German philosophy remained, well into the eighteenth century, bound to Wolffian metaphysics and only later introduced the French-connoted term Enlightenment. Thus, the confrontation between Enlightenment and Counter-Enlightenment was carried from France abroad and there transformed into a conflict between different nations.

Even though such attributions are common in the mutual reflections of national cultures, the Enlightenment of a particular nation should not be declared the norm by which other countries are measured. This applies especially to France, which by no means represents the model country of the European Enlightenment. Nevertheless, it must be acknowledged that the French Enlightenment in fact exerted the greatest influence in Europe, for which the *Encyclopédie* serves as a kind of emblem. It is equally mistaken to speak of a German "special path" that, in contrast to France, supposedly brought us the true Enlightenment. This gives the impression that one does not want to acknowledge the materialist and atheistic tendencies, in order to ideologically soften the epoch of the Enlightenment—along the lines of: It wasn't really that bad.

Instead of emphasizing the undoubtedly existing differences between the countries mentioned, I propose to focus more on the *commonalities* of the European Enlightenment. Although not all authors of the eighteenth century felt themselves to be part of this movement, and many, from today's perspective, stood far from it, the Enlightenment nevertheless marked a common point of reference by which both supporters and opponents oriented themselves in this era. This also applies to the Catholic apologists, who fought against the *philosophes* but at the same time made use of Enlightenment ideas to highlight the social function of religion. Therefore, it makes sense to speak of an overarching formation of the Enlightenment. Behind this attempt to emphasize affinities lies the current interest in recalling the unity of Europe. The Enlightenment was a genuinely European project, which continues to fascinate to this day and is capable of exerting political influence.

Europe in Self-Critical Discourse

The question now arises as to whether the representatives of the Enlightenment also made the continent of Europe a subject of discussion. This question is not so easy to answer, since corresponding statements are rather rare and mostly hidden in the texts. In this section, I will search for traces in the following discourses: a few titles with Europe, scattered passages in works on anthropology and philosophy of history, as well as in some treatises on peace. In these texts, judgments about Europe are very mixed, because they always include comparisons with other cultures: They range from praise to relentless criticism. Before resorting to the Eurocentric schema,[39] one should form a more differentiated picture.

One of the few texts in which Europe appears in the title is the article of the same name in the French *Encyclopédie*. In it, the author Jaucourt describes the physiognomy of Europeans and the geographical shape of Europe. With a subtle jab at Montesquieu, he emphasizes Europe's "power," which, however, consists mainly of military troops that are less useful than they are a display of ostentation. Jaucourt summarizes: "Moreover, it is of little importance that Europe, in terms of its extent, is the smallest of the four [sic] continents, for it is, thanks to its trade, its navigation, its fertility, the enlightened spirit and industry of its peoples, and its knowledge in the sciences, arts, and crafts, the most significant."[40] It is noteworthy, first, that by the "enlightened spirit" of Europe he does not primarily mean philosophy, but above all economic, technical, and scientific achievements. Furthermore, it must be noted that although the author designates Europe as the "most significant" continent, he writes only a very short article on it and shows no particular interest in the topic.

A different impression arises in *Italy*, where people lament their own backwardness and seek to overcome it through cooperation with Europe. With corresponding praise, they invoke participation in the European Enlightenment. Thus Beccaria describes Europe as "a great family" with a

---

[39] For example, Chakrabarty 2010; for a critical view see Beaurepaire 2019; likewise Lilti 2019, p. 43; see also Chap. 9.

[40] Jaucourt 1756, p. 212; cf. Pomeau 1966, p. 59.—The reference is to "four" continents, because Australia had not yet been discovered.

common heritage that does not belong to a single nation, but is to be used by all peoples. He understands his own work as a European project, since he aims to reform the legal system throughout Europe. Verri too praises the European "Republic of Letters," which produces not only works of taste but also practical benefits. When he calls Europe the "homeland of the Enlightenment," he does not fail to point out that its birth lies in the Italian Renaissance.[41] Incidentally, d'Alembert also notes this in his introduction to the *Encyclopédie*, when he admits "how deeply we are indebted to Italy: from there the sciences have come to us, which have since borne such rich fruit throughout Europe."[42]

Anthropology.—In this leading discipline, the topic of Europe is theoretically deepened. Thus Montesquieu, who is mentioned in Jaucourt's article on Europe, examines the influence of climate on the character of peoples. In doing so, he distinguishes between cold and warm countries, where people are accordingly more industrious or more lethargic.[43] The evidence comes from the entire then-known world: Europe, Africa, the Orient, Asia, America, China. Apparently, without expressly stating it, Montesquieu sees particularly favorable conditions for the development of Europe in the temperate climate. Yet the point of this theory is that these conditions of possibility are not granted to Europe alone, but also to other continents. This is made explicit for Persia, China and India.

In the *Persian Letters* (1721), Montesquieu describes the journey of two educated Persians to Paris, who master the local language, quickly adapt, and form their own thoughts on the European Enlightenment. In this way, he valorizes Persian culture and relativizes the supposed special status of Europe.[44] Françoise de Graffigny arrives at a similar result in *Letters of a Peruvian Woman* (1747), in which a princess from Peru is abducted to France. She recalls the Incas as a civilized people and preserves her own cultural identity. While she still has to acquire the French language, she criticizes the social ills and moral decay of France.[45] In his commentary on a travel account, Diderot compares the "natural customs" of Tahiti with European civilization, which he—probably under the influence of

---

[41] Beccaria 1966, pp. 52 f.; cf. Pomeau 1966, p. 123; Steinkamp 2000, pp. 119 f.; Rother 2005, p. 230.
[42] D'Alembert 1989, p. 65.
[43] Montesquieu 1951, vol. I, pp. 310–328.
[44] Montesquieu 1988, pp. 46 f., 68 f., 183 f.
[45] Graffigny 1999, pp. 9, 86, 120–126.—The social criticism is obviously modeled on Rousseau, see Chap. 8.

Rousseau—judges to be unnatural and decadent.[46] These examples show that, although a certain precedence is granted to European culture, Europe is by no means chosen as the central and sole standard of world cultures. And in the epistolary novels, not only are foreign cultures described, but European culture itself is viewed from a foreign perspective. Such a change of perspective is the opposite of a Eurocentric viewpoint.

A global typology, however, is offered by the *History of the Two Indies* (1770) by Guillaume Raynal and Denis Diderot. By orienting themselves on Montesquieu's theory of climate, they distinguish between the cultures of India, South America, Africa, and the Caribbean.[47] Although Europe is only one facet in this account, it nevertheless forms the starting point in the narrative, since it is Europe that discovered and conquered the foreign lands. The focus is on the reciprocal effects of colonization on the European continent.[48] In this case, Diderot considers the zenith of Europe to be past, while he promises a future to North America. Here, cultural development could begin anew, unimpeded by the disruptions of European civilization. In this way, colonization acquires a historical perspective.

Philosophy of history.—This new discipline is generally conceived as the history of all humanity, as is already signaled by titles containing the term *universal history*. Again, the question arises: What role does Europe play in this? Does Europe really, as is often claimed, appear as the origin and goal of world history? Upon closer examination, a much more differentiated picture emerges.

In his *Outline for Two Treatises on Universal History* (1751) Turgot sketches a general theory of cultural development with the stages of hunting and gathering, pastoralism, agriculture and industry. Since he relegates geography and chronology to mere auxiliary sciences, concrete places and times are mentioned only rarely and in passing; thus, Europe is not a topic at all.[49] Yet in his *Philosophical Account of the Gradual Progress of the Human Mind* (1750), Europe is already mentioned, as the narrative of progress begins in ancient Greece, continues with the Romans, and reaches its flowering in Italy: "The time has come when you, Europe, emerge from the

---

[46] Denis Diderot: *Supplément au Voyage de Bougainville* (1773/74); cf. Stenger 2013, pp. 528–530; Gumbrecht 2020, pp. 381 f.

[47] Raynal, Diderot 1988: Asia pp. 35–87, South America pp. 91–164, Africa pp. 195–236, North America pp. 239–300.

[48] Ibid., pp. 91 f.; cf. pp. 301–304; see the section on colonization in Chap. 9.

[49] Turgot 1990, p. 169; cf. Rohbeck 2010, pp. 75–79.—Rousseau proceeds similarly in his *Second Discourse*; likewise Kant in his philosophy of history; see Chap. 9.

night that surrounded you!" Finally, France follows as the "age of reason."[50] The position of Europe in Turgot's philosophy of history is thus ambivalent. In the earlier *Account*, which is more narrative and probably also apologetic, Europe is at the center. But in the theoretical *Outline*, the uniqueness of Europe is lost.

Shortly afterwards, Goguet publishes his multi-volume work *On the Origin of Laws, Arts, and Sciences* (1758), in which he maintains that the Greeks had adopted their civilization from the Egyptians.[51] Through the study of early high cultures such as Egypt and Babylonia, not only is the biblical creation story called into question, but also classicism, which had located the cradle of Western culture in ancient Greece. By placing the beginnings of ancient culture outside the boundaries of Europe, Goguet causes Europe to lose its position as the sole "origin" of culture. If one also considers the recognition of distant high cultures such as India and China, the old Eurocentric focus is replaced by a polygenesis of world cultures.

This also applies to Voltaire's *Essay on the Customs and Spirit of Nations* (1756), which begins with the history of China, followed by the history of India, Persia, and the Arabs.[52] By claiming that Chinese history is not only more civilized but also older than the culture described in the Old Testament, he has the civilization of humanity begin far from Europe. The peculiarity of European development becomes apparent in the comparison of cultures: while the Chinese reached a state of completion relatively early, which they could not surpass, Europe first had to endure a period of decline in order to reach a new peak under Louis XIV.

Once again centered on the history of Europe is the *Sketch for a Historical Account of the Progress of the Human Mind* (1795). In it, Condorcet considers the "universal history" of peoples as a continuum, within which the historical epochs from the beginnings up to the present century form an "unbroken chain."[53] While the beginning of the text is oriented toward Turgot's stadial theory, without naming specific places and times, from the "fourth epoch" onward the account focuses on the history of Europe, beginning with Greece and its philosophers. After the "decline" in the Middle Ages, Condorcet explicitly speaks of the "progress of the sciences after their restoration in the West" and names figures such as Bacon, Galileo and

---

[50] Turgot 1990, p. 160.
[51] Goguet 1758, vol. I, p. 67.
[52] Voltaire 1963, vol. I, pp. 33, 66–69, 186, 205.
[53] Condorcet 1976, p. 35.

Newton. From the perspective of the French Revolution, he acknowledges the emergence of the republic and the introduction of human rights. He even claims that "in Europe, all enlightened people already pay homage to the principles of the French constitution."[54] With this, he connects the hope that this form of government might become a model for other countries.

In contrast to this stands Constantin François de Volney with his work *The Ruins, or Meditations on the Revolutions of Empires* (1789). While Condorcet pushes the idea of linear progress to its extreme, with Volney the cyclical view of history returns. The occasion for his philosophical reflections on history is a journey to Syria.[55] The remains of an earlier culture observed there, which awaken the "memory of times past," painfully highlight the difference between former flourishing and today's lamentable desolation. They are a symbol of the "revolutions of empires" and thus of the cycles in history. When the "scepter of the world" passes from one people to another, the comparison with antiquity gives rise to the dreadful thought that Europe might lose its previously leading influence . As already Raynal and Diderot, Volney also considers it likely that the "torch of progress" will move on to North America. In this way, Europe remains only a transitional stage in history.[56]

The authors in the European neighboring countries. Adam Ferguson are rather skeptical towards the idea of progress. In his *History of Civil Society* (1767), Ferguson paints a picture of economic ascent and moral decline. In this context, it is interesting that he—like Turgot in the *Sketch*—conceives a general world history, but then draws on examples from all over the world: European countries such as Greece or Italy, but also China, India, Persia, Africa and America. When he speaks of the "temperate zones of Europe and Asia,"[57] he demonstrates that with Montesquieu's climate theory Europe is by no means privileged. A similar approach is taken by Robertson in his *History of the Discovery of America* (1777), Schlözer in his *Universal History* (1772) and Iselin in his *History of Humanity* (1779).[58] While the first five books on early history are kept general, three books follow with the concrete

---

[54] Ibid., pp. 113, 195.
[55] Volney 1977, pp. 20–31.
[56] This maxim is reminiscent of Hegel, who was familiar with Volney's work: "World history goes from east to west, for Europe is absolutely the end of world history, Asia the beginning." Georg Wilhelm Friedrich Hegel: Works in 20 Volumes. Ed. by Eva Moldenhauer and Karl Markus Michel, Frankfurt a. M. 1969, vol. 12, p. 134.
[57] Ferguson 1986, p. 242; cf. pp. 205, 399 f.
[58] Robertson 1841; Schlözer 1990; Iselin 2014, vol. IV.

history of specific countries and cultures. The eighth and final book concludes with an account of the "present-day European nations" with a moderate perspective on progress.[59]

Herder's position is completely at odds with the aforementioned philosophies of history of the European Enlightenment, even though he expressed his appreciation for Goguet. In his early work on the *Philosophy of History*, he initially employs the theory of climate and stages, but then, in a more narrative and poetic manner, turns to the history of the Orient, Egypt, Phoenicia, Greece, Rome, and Europe. Herder explicitly rejects the idea of progress, because he sees in it the danger of judging all peoples and epochs by a single standard. Instead, he advocates recognizing the intrinsic value of each culture: "Every nation has its *center* of happiness *within itself* just as every sphere has its center of gravity."[60] This famous dictum is directed first and foremost against France, which should not set itself up as the ideal for all of Europe. But beyond that, Herder polemicizes against the idea of a unified Europe in which "all national characters are erased."

While one might attribute a leveling tendency to the philosophies of history just described, it should nevertheless be noted that the idea of universal history was in fact the precondition for researching and presenting world cultures in their diversity, as well as for recognizing foreign cultures as distinct high cultures in their own right. In this context, the position of Europe in the world has proven to be highly controversial. On the one hand, Europe's special role is significantly relativized, as Europe is no longer regarded as the sole source of culture, no longer appears to be uniquely favored by a beneficial climate, and is no longer stylized as the goal of world history. On the other hand, there are some models that take Europe as their starting point and see in European, especially French, culture the provisional crowning achievement. Still other authors see in this precisely the danger for Europe, which threatens to lose its preeminence and cede it to America. Thus, if one wishes to maintain the charge of Eurocentrism, it must nevertheless be admitted that there have been numerous, and in some cases very prominent, examples of criticism of the privileging of Europe, which are sufficient to dispel any kind of general suspicion.

Discourses on Peace.—The Enlightenment era is characterized by the fact that several drafts for peace in Europe emerged—not only in Kant's famous treatise *Perpetual Peace* (1795), but, less well known, much earlier in France

---

[59] Iselin 2014, vol. IV, pp. 289–362: Orient pp. 215–231; Greeks and Romans pp. 235–286.
[60] Herder 1984, vol. I, pp. 611 f.

and Switzerland. In these earlier writings, Europe is at the center; only later does the horizon expand to a global order of peace.

The starting point is the *Projet pour rendre la paix perpétuelle en Europe* (1713) by the Abbé de Saint-Pierre.[61] In it, he asks whether the domestic model of contract can also be transferred to the international level. As one of the first, he proposes to prevent wars through a European confederation of states. His institutional design includes a permanent council with 24 member states. Each state is to remain autonomous, except in matters of international dispute resolution, foreign, customs, and military policy. Any amendment is possible only with the consent of all members.[62]

This draft was then made known by Rousseau in his *Extrait du projet de paix perpétuelle* (1756) and enriched with his own reflections. While Saint-Pierre dealt only with the legal aspects of a confederation of states, Rousseau also examines the economic, social, and cultural preconditions for lasting peace. According to him, Europe no longer needs to be constructed by legal means, but already exists as a real "system" with its own "force."[63] He sees the basis for this in the evenly distributed population, in the universally possible agriculture, in the high level of crafts and industry, as well as in the developed commerce, which favors peace. The rivers, which once separated nations, now serve both travel and the transport of goods. Rousseau also includes the "community" of scholars, the shared taste in literature, and the Europe-wide book market. According to him, these achievements have contributed to the "union of interests" and "concord of customs," so that the individual peoples are now in close relation to one another. In this way, Europe uniquely fulfills the conditions of a confederation. In the following *Jugement sur le projet de paix* (1756), Rousseau then explicitly aligns himself with the Saint-Pierre project, which he judges to be well thought out.[64] Nevertheless, he considers the project of lasting peace in Europe to be unrealistic. For he fears that the individual princes would resist it, as they would see their particular interests violated. Such peace, therefore, is not possible under monarchies, but only with politically free commonwealths.

---

[61] Saint-Pierre 1713; cf. Höffe 1995, pp. 255 f.

[62] This draft was followed by the Swiss Emer de Vattel (1758); cf. Cheneval 2002, p. 34; Frick 2020, pp. 114 f.

[63] Rousseau 1964, pp. 565, 567; cf. Faye 1992, pp. 115–146; Israel 2009, pp. 124, 127.—Raynal and Diderot also come to the conclusion in their *Histoire des deux Indes* (1770) that, after many wars and conquests, Europe has entered a phase "of calm and peace"; Raynal, Diderot 1988, p. 92.—Similarly Mercier 1982, pp. 162 f.; Mably 1975, pp. 120 f.

[64] Rousseau 1964, p. 591; see also Vattel 1758, p. 184.

Voltaire also judges in *De la paix perpétuelle* (1769) the peace project of Saint-Pierre skeptically, but for different reasons. He misses the inclusion of other states outside Europe, such as Turkey, Persia, Japan and China, without whose support no lasting peace would be possible.[65] By moving from peace in Europe to world peace, he gives the problem a global dimension.

In Spain, Gaspar Melchor de Jovellanos at the end of the 18th century drafted the utopia of a worldwide peace. He speaks of a "fraternal union" (unión fraterna), in which peace and justice overcome all hatred and terror. French, Africans, and Britons become brothers, Chinese and Lapps exchange their goods without guile. Humanity becomes "a single and great family," which in the end even speaks a common language.[66]

In his treatise *Perpetual Peace* (1795), Kant also by no means restricts himself to Europe, but from the outset adopts a cosmopolitan standpoint by aiming at a global order of peace, which is to supplement the existing state and international law.[67] Similar to Rousseau, he considers the project of lasting peace possible only on the condition that the constitutions of the participating states, if not democratic, are at least "republican."[68] In doing so, he does not propose a "state of nations" or a "world republic," but a "federation of nations" in the sense of a federation of autonomous states, to be realized by a "treaty of peace." Here it becomes clear that he initially focuses on the legal aspect.

But then Kant considers by what social "mechanism" people can be motivated to create and maintain peace. A corresponding motive that could help realize the desire for peace within a republic, he sees in the greed of the citizens. If the citizens are involved in the decision over war and peace, the state would be more likely to avoid wars, because the resulting "burden of debt" would be felt as unbearable.[69]

Finally, Kant names an economic reason: "It is the *spirit of commerce* which cannot coexist with war, and which sooner or later takes hold of every

---

[65] Voltaire: *Recrit de l'empereur de la Chine* (1762). In: Faye 1992, pp. 159–162; cf. Turgot 1990, p. 180; Condorcet 1976, pp. 196, 214.

[66] Quoted after Hans-Joachim Lope in: Rohbeck, Rother 2016, pp. 250 f.

[67] Kant 1965, vol. XI, p. 216.

[68] Ibid., pp. 204, 208, 2012; cf. Höffe 1995, p. 109; idem 1999, pp. 255–263.—In *Perpetual Peace*, Saint-Pierre and Rousseau are not mentioned, but they are in the treatise *Idea for a Universal History with a Cosmopolitan Purpose* (1784), published more than ten years earlier, which is also drawn upon here; Kant 1965, vol. XI, p. 42; cf. Rohbeck 2020, pp. 96–99.

[69] Kant 1965, vol. XI, pp. 47, 170.

people."[70] By this he means the interest of a nation engaged in commerce in the existence of other flourishing commercial nations. Peace in Europe is then no longer a purely legal task, but can build on the already existing basis of a division of labor in industry and reciprocal exchange of goods. It is based less on state treaties than on economic and social cooperation.

The Project of the European Union

Even if the topos of peaceful world trade has been refuted many times in the course of later history, one should not blame it for the catastrophes of the following centuries. The attempt to look for realistic factors for global peace remains understandable. This utopia can be applied especially to Europe, where after the Second World War the "common market" actually proved to be conducive to peace.

Peace in Europe and the world.—This connection is evidenced by formulations from the founding treaty of the *European Economic Community*. There, a "balanced trade" is regarded as a "means to an end"—and not solely with the aim of economic reconstruction, but as the basis for a lasting peace in Europe. The preamble states: The EEC is founded "in the firm will to lay the foundations for an ever closer union of the peoples of Europe."[71] This reads like an eulogy from the eighteenth century, in which the peace-promoting "spirit of commerce" was a commonplace—even reaching as far as Königsberg.

Within the European Union, this utopia has become reality and has proven itself for eighty years. Some observers even go so far as to claim that the principle of "change through trade" led to the collapse of the Eastern Bloc and thus to the end of the Cold War. Accordingly, it was the so-called soft power of consumer goods that gradually undermined the socialist states and ultimately brought about their downfall.

Since the Russian attack on Ukraine, these peace utopias have suffered a severe setback. With regard to the relationship between trade and war, a hybrid situation has emerged. On the one hand, the war brutally shatters the illusion that the mutual exchange of goods and services has the suggestive

---

[70] Ibid., p. 226.—Likewise Raynal and Diderot: "A spirit of exchange and barter is arising in Europe," which favors peace; Raynal, Diderot 1988, p. 92.—Similarly Montesquieu: "The natural effect of commerce is to incline toward peace." Montesquieu 1951, vol. II, p. 3; cf. the essay "Of Commerce" by Hume 1963, pp. 259–274, esp. p. 264.

[71] Quoted in Freiburghaus 2000, pp. 79 f.; cf. Cheneval 2003, p. 5.

power to prevent military conflicts. On the other hand, it is almost paradoxical that Russia has even exported gas and oil to Europe during the war in order to finance precisely this war. This is the perversion of "war through trade."

Conversely, the economic sanctions against Russia reveal the enormous impact that trade still exerts. Should Russia back down for economic reasons, this would be a negative proof of the power of the world economy. Global trade also has negative effects on Europe, as previously unknown bottlenecks in energy supply are becoming noticeable. Yet at the same time, new trade routes are being developed. Russia is intensifying the sale of coal, oil, and gas to China. And Europe is seeking the supply of liquefied natural gas from Arab and other countries. This does not mean the "end of world trade,"[72] as was read in the press; rather, global markets are shifting, as they always have.

For Europe, several practical consequences arise from the conflict with Russia. The economic and political union must now be supplemented by its own *military alliance*. The pacifist attitude is giving way to a defensive policy. In the long term, this will lead to a new world order in which the USA and Europe stand on one side, and Russia and China on the other. Yet with regard to free trade within Europe, the lively exchange with North and South America as well as with some Asian countries, it seems to me premature to completely abandon the motto "change through trade." This also applies to diplomatic efforts for fair peace treaties. At present, the war in Ukraine must be ended as quickly as possible in order to reach, through negotiations, a compromise that is bearable for both sides. With Kant, it is imperative never to give up hope for peace.

The problem of peace in Europe and the world points to a deeper level that is not limited to ceasefire and trade. It consists in the mutual *recognition of peoples and cultures*. Especially for this particular appreciation of foreign civilizations, the philosophy of the eighteenth century can serve as a model today. As shown, not a few authors described and valued the scientific, social, and political achievements in Persia, China and America.

The position of Europe has proven to be ambivalent: on the one hand as a high culture in its own right, on the other as threatened with decline. In our context, it is crucial that the widespread stereotype of Eurocentrism cannot be maintained. On the contrary, the position of cosmopolitanism and intercultural understanding can especially refer to the European Enlightenment.

---

[72] See the relevant passage on the supposed *deglobalization* in the ninth chapter.

This aspect will concern us again in the context of current *postcolonialism* at the beginning of the ninth chapter.

Enlightenment as legitimation.—At the same time, it has become clear how much the philosophers of the eighteenth century already possessed a *knowledge of Europe* that they expressed both literarily and practically. For all their diversity, they reflected more cultural commonalities than national differences would suggest. In the present day, the question arises as to what significance the memory of the European Enlightenment has for the social and political integration of Europe.

At this point, it suffices to summarize the provisional principles that have emerged from the comparison of the individual countries and that will be elaborated in detail. In doing so, I focus on the specifically *modern aspects* that developed in the second half of the eighteenth century.

At the beginning stands *religious tolerance*, which no longer primarily refers to theological dogmas, but aims at the recognition of the social function of religions. Corresponding to this is a claim to *truth*, which is based on scientific and thus empirical knowledge of reality. Furthermore, Europe is shaped by a *humanism* that owes itself to Enlightenment anthropology. It means understanding the human being holistically, with their thoughts and feelings, physical needs and labor, as well as their individual and collective claims to earthly happiness. The basis is a *civil society* that promises to guarantee economic prosperity and social justice. This also includes a *historical consciousness* that allows people to assure themselves of the changeability of their own culture and to entertain certain expectations for the future. Finally, Europe owes to its Enlightenment the validity of universal *human rights*. Even if the Enlighteners were not yet convinced democrats, they nevertheless set in motion the overcoming of authoritarian forms of government. In the core area of Europe, parliamentary *democracy* is still quite stable today.

More democracy.—Following from this, the problem arises as to how the *European Union* itself can be democratized. In order to dare more democracy in this sphere as well, *direct participation of citizens* is an option.[73] It would be possible, for example, to elect the European Parliament on the basis of transnational lists, in order to bring European citizens together politically across borders. Such a participatory democracy could be realized through referenda that would have a direct impact on certain political decisions of the European Union. Such a procedure would have to be harmonized across

---

[73] Goodman 1998, p. 357; Cheneval 2003, pp. 12 f.; Habermas 2008, pp. 123 f.; Verovšek 2020, p. 34.

Europe and limited to specific topics. This also includes the activation of a European public sphere, in which the issues at stake are debated. Those involved could be individuals, but also transnational organizations such as Amnesty International or social movements such as environmental activists, for example.

An already realized version consists in new forms of communication between political actors. A third way is intended to bridge the gap between the high pressure to solve problems and the limited political authorization of the European Union by the member states. In addition, it is meant to mediate between the two most important forms of decision-making: the "Community method," which requires unanimity, and the "intergovernmental method," in which national governments negotiate with each other. Because unanimity is difficult to achieve and the majority principle is not normatively justifiable, an additional method of *consensus formation* is needed.[74] Its purpose is to balance the social and cultural differences between the richer and poorer participants and to develop common guiding principles for market-correcting measures. This results in two different models of action, which are also philosophically interesting and can be traced back to the European Enlightenment.[75]

On the one hand, the European Union derives its legitimacy from *efficiency*, which consists in performance-oriented governance. This concerns both decisions and negotiations between the individual governments, which try to assert their national interests. Especially in the early days, this effectiveness was measured by the "logic" of the common market, then by the standards of political rationality. To solve problems here means to remove certain obstacles that stand in the way of economic and political integration. Technical regulations are used for this purpose, intended to increase the benefits for the member states.

On the other hand, there is *consensus*, which is to be achieved at the supranational level through deliberation oriented toward mutual understanding. Because the national starting points are very different and agreement on welfare-state content is hardly possible, binding decisions are avoided and the focus is on recommendations and opinions. In doing so, vertical hierarchies are avoided and emphasis is placed on argumentation and interaction. The participants are not only representatives of the

---

[74] This "Open Method of Coordination" (OMC) was developed in the 1990s and legally enshrined in the Treaty of Lisbon; see Lavenex 2006, pp. 100 f.
[75] See the social-philosophical passages in the seventh chapter.

European Council and governments, but also local state actors as well as non-state actors as representatives of the European public sphere. This also includes transnational movements or social networks for peace and the environment. The aim of these procedures is, not least, to implement new political content.

Goals.—These include a common *stability and growth package* with economic policy guidelines as well as a graduated harmonization of tax policy. As a reaction to the financial crisis of 2007 to 2009, in which the EU saved the major banks from collapse with tens of billions of euros, a tax on all financial transactions is being demanded. In addition, the European Central Bank should be required to offset inequalities in income and wealth. Furthermore, it makes sense to sanction persistent trade surpluses within the EU, so that countries like Germany have to pay penalties amounting to three percent of their surplus. Added to this is the recent intention to additionally tax extraordinary profits that result from energy shortages.

Equally necessary is a European *employment strategy*, which consists of an organization of the labor market, formulation of labor law with wage policy and co-determination, as well as a system of old-age security. As a result, every lawful resident of the EU receives a modest basic income, graduated by country. In particular, equality of the sexes in the workplace is ensured. Added to this are health and care policy as well as a common asylum policy with social inclusion.

The field of *science and education* is in particular need of support. Although Europe is the birthplace of the modern sciences, it is in danger of being pushed to the margins in global competition. Therefore, it must be ensured that Europe maintains its leading position in international competition. In the development of green and digital key technologies, Europe must not lose any time. Although Europe is a leader in basic research, it fails to develop market-ready products. This also includes the preservation of Europe's linguistic diversity. Therefore, publications should be promoted not only in English, but also in other European languages.

Recently, the *multiple crisis of energy supply* has been added. However, the shortages of fossil fuels are also an opportunity to accelerate the long-overdue ecological transformation. As early as the end of 2019, the European Commission conceived a "European Green Deal" with the goal of reducing net greenhouse gas emissions to zero by 2050 and thus becoming the first climate-neutral continent. There are even demands on the European Constitutional Convention to include the right of people to a healthy and protected environment in the European fundamental rights.

Given the current state of the European Union, this list may sound illusory. Recently, the disasters have been piling up to such an extent that their simultaneous management is hardly possible. Added to this are the political, social, and cultural differences between the member states, which make agreement difficult. Yet, due to the enormous external pressure, further *European integration* is required in the long term. Whether Europe should be limited to a "core country" that drives political integration forward may be doubted, since this would exclude other European countries. For Europe must assert itself as a whole against economic competition on the world market, which is only possible through increased economic cooperation. And it must also move closer together in foreign and military policy, which will probably result in a common foreign and defense ministry. Overall, a new European sovereignty is needed.

3

Critique of Religion

The European Enlightenment is closely linked to the process of secularization. At first, this is expressed in the *critique of religion*, especially of the doctrines of Christianity and the exercise of power by the Catholic Church. In addition, religion is opposed by its own principles, among which is the claim of *human reason*, to ground knowledge and ability in a secular manner. As we have seen, both the critique of religion and the self-foundation varied across the different countries of Europe. In Italy and especially in Spain, the clergy was so powerful that an open attack was out of the question. By contrast, the confrontation with the Anglican state church in Britain and with Protestantism in Germany was comparatively moderate. The critique was particularly radical in absolutist France, although atheistic positions were rather rare. While there was often agreement in philosophical matters, religious convictions diverged widely.

In the context of this book, the specific question arises as to what characterizes the Enlightenment critique of religion. As is well known, there had already been writings critical of religion since the early modern period, some of which were published or circulated in secret. The basic tenor consisted in a rationalist critique of the Christian faith as well as in the so-called priestcraft theory, according to which the clergy had "invented" religion in order to deceive and subjugate the people. Without doubt, these topoi continued in subsequent times.

Yet from my point of view, what is decisive is that the theoretical engagement with religion fundamentally changed in the second half of the 18th century. For, as already outlined, this period saw the emergence of entirely new subject areas and academic disciplines. And my thesis is that with these sciences, new theoretical means became available to criticize religion in correspondingly innovative ways and to establish an independent secular basis in its place. In *physics* of Newton, it now became possible to conceive of the cosmos as a self-dynamic system. The newly emerging *biology* with evolutionary approaches made it possible to explain the origin and development of human beings from natural causes. Entirely new as well was *philosophy of language*, with the help of which religious concepts such as God were discredited as a misinterpretation of human language. Thanks to *anthropology*, not only was the emotional basis of religion highlighted in order to create a "natural religion," but the idea of God was derived from the properties of human beings, thereby demonstrating anthropomorphism. In *social philosophy*, the Enlighteners were no longer content with accusations against "deceitful" priests, but investigated the social function of religion. This theorem was so successful that it was adopted by Catholic apologists. Finally, *philosophy of history* served to deconstruct the Christian origin myth, to investigate the political and cultural causes of sacred institutions, and thus to develop a genuinely historical consciousness of religion. I will attempt to show in detail how the aforementioned theories come to bear in this kind of critique of religion.

It is not an exaggeration to claim that this perspective on religion has, by and large, continued to develop into the social sciences and philosophy of the 20th century. Paradigmatic for this is the sociologist Max Weber, who summarized technical, scientific, and cultural modernization under the term "secularization" and described it as the "disenchantment of the world" or as the "rationalization" of all spheres of life.[1] Not a few authors explicitly placed themselves in the tradition of the European Enlightenment. To name just a few prominent examples: *The Philosophy of the Enlightenment* (1932) by Ernst Cassirer marked the beginning. In his main work *Man* (1944), Arnold Gehlen explicitly referred to Herder. Niklas Luhmann placed his entire life's work under the title *Sociological Enlightenment*. And the American social philosopher John Rawls developed his *Theory of Justice* (1971) on the basis of Enlightenment theories of the social contract. Jürgen Habermas's *Theory of Communicative Action* (1981) also stood in conscious tradition of Enlightenment and modernity, in particular of Kant's practical

---

[1] Max Weber: *The Protestant Ethic and the Spirit of Capitalism*. In: Collected Essays on the Sociology of Religion. Tübingen 1978, p. 93; cf. Lutz-Bachmann 2016, p. 81.

philosophy. Finally, the historian Reinhart Koselleck programmatically drew on Enlightenment historical thought for his theory of history.[2]

All this would hardly be worth mentioning if a drastic turn had not recently taken place. To be sure, there have always been conservative authors who recommended the Christian religion as a remedy for the allegedly ailing modernity. Likewise, some representatives of postmodernity flirt with religious ideas.[3] But suddenly, voices are multiplying that fundamentally question the fact of secularization. Strangely enough, this also includes authors such as Habermas, who in the 1980s still wanted to continue the "project of modernity" and now, since 2001, suddenly proclaims the "postsecular society" or even "postsecularism."[4]

The central objection to the diagnosis that today's societies are secularizing is that religion does not disappear completely in the process of secularization, but rather that articles of faith are transformed or displaced. Ultimately, the thesis of postsecularism contains the view that modernity requires a religious foundation. Because it allegedly *cannot* claim its own legitimacy, it is said to be dependent on premodern resources. It is even considered necessary to recover the semantic heritage of religions and to make their potential for meaning fruitful for today's lifeworld.[5] Here it becomes apparent that behind the discourses on secularization and postsecularism lies a deeper unease with contemporary civilization, which is perceived as deficient and in need of compensation.

In this chapter, I will take a position in this controversy by adopting the secular standpoint in the tradition of the European Enlightenment.

---

[2] Arnold Gehlen: *Man. His Nature and Place in the World*. Wiesbaden 1986, pp. 31–34; Luhmann 1970; Rawls 1975, pp. 27–34; Jürgen Habermas: *The Theory of Communicative Action*. Frankfurt a. M. 1981, vol. I, pp. 210–218; cf. Karl-Otto Apel: *Transformations of Philosophy*. Frankfurt a. M. 1973, vol. 2, p. 157; Koselleck 1979, pp. 17–37.

[3] Lübbe 1986, p. 9.—Giorgio Agamben: *Homo sacer*. Frankfurt a. M. 2002; Julia Kristeva: *This Incredible Need to Believe*. New York 2009; Terry Eagleton: *Reason, Faith, and Revolution*. New Haven 2010.

[4] On modernity: Habermas 1981, pp. 444–464; idem 1985, pp. 390–425; idem 1988, pp. 11–17.— On postsecularism: Habermas first in 2001 in *Faith and Knowledge* in his Peace Prize speech at the German Publishers and Booksellers Association; then Habermas 2005, pp. 119–154, 216–257; cf. Asal 2007, pp. 9 f.; Casanova 2016, pp. 16 f.; Lutz-Bachmann 2016, pp. 79–96; Renner 2017, pp. 103–109.—See also Rorty, Vattimo 2006; Taylor 2007.—On this topic complex also Ludwig Nagl (ed.): *Religion after the Critique of Religion*. Vienna, Berlin 2008; Herta Nagl-Docekal and Friedrich Wolfram (eds.): *Beyond Secularization*. Berlin 2008; Thomas Schmidt and Anette Pitschmann (eds.): *Religion and Secularization*. Stuttgart 2014.

[5] Habermas 2005, pp. 137, 218, 247, 255; Renner 2017, pp. 107 f.—Cf. previously Lübbe 1986, pp. 16 f., 133, 287–291; Casanova 2016, pp. 10–15, 18 f.; Lutz-Bachmann 2016, pp. 79 f.; Harari 2018, pp. 207 f., 216 f., 318 f.

In the first section, I will examine the *factual situation* in Europe and the world. Then I will address the *arguments* that are brought against the secularization thesis. In the fourth section, I will discuss the problem of how civil interaction between religious and secular citizens can be regulated. In the two intervening sections, I will address critique of religion during the Enlightenment era as well as the relationship between Enlightenment and Counter-Enlightenment. Not least, the limits of Enlightenment must also be taken into account. But such self-reflection does not necessarily lead to a postsecular rehabilitation of religion. The alternative that seems more convincing to me consists in a strengthening of Enlightenment in the sense of a critical and reflexive continuation of the secularization process.

Postsecular Society?

First, some *empirical data* on the current situation: In *Europe*, the process of secularization is quite obvious when one considers the individual attitude of citizens toward religion. The number of members of Christian denominations has been continuously declining for decades and, according to all forecasts, will continue to decrease. *France*—where the tradition of Enlightenment is particularly present—now has only about 60% Christians and about eight percent Muslims, while a quarter of the population considers itself unaffiliated. This trend has also taken hold in *Canada, Australia*, and *New Zealand*. Whereas in *Germany* in 1950, 95% of the population still belonged to one of the two Christian denominations, after reunification it was 72%; today it is just under 50% of the population. As a result of the abuse scandal, church departures have risen sharply, with more than 350,000 deregistrations in 2021 alone. A study commissioned by the churches predicts a further halving of memberships by the year 2060. As soon as the churches no longer represent the majority of the population, the previously self-evident sense of belonging turns into skepticism. Even in the southern countries, Italy and Spain, attachment to the Catholic Church is declining. Especially in *Spain*, where the Inquisition raged until the 18th century and where Franco's dictatorship was able to rely on the Catholic Church, just under 60% still feel affiliated with the Church, but only 20% practice their religious faith.[6] This specifically European secularization is undisputed.

---

[6] Pollack, Rosta 2015, pp. 89–195, 437 f.

When, on the other hand, there is talk of a "postsecular age," reference is made to countries outside of Europe, which is thereby declared the exception. As exemplary for this, are considered the *United States of America*, which are described as a religiously shaped country.[7] But even there, the connection to the churches is waning. Whereas fifty years ago two-thirds of adult Americans felt connected to a Protestant church, today it is less than half, while at least twenty percent now identify as "nones" with no denomination. In South America, too, where the Catholic Church has colluded with some military dictatorships, the number of church members is gradually declining. By contrast, in recent years the proportion of Christians has been rising in Africa and Asia. Overall, Islam is on the rise: currently, a quarter of the world's population are Muslims, and by 2030 it will probably be 35%. As a result of migration, the proportion in Europe is also rising from four to six percent. Nevertheless, these indications by no means refute the secularization thesis. For secularization is by no means a homogeneous process that does not allow for asynchronicities.

The frequently invoked USA strikingly demonstrate the other side of secularization when one considers the *constitution* of the American state. Here, the historical peculiarity becomes apparent that this nation has never been a theocratic state from which citizens first had to liberate themselves. On the contrary, since its founding, not only has there been freedom of religion, but—similarly to France—an absolute separation of state and religion. Conversely, this case shows that state autonomy and neutrality toward religions are fully guaranteed, entirely independent of the degree of religious practice among citizens. And it is precisely such independence of the state from religion that actually exists in most countries of the world, including Africa. This also applies to legislation and jurisdiction, which are no longer religiously grounded. Likewise, the sciences remain untroubled by ecclesiastical interference. Even in Great Britain, where there is a state church, political decisions are made independently of religion. In addition, there are only a few religiously motivated dictatorships, such as in Iran, the United Arab Emirates, and, to some extent, Turkey. From this perspective, secularization is a global success story, which is not even questioned by the proponents of so-called postsecularism.

Now, the postsecular counter-thesis is not only a matter of empirical facts, but above all of *normative evaluation*. Here, I have the impression that

---

[7] Graf 2004, pp. 14–16, 106–115; Habermas 2005, p. 123; Pollack, Rosta 2015, pp. 327 f., 401 f.; Casanova 2016, pp. 21–25; Reinalter 2016, p. 113; Renner 2017, p. 267.

the supposed resurgence of religions is somehow positively connoted. This may be understandable from a religious and theological perspective, since not a few theologians believe themselves to be experiencing a new upswing. How one-sided these judgments are is already evident in the fact that the negative flip sides of the new religious movements are ignored. It is almost macabre when, as evidence, the attack by Islamist terrorists on the towers of the World Trade Center in New York in September 2011 is repeatedly cited. Likewise, it is overlooked that it was the American evangelicals who, to a considerable extent, helped Donald Trump to power, ultimately even putting American democracy in jeopardy. Similar phenomena could be observed in Brazil among the supporters of Jair Bolsonaro. In addition, many COVID-deniers and anti-vaxxers often come from religious sects. So, if one is going to praise postsecularity, one is equally obliged to point out the new dangers to democracy, health, and peace.

In this normative context, I consider it worthwhile to investigate the deeper reasons that are supposed to support the sociological claim of a postsecular society. By also drawing on earlier justifications from the philosophy of religion and the history of philosophy, I would like to attempt to refute the corresponding *argumentation.*

The *first* argument advanced against the secularization thesis is that, in the social process, *religion* is *not simply superseded*, but rather persists in multifaceted ways. The process of secularization does not consist in a linear or even teleological development—which would amount to a poor philosophy of history—but must be understood in a differentiated way as transformation, recoding, or displacement.[8] Consequently, "residues of tradition" in religious dispositions always remain, which should not be abandoned but preserved.

However, I consider the notion of a purposeful and inevitable secularization, at the "end" of which all religions would have disappeared, to be a *polemical misunderstanding.* This already applies to the process of modernization, which has proven to be highly multifaceted. The same holds for the relationship between modernization and secularization, which are not automatically linked. Finally, secularization is not simply followed by a phase of a "return of religion." For even the term "postsecular" is problematic, as it suggests a chronological sequence from the religious to the irreligious and back again to the religious. Paradoxically, this would only apply to countries

---

[8] Asal 2007, pp. 9 f., 99; Lutz-Bachmann 2016, p. 81; Gabriel, K. 2016, pp. 218 f.—The philosophy-of-history dimension of the secularization thesis is emphasized by Charles Taylor, who speaks of a historical "stage-consciousness" of the secularizing modern age; Taylor 2007, p. 458; cf. Casanova 2016, pp. 16 f.

like Europe, which had been "previously" secularized. Rather, the history of religions is to be understood as a complex, multiple, and contingent process. In the following section, I will illustrate precisely this characteristic in the beginnings of secularization during the Enlightenment as an example.

Despite all the complexity and contradictions, I would also like to adhere to the *concept of secularization* for the present day. Among the reasons for this is, first of all, the existence of secular states throughout the world and the global practice of science independent of religion. Furthermore, the declining number of church members in several continents should not be marginalized. Finally, greater account must be taken of the internal transformation of religions. Members of religious communities tend to turn away from ecclesiastical authorities and theological doctrines. The much-demanded Catholic and Protestant ecumenism, which can only be implemented against the resistance of some church leaderships, is an example of how catechetical differences are being smoothed out in order to reach pragmatic arrangements. Increasingly, believers are developing individual convictions in which they combine elements from world religions and create their own *patchwork religion* or religious *bricolage*. In this way, religions become less confessional, clerical, dogmatic, and sacral. All these phenomena can rightly be characterized as secularization.

The *second* argument comes from Hermann Lübbe, who, for *philosophy of religion* reasons, doubts the *separation of social function and truth claim* of religions.[9] Therefore, it is not possible for believers to benefit from the effects of their religion on everyday life without being convinced of its religious content. This is comparable to the placebo effect of medications, which only work if the patient believes in their efficacy. Lübbe laments the loss of religious faith because he considers the social function of religion indispensable for the existence of any community.

Against this, it can be objected that in modern societies, this very case has long since become the norm: religions fulfill their *social functions*, while the contents of belief recede into the background. This is already evidenced by the dominant sociological interest in religious, secular, and postsecular societies. This is also reflected in the actual behavior of members of religious communities, who practice their religion without being interested in theological dogmas. What is central are the emotional experiences in the communities and social engagement, that is, the communication and interaction

---

[9] Lübbe 1986, pp. 60, 219 f.; cf. Luhmann 1977, p. 123; Kondylis 1981, p. 495; Renner 2017, p. 156; Frick 2020, p. 100.

of those directly involved. Young people flock to church conventions primarily to experience a sense of community. This also includes the commendable engagement of churches in kindergartens, schools, nursing homes, and hospitals. This trend is further reinforced by new social media. In this fact as well—that religion is retreating to its pragmatic side—I see further evidence for the process of secularization.

The *third* argument is situated in the context of the *history of philosophy* of Hans Blumenberg. In *The Legitimacy of the Modern Age*, he indeed impressively confirms the secularization of European culture in the transition from the late Middle Ages to the early modern period. He includes in this the sciences since Galileo and Descartes, which take the place of biblical revelation; the modern work ethic, which replaces the asceticism of Christianity; as well as the new philosophy of history, which supersedes Christian eschatology. But at the same time, Blumenberg criticizes the thesis of secularization, because he does not see in it a dissolution of religion, but rather a "transformation" or "reconfiguration" of religious contents.[10] Ultimately, he presupposes an identically persisting "substance" that is merely reassigned to new positions. According to this reading, all that remains of religion is a "substitute." The concept of secularization thus acquires the negative meaning of a failed transformation, because the religious substratum is lost.

Against the still widespread thesis of "substitute religion," I object that the construction of a spiritual substance that is, so to speak, eternally preserved through all ages is highly problematic. This is more reminiscent of antiquated metaphysics, which does not allow for any profound change. In principle, nothing genuinely new can then arise after religion, neither in the modern age nor in the Enlightenment and modernity. Moreover, I see in this an inadmissible origin myth, because Christianity is declared the source of all possible cultural phenomena. In loose adaptation of Hegel, the religious appears as an overarching universal, so that even the irreligious ultimately represents a distorted form of religiosity. Even atheism can then count as religion, because something is always believed, even if in this case the belief is that God does not exist. In determinate negation, the religious endlessly persists. Apparently, in this bad dialectical sense Blumenberg claims a "negative continuity" of religion.

---

[10] Blumenberg 1966, pp. 9–34.—Expanded, revised, and partially newly written versions appeared under separate titles: *The Process of Theoretical Curiosity* (1973) and *Secularization and Self-Assertion* (1974).—See also Rüdiger Zill: *The Absolute Reader. Blumenberg. An Intellectual Biography*. Frankfurt a. M. 2020, pp. 292, 475–489; cf. Habermas 1985, p. 16; Renner 2017, pp. 133 f.

Ultimately, this insinuates that no one is ever able to escape the sphere of religion. No matter what he or she says or does, they always produce nothing more than a religious substitute. Traditionally, capitalism and especially the pursuit of money are considered a modern religion. Recently, opponents of Europe have claimed its "sacralization." In the arts section, it is said that even a football match constitutes a worship service, in which the devoted fans form opposing congregations. Or the climate catastrophe is declared the new apocalypse, just as the activists against it become pietistic guardians of virtue or fanatical missionaries. This is also said of the protagonists of the new identity politics, which is said to have a pseudo-religious character. In any case, only surrogates result, which are treated quite ambivalently. On the one hand, they are supposed to demonstrate how inescapable religion is; on the other, the connotation with the religious turns into polemic. The secularized becomes a term of abuse. In view of such absolutist claims of the religious, I consider the secularization thesis to be an important corrective. It will also serve as a standard in the following account of the transition from the modern age to the Enlightenment.

The Social Function of Religion

The critique of religion in the Enlightenment has many facets. Only rarely did the Enlighteners advocate a consistent atheism; most of the time, they favored an enlightened religion in the form of deism. Thus, the spectrum of religious criticism ranges from the radical claim that the Christian religion is incompatible with human reason and therefore to be completely rejected, to the more moderate position of a separation of reason and faith, so that politics and science can no longer be troubled by the Catholic clergy. Basically, these attitudes continue the rationalist critique of religion of Pierre Bayle in the modern age.[11] But what is truly new compared to the critique of religion in the seventeenth century is that, in the European Enlightenment since the mid-eighteenth century, fundamentally different forms of critique of religion emerged, which are owed to the already mentioned new sciences of philosophy of language, anthropology, philosophy of history, and social philosophy.

---

[11] In the *Dictionaire historique et critique*, Pierre Bayle criticizes a number of Christian articles of faith; Bayle 1687.—On this see Schröder 1998, pp. 162 f., 254 f., 346 f.; Forst 2003, pp. 312–351; Mulsow 2006, pp. VII f.

Reason and faith.—I begin with the traditionally rationalist critique, which of course continues to live on until the end of the century. The sharpest objections come from Paul Thiry d'Holbach, who in his work *Christianity Unveiled* (1768) summons the Christian religion before the "tribunal of reason" and subjects it to rational scrutiny.[12] In doing so, he is not only troubled by the doctrine of the Trinity or the immortality of the human soul, as well as the tradition of miracles such as Jesus's resurrection. Rather, he grounds his critique much deeper, by criticizing the belief that an omnipotent God created the universe out of nothing—for him, an "incomprehensible act." Overall, he considers the Christian religion to be a construct of "absurdities, incoherent fables, senseless dogmas, childish ceremonies," and "superstition." For this reason, he demands that this "veil" of ignorance, credulity, and prejudice be torn apart.

The most well-known is probably the critique of religion by Voltaire, who has nothing but biting mockery left for Catholic doctrine. Added to this is his criticism of theodicy as formulated by Leibniz, which he ridicules in several stories.[13] Famous in this context is his motto "crush the infamous thing" (écrasez l'infâme), with which he expresses the hope: "Reason is advancing further in France every day."[14] Nevertheless, Voltaire distances himself from d'Holbach's atheism and aligns himself with deism. Denis Diderot too, in his *Philosophical Thoughts* (1746), criticizes biblical belief in miracles and Christian dogmatics.[15] He even considers superstition more dangerous than atheism. Yet, in contrast to d'Holbach, he ends with a surprising avowal of Christianity. Ultimately, Diderot aims at a rational religion that reconciles reason and faith.

An explicitly skeptical stance is taken by David Hume in his *Dialogues Concerning Natural Religion* (published posthumously in 1779). He fundamentally questions whether God created the world according to a plan.[16] It is difficult to determine whether his epistemological skepticism is inspired

---

[12] D'Holbach n.d., p. 55; for the following pp. 79, 84, 89, 99, 459 f.—See also *Letters to Eugénie* (1768); ibid., pp. 295–467. In the *Pocket Theology* (1768) there are satirical and blasphemous remarks about the Catholic Church; ibid., pp. 173–29. Also in the main work *System of Nature* (1770), the second part deals with "On the Deity"; d'Holbach 1960, pp. 273–559. See also *On Prejudices* (1769).—Against scholasticism Helvétius 1976, pp. 14 f., 42; Morelly 1964, p. 128.—Cf. Cassirer 1932, pp. 178 f.; Porter 1991, pp. 45–52; Schröder 1998, pp. 86 f., 171 f., 235 f.; Reinalter 2016, pp. 55, 59; Frick 2020, pp. 86 f.

[13] See Voltaire's critique of Leibniz in the context of the Lisbon earthquake in Chap. 5.

[14] Voltaire 1994, p. 282.

[15] Diderot 1961, vol. I, pp. 267 f.; cf. Schröder 1998, pp. 79 f.; Stenger 2013, pp. 190–204.

[16] Hume 1968, pp. 7, 12, 16; see also Stollberg-Rilinger 2000, pp. 94–97; Thoma 2018, pp. 149–153.

by his critique of religion, or whether his conception of natural religion is influenced by his epistemology. In my view, philosophical skepticism was decisive, so that the theoretical foundation predominates. Skepticism here means the critique of a doubting agnostic.

The rigorously rational standpoint toward religion is represented by Immanuel Kant in his work *Religion within the Bounds of Mere Reason* (1793). As the title suggests, he is concerned with the separation of human reason and religious faith. And, like a thunderclap, he immediately makes clear: "Morality, insofar as it is based on the concept of the human being as a free being, and therefore as a being that binds itself by its own reason to unconditional laws, needs neither the idea of another being above him [...]".[17] This also applies to the sciences, which should not be destroyed by the presumptuous "censorship" of the clergy. Conversely, biblical and philosophical theology as practiced at the faculties should "move only within the boundaries of mere reason." In this, he sees a guarantee for "tolerance," which should not be limited to an "arrogant name," i.e., to the condescending contempt of a prince, but should consist in the mutual recognition of citizens.[18] A reason-guided critique of religion could hardly be more explicit.

Now I will show that the later Enlightenment offers significantly different and less well-known critical potentials, which one must actively seek out.

Religion as a problem of language.—While John Locke had already supplemented his investigation of human understanding with some reflections on the philosophy of language, it was Étienne Bonnot de Condillac who, in his *Essay on the Origin of Human Knowledge* (1746), placed human language at the center of epistemology.[19] Since he himself was a clergyman, his philosophy of language contained little criticism of religion. But soon other Enlightenment thinkers such as d'Alembert, Helvétius and Diderot recognized its critical potential by holding the "abuse" of language responsible for the emergence and spread of religious "prejudices."[20]

It was only d'Holbach who explicitly made the philosophy of language into a new theoretical tool of his critique of religion.[21] He accuses Catholic

---

[17] Kant 1965, vol. VIII, p. 649; for what follows, pp. 654 f.—Cf. Möller 1986, p. 71; Godel 2007, p. 94; Habermas 2005, p. 216; Forst 2003, pp. 418–436; Reed 2009, pp. 9 f.

[18] Kant 1965, vol. XI, p. 60; cf. Reed 2009, p. 214.

[19] Condillac 2006, p. 58.

[20] D'Alembert 1989, pp. 33, 36, 59; Helvétius 1973, pp. 95–101; idem 1976, pp. 14 f., 78, 126 f.; Diderot: article "Encyclopédie," in: Encyclopédie 1972, p. 417.

[21] Not yet in *Christianity Unveiled*, but in the later works *Letters to Eugénie* and *The System of Nature*: d'Holbach n.d., p. 257; idem 1960, pp. 273, 278, 283, 300 f.

priests of using "only meaningless words," and complains that the terms used in religious discourse do not correspond to any clear ideas. Thus, the word "God," which refers to an unknown cause of the world, remains incomprehensible and obscure. The words "incorporeal substance" and "infinity" are also abstract and indeterminate expressions. From this, he derives the demand that all concepts of human language should be linked to clear ideas, i.e., to sensory perceptions and established experiences. From his perspective, this means that religious belief cannot withstand not only the test of mere reason, but also that of linguistic scrutiny.

Among the authors of a critique of religion grounded in the philosophy of language is also Hume. Toward the end of his *Dialogues*, he complains that in debates about religion there is a "dispute about words" that can only be resolved by precisely determined ideas and clear definitions.[22] He is therefore of the opinion "that the dispute concerning theism [...] is merely verbal in nature." Because he adopts an agnostic position, he concludes that a clear decision about such disputes over words is not possible. What is remarkable about this statement is that he now adds a critique of language to his originally epistemological skepticism. And what is particularly interesting is that this extension of his argumentation occurs in the context of the critique of religion.

Anthropological Foundation and Anthropomorphism.—The anthropological turn also decisively shaped the critique of religion in the eighteenth century.

First, the *foundation of religion* undergoes a fundamental transformation. Now, it is no longer solely human reason that guarantees clear boundaries are drawn between church dogma and popular superstition. Instead, the resulting void is filled by the new *theory of the affects*, which is now declared the basis of religious belief. Thus, it soon becomes a topos of the Enlightenment that humans have a "need" for religion, which ultimately rests on certain "feelings." In the radical variant of a d'Holbach, this insight serves to dismiss religious belief as "consolation" and "habit."[23] Among the deists, by contrast, there is consensus that humans have, in a positive sense, a "natural inclination" toward religion. This is the core of the many conceptions of a "natural religion."[24] Even in this turn toward human nature, the tendency toward secularization is confirmed.

---

[22] Hume 1968, pp. 108 f.; for what follows, p. 111.

[23] D'Holbach n.d., pp. 65, 75, 170; idem 1960, pp. 274, 278, 285.

[24] Hume 1968, pp. 79, 89, 105, 113; Diderot: Article "Irreligious," in: Encyclopedia 1972, p. 712; Rousseau 1976, p. 107.—With some distance, also Kant 1965, vol. VIII, pp. 649, 652; cf. Himmelfarb 2004, p. 25.

More important to me seems the theorem of *anthropomorphism*, which can be traced in the second half of the eighteenth century. It consists in the claim that it was not God who created humans in his "image," but rather that it is humans who, after their own model, form a conception of God.

Again, already in d'Holbach we read about religion: "Humans thus drew these ideas from themselves; their soul served as the model for the universal soul [God]; their mind was the prototype of the mind that governs nature [...] finally, the qualities that humans call *perfection* in themselves, in miniature, were the prototypes for divine *perfection*. Thus theologians were and always will be *anthropomorphists*; for they can always make only humans the sole model for the deity."[25] In this sense, for him God is a "human-like being" in whom all human qualities are united and heightened. What is entirely new in this critique, which anticipates the nineteenth century,[26] is that the human being is declared the sole center of the critique of religion.

It may be surprising that this kind of critique of religion also appears in a skeptic like Hume, albeit in the *Dialogues* in the form of a salvific critique. In order to keep open the possibility of religious belief, people, to whom the attributes of God are "hidden," should beware of imagining God "with a human body or human mind."[27] Accordingly, there is no "similarity" whatsoever between God and humans. Thus, one must abandon the idea that God created the world "like a builder." Likewise, one should not project human qualities such as "justice, benevolence, or mercy" into the essence of God. Hume repeatedly uses the term "anthropomorphism," which is very rarely attested in other authors.[28] In this case, he makes defensive use of it, which affirms the primacy of anthropology.

Directly in relation to Hume, Kant distinguishes in dealing with "anthropomorphism" between a *dogmatic* and a *symbolic* use of the term. With Hume, he shares the concerns about transferring predicates from the human sensory world to a being entirely distinct from the world. But against Hume, he considers it unobjectionable and even advantageous that people imagine the world "*as if* it derived its existence and inner determination from a

---

[25] First in the *System of Nature*: d'Holbach 1960, pp. 299f.; cf. pp. 311, 322, 328; likewise idem n.d., p. 79; cf. Helvétius 1976, p. 42.

[26] This points to Ludwig Feuerbach: *The Essence of Christianity* (1841), in: Collected Works, ed. by Werner Schuffenhauer, vol. 5, Berlin 1984.

[27] Hume 1968, pp. 18f., 40, 85, 102.

[28] In addition, Hume also mentions the "anthropomorphites," members of a religious sect who still used the term affirmatively; Hume 1968, pp. 18, 39, 40, 42, 46, 50, 54, 71, 85, 87.—A deeper justification is already found in the *Treatise of Human Nature*, where Hume criticizes "that the mind has a great tendency to project itself into the objects of the external world"; Hume 1973, vol. I, p. 226.

supreme reason."²⁹ In such a mode of speech, he sees a "middle way" to avoid Hume's agnosticism and at the same time to ensure a religion suited to human beings. This compromise, too, once again confirms the anthropological approach in a double sense, by rejecting theoretical anthropomorphism and at the same time pragmatically accommodating the sensual character of human nature.

Religion and history.—In the course of the new historiography and philosophy of history that emerged around the middle of the eighteenth century, religion too acquires a history—but no longer as a traditional history of salvation, rather as a component of a general development of culture. A fitting example is Hume's *The Natural History of Religion* (1757), which makes the emergence of polytheism dependent on the "progress of human societies" such as animal husbandry and agriculture. The prerequisites for the subsequent monotheism, he sees in further cultural achievements such as writing, technology, science, and enlightenment. However, Hume breaks this developmental line by depicting non-simultaneities and mutual intermixtures.[30] Moreover, he sees in theism the danger of dogmatism, intolerance, and inquisition.

This parallel between profane and sacred history is broken by Condorcet. He adopts the then-common cliché of the "dark Middle Ages," which followed the flourishing of antiquity and was overcome by the Renaissance, modernity, and the Enlightenment. Thus, in the fifth epoch of his *Historical Sketch of the Progress of the Human Mind*, he lets a period of cultural "decline" follow, for which he holds Christianity responsible.[31] Christianity, he argues, arose because the secular empires became weaker; but likewise, Christianity contributed to cultural decline through its "contempt for human knowledge." For Condorcet, the critique of religion consists in the fact that Christianity is, as it were, classified as a disruption of the universal process of civilization.

Already forty years earlier, Turgot had attempted to prove the exact opposite, namely in his then still unpublished *Lecture on the Advantages that the Emergence of Christianity Has Brought to Humanity*.[32] Like Condorcet, Turgot is one of the staunch supporters of the idea of progress, but precisely

---

[29] *Prolegomena*, Kant 1965, vol. V, pp. 235f.

[30] Hume 1984, pp. 2–14, 44.—D'Holbach's second part of the *System of Nature* (On the Deity) also consists in a history of religion: from natural religion to polytheism, theism, and deism; he even lets "atheism" follow; d'Holbach 1960, pp. 472–545.

[31] Condorcet 1976, pp. 81–113; cf. Im Hof 1993, p. 223.

[32] Turgot 1990, pp. 117–139; cf. my introduction ibid., pp. 32–36.

for this reason, in contrast to Condorcet, he seeks to bridge the cultural-historical valley caused by Christianity between the two peaks of Antiquity and Modernity, in order to be able to claim an unbroken continuity of civilizational progress. For these reasons, Turgot is eager to enhance the cultural value of Christianity by pointing to civilizational achievements in this era as well, especially in metaphysics. Again, it is not about theological content, but solely about the practical "utility" of religion.

Without being able to refer to Turgot, Herder also pursues the same goal of revaluing the Christian Middle Ages. Yet the irony now is that in doing so, he does not adopt a perspective of progress, but on the contrary, demonizes the idea of progress: "The *dark* sides of this period are in all the books: every classical beau penseur who considers the policing of our century the non plus ultra of humanity has the opportunity to belittle entire centuries as *barbarism* [...] and to exult over the *light* of our century [...]. All the books of our *Voltaire* and *Hume, Robertson* and *Iselin* are full of this."[33] In this case, the Christian religion serves as a discursive plaything in a fundamental confrontation with the European Enlightenment.

However diverse the voices may be, the common tenor is still perceptible: religion is treated as a secularized phenomenon. The theological articles of faith, which were central to rationalist critique, shift to the periphery. Much more important now is the effect Christianity has had on the development of society, state, and culture. This adaptation to a profane philosophy of history goes so far that the world religions are not only set in parallel to the historical epochs of civilization, but are even themselves understood as civilizational stages. The criterion is not the increase of religious certainty, but the role of religion in social development.

The social function of religion.—The Enlightenment's critique of religion is indeed a double-edged sword. If the theological claim to truth is disputed, it would only be consistent to dispense with religion altogether. However, only very few Enlightenment thinkers draw this consequence. Instead, most authors of the eighteenth century adhere to Christianity because they do not want to forgo its *social functions*. While Pierre Bayle had claimed that a false religion is worse than no religion at all and that a society of virtuous atheists is quite conceivable,[34] most representatives of the Enlightenment shy away from such a radical step. With different interpretations, they consider

---

[33] Herder 1984, vol. I, pp. 629 f.

[34] Notably, in explicit distance from atheism; quoted in Schröder 1998, pp. 162 f.; cf. Forst 2003, p. 312;

bourgeois society not stable enough to assert itself entirely independently in economy, politics, and morality. In place of theology and metaphysics arise an empirical *sociology* and *comparative study of religion*.

The sociological and comparative approach to the topic of religion is best studied in Montesquieu, who, with his *Spirit of Law*, is among the founders of modern sociology. He explicitly emphasizes that in his work he speaks "not as a theologian, but as a politician" and wants to "examine the various religions in the world only with regard to their utility." In this sense, he opposes Bayle by turning Bayle's provocative thesis on its head, arguing that "religion, even if it is false, offers people the best guarantee of their honesty toward one another."[35] Therefore, it is less a matter of "the truth or falsity of a doctrine of faith" than of its useful or harmful application. Thus, even the "most erroneous doctrines of faith can have excellent consequences." Here, Montesquieu sees the deeper reason for "religious tolerance," to which he devotes a separate chapter. In it, he distinguishes between "toleration" and "recognition" of a religion, considering it sufficient that citizens tolerate one another or "do not disturb" each other.[36] As a positive example, he cites the "religion of Confucius." In this way, the hiatus between religious content and social function is taken to its extreme.

In concrete terms, Montesquieu attempts to show that it is people alone who create their own religion, and that they do so under certain *climatic, geographical, and political conditions*. Thus, Catholicism arose in southern countries, where monarchies generally prevail, and Protestantism in northern regions with republics.[37] Here, function and genesis are mutually dependent. In order for religion to fulfill its task, it must be adapted to the respective conditions of its emergence. Once again, religion is placed in a profane context, now less in terms of the philosophy of history than of social science.

In a similar way, Hume also justifies the social function of religion in his *Dialogues*: "Religion, however corrupt it may be, is still better than no religion at all."[38] Here, he emphasizes more the *moral-philosophical* aspect, highlighting the positive influences of religion on the "heart of man." At this point, Hume's anthropologically grounded theory of emotion and motivation comes into play once again. In a similar vein, Helvétius proposes

---

[35] Montesquieu 1951, vol. II, pp. 168, 177; cf. Forst 2003, pp. 359 f.; Himmelfarb 2004, p. 116.
[36] Montesquieu 1951, vol. II, book XXV, Chap. 9 : "On Religious Tolerance," p. 196; cf. Helvétius 1976, pp. 46, 208–218.
[37] Montesquieu 1951, vol. II, p. 165.
[38] Hume 1968, p. 112.

a "world religion" whose only "cult" should consist in the realization of human happiness. In a more attenuated form, this also applies to Kant's moral philosophy of reason, who certainly appreciates religion "for strengthening the moral incentive."[39]

The radicalism of d'Holbach's critique of religion is also evident in this social-philosophical context. First, he employs the classical priest-craft theory: "Religion seems to have been invented only to make rulers and peoples alike slaves of the priesthood," thereby exploiting the "ignorance and gullibility" of people.[40] In this way, he opposes the widespread view that the common people need religion in order to maintain the state order. More than that: d'Holbach not only denies any benefit of religion, but even considers religious practices to be harmful, because they undermine industriousness, promote priestly celibacy, and sow discord in society. Since he thus denies the Christian religion any moral gain, he argues that states and peoples should abandon all forms of religion and establish only secular laws. In this way, he dissolves the traditional alliance between religion and politics, or church and state. Even if one does not share this atheism, it must be conceded that it is more sincere than a merely instrumental use of religion.

Against d'Holbach's atheism it is above all Voltaire who takes up the fight, although he is among the most well-known critics of the Catholic Church. His reasons are exclusively utilitarian in nature, because he is not willing to give up the social function of religion. Thus, in his *Philosophical Dictionary*, he distinguishes between "bad" and "good prejudices," which serve the public interest.[41] When Voltaire advocates religious tolerance, he insists on the usefulness of religion for politics and morality. This also applies, in a more moderate form, to Diderot, who vacillates between the extremes: He is aware both of the disadvantages of the Christian religion for society and of the advantages of the disciplining effect of religious rituals. In his article "Intolerance" in the *Encyclopédie*, he advocates both ecclesiastical and state tolerance,[42] which he considers the only path to greater humanity.

In contrast, Jean-Jacques Rousseau occupies a special position. While other Enlightenment thinkers were content with the existing religions

---

[39] Helvétius 1976, pp. 44 f.; Kant 1965, vol. VIII, p. 652.

[40] D'Holbach n.d., pp. 68, 70, 134; likewise pp. 315, 437.—See also Helvétius 1976, pp. 133–138, 454–465; Morelly 1964, pp. 128–131.—Cf. Kondylis 1981, p. 361; Schröder 1998, pp. 86 f.; Asal 2007, pp. 80 f.

[41] Voltaire 1994, pp. 271 f.; cf. Saul 1992, pp. 10 f.; Forst 2003, pp. 383 f.

[42] Encyclopédie 1972, p. 710.—In the article "Celibacy" Diderot criticizes its unnaturalness and uselessness; ibid., p. 191. In his novel *The Nun* (1796) he imagines sadistic practices in convents.

because they considered the prevailing conditions to be reasonably stable, in his *Discourse on Inequality* he fundamentally questions bourgeois society. Therefore, his later work *The Social Contract* (1762) contains a contract intended to constitute a new state. In the final chapter, "On Civil Religion," Rousseau devises his own "catechism of the citizen." The first two principles, concerning the existence of God and life after death, correspond to Christian doctrine; the third principle, concerning the "sanctity of civil laws," adds a political element. Apart from the fact that the religious truth content remains open even in this case, this draft is not without contradictions: On the one hand, the principles are so general that citizens of different confessions can agree to them. On the other hand, however, these articles of faith, established by the sovereign and by no means religiously neutral, are so binding that dissent, especially atheistic reservations, are no longer tolerated, whereby this conception takes on totalitarian features.[43] Obviously, in Rousseau's case, this is not a general problem of political legitimacy in modernity,[44] rather, his concept of "civil religion" is essentially nourished by his critique of civilization.

Ideology critique.—In summary, I note that this more or less radical critique of religion is at the same time also various forms of a genuine *critique of ideology*. This is not only to be understood as the demonstration that certain religious beliefs are "false" because they contradict the truth; beyond that, the *reasons for the corresponding errors* are also to be demonstrated. The first approaches to this can be found in Francis Bacon's "doctrine of idols."[45] But since the mid-18th century, the aforementioned sciences have been added, which give religious criticism new dimensions. Through *philosophy of language*, religious concepts such as God can be traced back to an inappropriate use of linguistic signs. Thanks to *anthropology*, religious ideas prove to be projections of human characteristics. In the course of the emerging *sociology*, the content of belief is replaced by the interest in the social function of religion. Specifically social-scientific is also the attempt to explain the emergence of religion not only as an "invention" of priests, but to investigate the climatic, social, and mental factors of populations.

---

[43] Rousseau 1977, pp. 195–208; similarly Volney 1977, p. 210.—Cf. Im Hof 1993, p. 219; Forst 2003, pp. 368 f.; Asal 2007, pp. 13, 100 f., 111; Pečar, Tricore 2015, p. 63.

[44] Rousseau's solution is therefore not "premodern," intended to compensate for a general "deficit" of modernity, as Sonja Asal claims; Asal 2007, pp. 85 f., 97.

[45] Francis Bacon: *New Organon of the Sciences* (1620), in which he examines certain "prejudices." Bacon 1971, pp. 32–45.

Enlightenment and Counter-Enlightenment

If one considers philosophy in the second half of the 18th century in Europe, one should not overlook the fact that not all philosophers saw themselves as Enlighteners and that quite a few authors opposed this movement.[46] In response to the critique of religion of the Enlightenment, a counter-critique immediately arose, put forward by the *apologists* of the Catholic Church. This so-called *Counter-Enlightenment* had relatively great influence in France and especially in Italy and Spain.

Counter-Enlightenment.—In this context, extensive critiques of the works of Voltaire, Rousseau, d'Holbach, Helvétius and others emerged, whereby the differences were leveled out. In the polemics, the criticized positions appeared much more radical than they actually were, for example when deists were labeled as atheists or natural philosophers as materialists. A closer examination of the apologetic writings shows that many of these critics indeed operated within the discursive field of the Enlightenment, explicitly employing its arguments in order to measure their opponents by their own standards and to fight them with their own weapons. With their often precise criticism, they also drew attention to the weaknesses and contradictions of the Enlighteners. In this way, a complex and differentiated context of Enlightenment and Counter-Enlightenment emerged. Thus, it seems more appropriate to speak of an overarching Enlightenment culture.

One of the best-known and probably also most capable representatives of Catholic apologetics in *France* was Nicolas-Sylvestre Bergier, who was indeed respected by Enlighteners such as Voltaire, Diderot and d'Holbach.[47] His writings were translated into Italian and Spanish and thus indirectly contributed to the dissemination of Enlightenment ideas.

In our context, it is particularly interesting how Bergier employs the same scholarly disciplines that had already been used in the religious critiques he criticized. At first, he presents a rational counter-critique by attempting to show that Christian revelation can indeed be reconciled with human reason. Since this is hardly feasible for certain dogmas such as the doctrine of

---

[46] In Ireland, the Protestant bishop George Berkeley had already earlier criticized Newton's physics. Like Hume later, he doubted that the force of gravity could be directly perceived. But instead of resorting to skepticism, he believed that God was the cause of mechanical movements. Berkeley 1964, p. 60.—For a critical view, see Hume 1973, vol. I, pp. 216 f.

[47] Sylviane Albertan-Coppola in: Rohbeck, Holzhey 2008, pp. 731–750; cf. Albertan-Coppola, McKenna 2003, p. 1 f.; Reinalter 2006, p. 281 f.; idem 2016, p. 20, 143; Gerrard 2006, p. 17; Asal 2007, pp. 13–17; Jung 2012, p. 89.—On "Catholic Enlightenment" in Germany, see Schmitt-Maaß et al. 2022, Introduction, pp. 7–16.

the Trinity, in the *Traité historique de la vraie religion* (1780) he turns to a historiographical mode of argument, embedding the history of Christianity within the entire history of humanity. Finally, in his *Apologie de la religion chrétienne* (1769), which is directly aimed against d'Holbach, Bergier emphasizes the social function of the Christian religion for the preservation of society and the state. He even refers to religious rites and ceremonies as "social glue."[48] Even with such a cleric, the argument shifts from metaphysically oriented theology to a theory of the sociology of religion.

In *Spain* the Catholic Church exercised such a rigorous rule that even the most moderate religious criticism was impossible.[49] The apologists primarily criticized the French authors such as Voltaire, d'Holbach and Rousseau, whereby Rousseau's contrary position appeared incidental. The critics presented their works, which they had apparently read in the original, so thoroughly and precisely that Spanish intellectuals could inform themselves quite well and even take an interest in them. Here, too, a similar tendency as in French apologetics becomes apparent: not only are the theological "errors" of the deists and atheists listed, but the "utility" of religion for the maintenance of political and social order is also emphasized. It is precisely in strictly Catholic Spain that this kind of internal secularization of religion is striking.

A somewhat different situation is found in *Italy*, where the Catholic Inquisition did not rage quite as fiercely as in Spain. Accordingly, the position of the northern Italian Enlighteners such as Pietro Verri and Cesare Beccaria was ambivalent. At first, like the Spanish, they condemned every form of atheism and maintained their Christian faith, which they regarded as a private matter; but then they sharply criticized the Catholic Church—not only its theological dogmas, but above all the *Church as a social and political institution*.[50] They demanded the limitation of the Church's power, specifically the curtailment of the decadent papacy, the abolition of clerical privileges, and even the dissolution of religious orders. Beccaria denounced the torture and death penalty of the Inquisition. Here, too, it becomes clear that the social-critical and thus ultimately secular aspects gain significance.

Summary.—At the end of this overview of Enlightenment religious criticism, it can be summarized that the positions are highly diverse: they range

---

[48] Quoted in Albertan-Coppola in: Rohbeck, Holzhey 2008, p. 784.
[49] Francisco Sánchez-Blanco in: Rohbeck, Rother 2016, pp. 324–344.
[50] Carlo Borghero in: Rohbeck, Rother 2011, pp. 207–243; likewise Rother 2005, pp. 187–224.

from theism and deism to atheism and even to a specifically constructed state religion. Since Catholic apologetics also adapts to the new discourses, it can be included in this ensemble. What is decisive are the forms of criticism that are indebted to the aforementioned sciences. For the controversy discussed at the outset between the secularization thesis and postsecularism, this has several consequences.

First, secularization from the very beginning involves the *separation of the social function of religion from its religious content*. All currents share the feature that the truth claim of religion fades, and the demonstration of practical functions in society and the state comes to the fore. While the apologists still insist on religious faith, the other Enlighteners consider theological content to be rather secondary.

Second, the *motives* for such instrumentalization are very different. The apologists are obviously concerned with saving the power of their church, even if they have to make secular concessions to do so. Atheists like d'Holbach believe they can do without the stabilizing influence of religion. The other Enlighteners consider this too risky and want to secure bourgeois society in terms of worldview. Rousseau, in turn, who criticizes this social system, designs a new state, which he wants to flank with corresponding confessions of faith. Thus, behind the plea for or against religion there is no abstract deficit *of* modernity, but rather the concrete affirmation or critique of specific phenomena of modern civilization.

Thirdly, it was shown that the *process of secularization* has taken place through various transformations and shifts. Thus, there can be no talk of a "complete" dissolution of religion. This is demonstrated by the very concepts of a "natural religion" of Hume, Diderot and Rousseau. Nevertheless, tendencies toward deconfessionalization, desacralization, and functionalization for secular purposes can be identified. Secularization is therefore by no means a mere "thesis," but rather a sufficiently documented fact of this epoch.

Fourthly, from this development arises the ethical and political principle of *tolerance*, in which one can see the common denominator of the European Enlightenment. Yet here, too, there are significant differences. As noted, Rousseau allows the commandment of tolerance only within the Christian confessions, which he levels dogmatically, while he behaves with pronounced intolerance toward atheism. Other authors are much more consistent in this regard. Montesquieu distinguishes between toleration and recognition, giving preference to politically motivated toleration. Diderot tends more toward recognition, in order to ensure a deeper sense of humanity. And when Kant opposes the arrogance of princes disguised as tolerance, he too advocates for social and religious recognition. In place of a top-down tolerance, he puts mutual understanding among citizens.

Religious and Secular Tolerance

Now I will build a bridge from the 18th to the 21st century by continuing the discourse of secularization. Here, the focus is neither on empirical data nor on the fundamental objections to the secularization thesis, which were already discussed in the first section, but rather on the current conceptions that are being developed for the practical handling of religion. Religious tolerance means that citizens bound to a confession, as well as atheists, respect the various religions. Secular tolerance here is to mean that atheists are also respected by society and are officially represented in its cultural institutions. From this horizontal level, the following discussion distinguishes the vertical level, which refers to the ideological neutrality of the liberal constitutional state.

Following the types of Enlightenment criticism of religion analyzed above, the following *transformations* initially result.

Separation of reason and faith.—This principle has now become standard. This applies especially to scientific knowledge, which is no longer fundamentally questioned from any side, not least because this would mean forgoing technological and economic effects. One of the few exceptions is creationism in the USA, that is, the belief in the biblical creation myth taken literally, which results in the rejection of the biological theory of evolution. Although this does not restrict academic research, in some states the teaching of Darwin is not permitted in general education schools.[51] The creationists are thus today's counter-Enlightenment thinkers. Conversely, theology has long since abandoned the claim to justify religious faith by means of reason. Ultimately, this would mean denying the irreligious the capacity for rational knowledge. Therefore, the focus is limited to hermeneutic, historiographical, sociological, and pastoral aspects.

For the relationship between *human beings and history*, it still holds today that religion cannot be separated from the needs and ideas of people and has its own history, which is embedded in general history. With regard to

---

[51] Creationism is by no means limited to the USA, but is widespread worldwide. As recently as 2006, the Catholic philosopher Robert Spaemann, at Ratzinger's request, organized a symposium at the University of Munich to criticize the theory of evolution. Graf 2004, pp. 166–202, especially p. 192.

the process of secularization, two problems arise. On the one hand, radical Enlightenment can be extended so that polytheism is followed by monotheism, deism, and finally even atheism. Especially in France, this tradition culminates in laïcité, which has now entered a crisis. On the other hand, as mentioned, the recent slogan is "post-secular society," according to which religion has returned on a global scale. But when Habermas agrees with this diagnosis, he does not claim that modern societies are turning their backs on the secular. More precisely, he means a "changed self-understanding of a largely secularized society,"[52] that is, a *change in the consciousness* of religion. This also includes the *social function of religion*, which has by no means lost its relevance. Habermas here recalls Enlightenment thinkers such as Hume, Montesquieu and Voltaire, for whom the religious content was indifferent and who were interested solely in the social effects.

Finally, the theories about the *language of religion* are transformed. As has been shown, in the 18th century, religion was for the first time declared a problem of language, by criticizing the "incorrect" use of religious concepts. In the 21st century, by contrast, the focus is on linguistically mediated communication between religious and secular citizens. The new topic, then, is the significance of religion in *public discourse* in liberal societies.

In order to discuss the difficulties that arise here in more detail, I will refer to Habermas, who in turn engages with the American social philosopher John Rawls.

Religion in social dialogue.—In *Political Liberalism* (1992/93) Rawls demands of the citizens of a liberal society that they justify their political aims normatively.[53] While citizens are permitted to express their religious opinions privately, in public political discourse *all* citizens are to refrain from invoking religious reasons. Here, only secular arguments are to be accepted, presented in a generally comprehensible language. This creates an asymmetrical challenge for the participants. While for secular citizens the private and public language coincide, religious citizens are confronted with the epistemic demand to view their religious convictions, as it were, from the outside and to translate them into the language of public reason.

Habermas considers Rawls' proposal to be "secularist," because he believes that it does justice neither to religious nor to secular citizens.[54] For *religious*

---

[52] Quoted from an interview in Casanova 2016, p. 17; Habermas 2005, p. 118.
[53] Rawls 2003, pp. 314–316, 321 f., 349 f.; see also Rawls 1975, p. 140; cf. Lutz-Bachmann 2016, pp. 86–88.
[54] Habermas 2005, pp. 129–137; Lutz-Bachmann 2016, pp. 88, 90; Renner 2017, p. 133.

citizens, this means that they should *not* be expected to translate their religious convictions into secular arguments for the liberal public. One cannot demand of them that they justify their political positions independently of their religious faith. For *secular citizens*, according to Habermas, this means that they should show solidarity with religious citizens by helping them to formulate their certainties of faith in the language of public discourse.

However, this argumentation by Habermas is not very convincing.

The claim that *religiously oriented citizens* are not at all able to articulate their judgments and actions in a generally comprehensible and secular language does not correspond to public perception. That may apply to some sects or isolated religious communities, perhaps also to migrants who do not master the national language, but in reality, modern societies are already so secularized that political aims and measures are negotiated in a general discourse. I consider it a misguided consideration and an arrogant underestimation to deny believers such competence. For example, someone who supports the prohibition of abortion for religious reasons is required not to appeal to divine revelation, but to invoke a universally valid "right to life." Such a discourse is not only "rational" but explicitly also "secular," since only a worldly mode of legitimation is permitted.

The same applies to *secular citizens*, of whom Habermas draws an equally unrealistic picture. These people remain curiously abstract, as if they were guided solely by reason and used only rational arguments. Yet we know that even irreligious people have certain worldviews that do not necessarily have to be rational. Psychological research on prejudice has shown that moral problems are mostly solved with irrational intuitions. In addition, there are unpleasant resentments against homosexuals, foreigners, people with disabilities, or the impoverished, which are not acceptable. It is therefore only consistent to require secular citizens as well to translate their private convictions into publicly recognized arguments and into a language capable of consensus.

With regard to the topic of secularization, a further distinction must be made. On the *horizontal level*, secularization, as just discussed, means that secular citizens can and should communicate with the remaining religious citizens.[55] Following the European Enlightenment, this concerns the topic of *tolerance*. Instead, Rainer Forst today proposes the concept of *respect* to characterize the desired behavior between persons who employ rational

---

[55] Taylor 2007, pp. 531 f.; Casanova 2016, pp. 10–15, 18 f.; Lutz-Bachmann 2016, pp. 79 f.

arguments.[56] By tolerance, he understands the overarching principle of practical justification, which should apply generally and reciprocally among citizens.

State and religion.—On the *vertical level*, the process of secularization and the principle of tolerance aim at a *liberal constitutional state* that is separated from religion and maintains a neutral stance toward religious communities. The more diverse the existing religions, the more important the neutrality of the state becomes in order to ensure peaceful coexistence. The question arises here: Should it adhere to its strictly secular stance, thereby incurring the accusation of "secularism," or should it make special concessions to religious citizens, as the advocates of "postsecularism" demand? In this case, both Rawls and Habermas presuppose a liberal constitutional state. Accordingly, state laws and regulations may not contain any religious justifications whatsoever. In concrete implementation, this separation varies in different countries: from French laïcité to the "limping separation" in Germany and the cooperation model in Italy and Spain.[57]

The version of the "Charter of Laïcité," which stems from the French Enlightenment and Revolution, was only adopted in *France* in 1905.[58] The strict separation of state and church is manifested above all in the fact that the state does not collect church taxes and that no religious symbols are permitted in state institutions such as schools and courts—neither the Christian cross nor the Muslim headscarf. This also includes the right to criticize religion up to the point of blasphemy. Most recently, this line was reaffirmed in a law "to strengthen republican values," which even extends into private life, for example when polygamy or forced marriages are prohibited. Such measures are intended to curb the "separatism" of religions. But they also carry the risk, conversely, that Muslim citizens are stigmatized and that religious communities such as Islam withdraw from the public sphere and become radicalized. This in turn leads to a counter-reaction by left-wing intellectuals who attempt to justify radical Islam (islamogauchisme), and to whom the French state is helplessly opposed. Because such opposing tendencies are gradually gaining the upper hand, further, especially social, reforms are needed in France to contain religious radicalization.

---

[56] Forst 2003, p. 21; cf. Renner 2017, pp. 175–177.
[57] Graf 2004, pp. 103 f.—In Spain, it is still not possible to leave the Catholic Church, because neither the Church nor the state has a legal procedure for this.
[58] Graf 2004, p. 118; cf. Frick 2020, pp. 99 f.

In *Germany* there prevails a combination of separation and cooperation. Conservative politicians invoke the Christian West, not infrequently also in legislative proposals such as those concerning assisted suicide. The closeness to the churches becomes manifest in the fact that the state administration collects taxes for them. Furthermore, it is a criminal offense to offend the "religious feelings" of believing citizens. German governments are also inconsistent in their approach to the admission of religious symbols in public spaces, as in Bavaria, where it was even ordered that crucifixes be placed at the entrances of state buildings, and where Muslim women are permitted to wear a headscarf as teachers or judges in public service. Yet recently, the German Bundestag has been planning a "Law Regulating the Appearance of Civil Servants," which prohibits "non-neutral" religious clothing if it "objectively" endangers the conduct of official duties. This is likely to be the case, for example, if a Muslim female judge has to rule on a crime motivated by Islam.

Conversely, it is prudent for the state in all countries not to allow religious communities to act entirely at will in a strictly laicist sense, but rather to control certain religious institutions that are in the public interest within tolerant limits. This concerns church educational institutions, whose curricula and forms of instruction must conform to the constitution. The same applies to the training of religious education teachers, who must present a state-recognized examination that guarantees academic standards. In this respect, it is to be welcomed that Islamic religious teachers in originally Christian states are also to be trained at universities or corresponding institutions.

If one takes this consequence a step further, laicism does not even represent the supposed end or even the pinnacle of the secularization process. Politically necessary, however, is a secularization through which governments exert such influence on religious institutions that the secular rule of law and the liberal public sphere remain secured. Precisely the enforcement of such a process of secularization stands in the tradition of a European Enlightenment that has placed the social function of religion at the center. Even here, one can learn that religion can only serve the community if it has itself been secularized by state measures. This should not be a civil religion à la Rousseau, but rather a civilized religion, within which the rules of a democratic constitutional state are observed.

In this context, the special relationship of the German state to the *Catholic Church* must also be reconsidered. Of course, the imperative of tolerance toward religious belief and the free exercise of religion applies here as well. But at the same time, new limits must be set to tolerance when one considers this church as an *institution*. Thus, employees there must be granted the usual labor rights, including protection against dismissal and the right to strike. It is also not justifiable for a secular state to finance the salaries of pastors and bishops. Also problematic is the fact that the German federal states still pay millions of euros annually to the churches as compensation for the expropriation of church property in the nineteenth century. The necessary criticism of the Catholic Church concerns above all its hierarchical structure, which explicitly does not tolerate democratic opinion- and will-formation. Equally intolerable is the discrimination against women, who are categorically excluded from the priesthood. The widespread sexual abuse, which is hardly prosecuted by German courts, must be prevented under civil law. While such a crime is usually punished with imprisonment, priests—if at all—get off with pastoral admonitions. With such special rights, the Catholic Church violates the constitutions of democratic and constitutional states. Apparently, it is not capable of reforming itself from within. It is therefore time to exert more political pressure from outside and to push for reforms. For in a constitutional state, there must be no lawless, misogynistic, and unconstitutional spaces.

Freedom of religion also means the freedom *from* religion. If tolerance is demanded everywhere toward denominationally affiliated citizens, then *non-religious citizens in the public sphere must also be granted more rights*. Just as the political discourse between religious and secular citizens should be structured symmetrically, so too does the position of atheists in state institutions require a corresponding balance. In state and public bodies, the Christian denominations are represented, but the "unbelievers" have no place in them. This concerns, for example, the composition of *broadcasting councils*, which include church officials but no atheist representatives. This also applies to the German *Ethics Council*, which includes some Protestant and Catholic theologians, but no philosophers or ethicists who explicitly represent an atheist position. Furthermore, in most *curricula* of general education schools, the topic of criticism of religion and atheism is missing. A suitable framework for this is provided by the ideologically neutral *school subject Philosophy and/or Ethics*, in which students of all religions—and thus also non-religious children and adolescents—can participate and compare and evaluate their convictions through argumentation.

4

Human and Nature

Under the title "Diversity and Unity of the Enlightenment," I have already mentioned the new sciences that emerged in various European countries over the course of the eighteenth century. In the discussion of the critique of religion, I was able to demonstrate how these scientific disciplines were put to use: anthropology, philosophy of language, sociology, history. Now follow systematic investigations of these fields, each of which is given its own chapter.

I begin with *anthropology*, which represents the leading science of the Enlightenment. At first, the focus is on the natural constitution of the human being and their position in relation to external nature. This discourse is then continued with the topics of knowledge and language. Finally, the social and historical dimensions of the modern way of life are addressed. Here, the limits of the anthropological approach become apparent. Whereas the Enlighteners originally promised a new creative power of humanity, now the contingent conditions of human action come to the fore. It should be noted that this is no longer a dependence on a divine plan of salvation, but rather a heteronomy through self-created circumstances.

The *natural history* that emerged in the eighteenth century places the human being within a broader context of development. This raises the question of the relationship between humans and animals: is it a qualitative leap, or merely a gradual transition? Already the naturalist Buffon integrated the emergence of humanity into his "Natural History," which in turn served as a model for the Enlightenment philosophers of history. Thus, historiographers such as Ferguson in England and Herder in Germany quite naturally began with a genesis of animals, which is then superseded by human history. Other Enlighteners such as d'Holbach and Kant drew the opposite conclusion from this, namely that humanity could also disappear from the globe once again. In both extremes, humanity forfeits its central position in creation. When Sigmund Freud diagnosed a "biological humiliation" by Charles Darwin, it can be added here that this humiliation had already begun during the historical epoch of the Enlightenment.

In the course of *medicine*, research into the physical nature of the human being was taken to a new level. Now, the human being is understood as a being primarily guided by bodily instincts. This also calls into question the traditional dualism of body and soul. Ultimately, the issue is whether there is an independent mind at all, or rather a sentient and thinking matter. Whereas the philosophers of the early modern period depicted the human body as a mechanical apparatus, the Enlighteners increasingly understood the human being as a living organism.

The new medicine brought the *female body* into focus. As a result, the biological differences between man and woman, especially the particular nature of woman, became the center of interest. This difference is further reinforced by the social context, in which women are reduced to their familial role and kept away from social, political, and scientific life. Yet, since the early modern period up to the French Revolution, the following also holds: all human beings are equal. This also concerns the relationship between the sexes, to whom, since Descartes, a fundamentally equal intellect has been attributed. The resulting demand to provide women with greater access to education can be traced up to the end of the century. In this sense, one can speak of a *feminist Enlightenment*.[1] This dilemma can be taken up by current gender debates, which continue the alternative between *equality* and *difference* to this day.

In current debates, the Enlightenment is often criticized as *anthropocentric*, which is linked to the accusation of environmental destruction. The new counter-concept is *Anthropocene*, which refers to the epoch of the Industrial Revolution and contains the demand that humanity should once again live in harmony with its natural environment. Since this causes humanity to lose its former supremacy, there is even talk of a *posthumanism*. However, it will become apparent that it was precisely the anthropologists

---

[1] Karremann, Stiening 2020, pp. 8 f. However, in their own contributions, the authors refer only to the early modern period and less to the Enlightenment since the second half of the eighteenth century. See especially Steinbrügge 2020, pp. 225–226.

of the Enlightenment who emphasized the closeness of humanity to nature. This refers both to external and to internal nature, which points to a natural and thus material character of the human being.

The problem of *materialism* remains relevant to this day. After dialectical materialism has lost its credibility, the topic can be renegotiated. Already in the discourses on the Anthropocene, materialist tones can be heard. The difficulties with brain research lie less in materialism than in an encroaching naturalism that excludes cultural factors. Finally, the transition from the rationalism of the early modern period to the anthropology of the Enlightenment is repeated in the question of how human beings differ from computers, in that it is not rational calculation but human emotions that come to the fore.

Era of Posthumanism?

Anyone who today reflects on the position of the human being in the world feels a great unease. This concerns, first of all, external nature, which is being destroyed to a considerable extent by human civilization and is on the verge of collapse. This includes, as is well known, climate change, the extinction of species, and the accumulation of toxins and waste. There is no doubt here that these ecological crises are caused by humans.

To describe this phenomenon, the term *Anthropocene* has become established over the past twenty years or so.[2] What is meant is the epoch in which humans have intervened so deeply in their natural living conditions that the surrounding nature is their own product, just as they themselves have become an unpredictable force of nature. This renders the traditional distinction between human and environment obsolete. This diagnosis is linked to a fundamental critique of the human self-conception. The idea that humans could rise above nature and dominate it according to their own purposes has proven to be presumptuous and disastrous. In contrast, a "new materialism" is being advanced, in which a world is described where the entire material wealth interacts.

This position is sharpened by the demand by Clive Hamilton for a *posthumanism* that is intended to shake the modern image of humanity.[3] For

---

[2] Horn, Bergthaller 2019, p. 9, 19 f.; cf. Hamilton, C. 2017, p. 110; Schneidewind 2018, p. 132; Büttner, Richter 2021, p. 12; likewise Davies 2016; Elis 2018.
[3] Hamilton, C. 2017, pp. 116–118; Horn, Bergthaller 2019, p. 62 f.; cf. Žižek 2001, p. 7 f.

it means that humans have long since lost their former agency and special status. Instead, it is now emphasized that they are interwoven with and dependent on external nature. As a result of biological evolution, their inner nature differs from that of animals only by degree. For this double reason, the boundary between culture and nature has dissolved, which now constitute a hybrid entity.

The Spanish philosopher Marina Garcés goes a step further and posits a "posthumous condition," which she characterizes as the time after the death of humans or of humanity as a whole.[4] It is the time of "catastrophe," which consists in the irreversible destruction of our living conditions. Garcés already counts the Chernobyl reactor disaster of 1986 among these, as well as the long-term global warming that threatens our natural environment. She also considers present-day capitalism, which widens the gap between rich and poor, to be equally unsustainable. The numerous wars lead to famines, mass flight, and terrorism.

Both the concept of the Anthropocene and that of posthumanism are directed explicitly against the philosophy of the *Enlightenment*. It is accused of having initiated all the calamity by postulating a rational and autonomous subject. This accusation corresponds quite closely to the chronological dating. For the epochal threshold of the Anthropocene coincides with the beginning of industrialization around the middle of the 18th century, that is, with the period in which the era of the Enlightenment began. As should already have become clear and will be further elaborated, Enlightenment and industrial society are closely interconnected.

For these reasons, it seems plausible to hold, not least, the European Enlightenment responsible for the problems of the Anthropocene. This applies in particular to *anthropology*, which indeed forms the core of the Enlightenment. For if one wishes to blame the construction of an all-powerful human being for the current predicament, it is precisely the theory to which such a conception of humanity is attributed that becomes the target of critique. The concept of the Anthropocene thus radically calls into question anthropology since the Enlightenment.

Against this contemporary background, this passage on the *anthropology of the Enlightenment* is to be conceived. As so often, the critics equate the Enlightenment with the rationalism of the modern era and construct from this their distorted image of a subject detached from nature. The opposite, however, is the case, for the anthropology under discussion here

---

[4] Garcés 2019, p. 12, 31, 33, 40 f.

has from the outset regarded the human being as a natural being, embedded in the overarching process of natural history. Likewise, physicians studied the physiological character of the human body. If, therefore, a so-called posthumanism is currently being called for, it must be countered that the nature-connectedness propagated therein was already advocated by the anthropologists of the 18th century. In this I see the ecological potentials of the Enlightenment. Here it becomes strikingly clear that an appropriate relationship between human and nature is also conceivable within modern humanism.

Anthropology as Leading Science

The *science of the human being* forms a new paradigm in the second half of the 18th century. Quite generally, such an elevation means that humans become aware of their position in the world. This concerns their origin from natural history, which takes the place of biblical creation. From this it follows, in turn, that humans primarily understand themselves as embodied beings, driven by emotions such as pleasure and pain. Thus, the controversial position of atheism shifts to the problem of materialism. While anthropology as a new foundational science was common property of the European Enlightenment, its representatives again proved to be divided on the materialist question.

Anthropological Discourses.—The extent to which *anthropology* advanced to become the leading discipline of the Enlightenment is evident in the French *Encyclopédie*. In the article of the same name, the editor Diderot declares the human being to be the center of the entire work: "Why should we not make him the common center?"[5] And in the article "Man" (homme moral) he writes: "Man is the unique concept from which one must proceed and to which everything must be referred."[6] The author knows that the human being is "assigned to the class of animals," without, however, overlooking the distance between animal and human. Thus, the human is considered "the being that thinks, wills, and acts," whereby human actions arise from natural

---

[5] Article "Encyclopédie," in: Encyclopédie 1972, p. 452.—This is also evident in the programmatic division, which (in the tradition of Francis Bacon) is oriented toward three human faculties: memory, reason, and imagination; d'Alembert 1989, p. 48.

[6] Encyclopédie 1972, pp. 674–676; Diderot 1961, vol. I, p. 187; for the following see ibid., pp. 674 f.—Cf. Duchet 1971, p. 17; Schneiders 1997, p. 11; Reinalter 1997, pp. 22 f.; d'Aprile, Siebers 2008, p. 77.

drives. In order to set limits to human hubris, his "baseness and cruelty" are also addressed. The anthropological turn could hardly be formulated more clearly.

In the posthumously published work *On Man* (1773) Helvétius makes the human being the central theme. Previously, he had published *On Mind* (1758), which deals solely with the intellectual faculties of the human being.[7] The human being appears as a primarily natural and sensual being, who above all strives for earthly happiness. The same is true of the *System of Nature* (posthumously 1791) by d'Holbach, for whom the human being is above all a physical being. Despite the provocative title *Man a Machine* (anonymous 1748) La Mettrie does not differ significantly from this. These authors were very soon received by the representatives of the Italian Enlightenment Pietro Verri and Cesare Beccaria.[8]

The step toward *anthropology* is already taken by David Hume in his early major work *A Treatise of Human Nature* (1739/40), which he later reformulated in separate publications on epistemology (1748) and moral philosophy (1751).[9] His conception is innovative because, for the first time, he presents the human being in his entirety. In doing so, he lays claim to the not exactly modest ambition to become the Newton of a new "science of man." After physics from Galileo to Newton had explored external nature, the nature of the human being now comes into the focus of philosophical interest.

Here, the concept of nature is used not only metaphorically, but also substantively in the physical sense. For in the middle of the *Treatise* is found the book "Of the Passions," which is intended to ground the following book "Of Morals." Among these passions, which people perceive within themselves, are the selfish feelings such as pleasure and displeasure, love and hate, as well as the altruistic emotion of compassion or sympathy, which is supposed to lead to moral behavior. What is decisive now is that Hume sees these passions, which also consist in direct willing and desiring, as grounded in an "original instinct" or "natural impulse."[10] In this I see the beginnings of a natural-historical grounding of morality. But at the same time, it becomes clear here that these passions are culturally shaped, in that they are

---

[7] Helvétius 1973, p. 81; idem 1976, p. 11.
[8] D'Holbach 1960, p. 66; La Mettrie 2015, p. 27; Verri 1996, pp. 4 f.; Beccaria 1966, p. 44; cf. Rother 2005, pp. 65–79.
[9] Hume 1973; idem 1964 and 1962; for a detailed discussion of Hume's epistemology and moral philosophy see chap. 6 and 7.
[10] Hume 1973, Book II, pp. 177 f.

directed as emotions toward particular states of affairs in the world and represent them.

Although Kant with his epistemology and doctrine of morals rather executed a volte-face toward rationalism, in his last work he nevertheless provides an *anthropology from a pragmatic point of view* (1798). In it, he gathers all those features of human nature that he, in old age, had received from the European Enlightenment.[11] Nevertheless, he is beset by a certain unease that the "Leidenschaften" (passions) could not be governed by reason and therefore threatened to become "morally reprehensible" and to turn into "disease of the mind, intoxication, madness." A fundamental distance is evident in the coinage "anthroponomy," which, in contrast to empirical anthropology, is once again oriented toward reason.[12]

Nevertheless, these examples show the common form and function of Enlightenment anthropology. As Kant indirectly makes clear, the new discipline understands itself as an *empirical science* in contrast to earlier metaphysical speculations. In doing so, the *unity of human nature* is emphasized against the rationalist dualism of mind and body, even if the materialist tendency is not always unambiguous. Finally, the new anthropology fulfills an *integrative function* by bringing together the fields of knowledge, morality, and politics in a single discipline that almost assumes encyclopedic proportions. Kant's formulation "from a pragmatic point of view" subsequently indicates that he assigns this anthropology a *practical task*, even understanding it himself as a philosophy of praxis.

Natural History of Man.—In his *Natural History* (1749–1767), the naturalist Georges Louis Leclerc de Buffon described the emergence of humans from the animal kingdom, raising the heretical question of whether humans are descended from apes.[13] He then attaches to this a cultural history, in which humans develop their practical, cognitive, and emotional abilities. In accordance with a long tradition of political thought, he considers humans to be a social animal (zoon politikon), which, like other animals, lives in community from the outset.

Hardly any philosopher oriented himself so closely to Buffon as Rousseau. In his *Discourse on the Origin of Inequality*, he sketches a *history of the*

---

[11] Kant 1965, vol. XII, p. 580.
[12] *Metaphysics of Morals*, in: Kant 1965, vol. VIII, p. 573.
[13] Buffon 2008, p. 72.—Rheinberger, McLaughlin in: Rohbeck, Holzhey 2008, pp. 399–401; Rheinberger in: Rheinberger, McLauphlin 2021, pp. 167–203; cf. Rohbeck 2010, pp. 125–138.

emergence of man from physical nature, which consists in a chain of accidents.[14] In order to characterize the "natural man," he describes in detail the physiological characteristics of the orangutan. But in contrast to his model, Rousseau considers man in the so-called state of nature to be a solitary being without any social bonds. Moreover, he maintains the fundamental difference between animal and human. This also applies to Ferguson, who derives the history of humanity from natural history but shrinks from the ultimate consequence. Only Henry Home in Scotland dares to draw a direct line to the orangutan.[15]

Yet these attempts at connection should not obscure the fact that zoology at the time possessed *no theory of development* in the modern sense of evolution. The prevailing model consisted in the growth process of plants and animals, which merely need to unfold their natural dispositions. According to the theory of preformation, this means that all later forms and functions are contained *en miniature* in the germ. According to the theory of epigenesis, it is "internal molds" (moules intérieures) that guide the organism in its growth.[16] Thus Rousseau presupposes in humans the capacity for perfectibility (perfectibilité). Similarly, Ferguson assumes an "ability to progress" (faculty of improvement) inherent in human nature. Kant aptly describes this developmental form as a process in which the natural potentials are to be "unfolded."[17]

Again, in d'Holbach one finds a surprising reflection on the relationship of humans to nature. He regards humans as "a product that has arisen in the course of time," i.e., as a "consequence of the development of our globe," without beginning or end being known.[18] From this natural-historical fact, he draws the conclusion that humans are nothing more than an "ephemeral being," subject to constant change. He even denies that humans are in any way a "privileged being in nature." By subordinating humans to nature, he connects anthropology with ecology.

Even Kant considers the end of humanity on earth. In his early work *Universal Natural History and Theory of the Heavens* (1755), he speculates

---

[14] Rousseau with extensive quotations from Buffon: 1978, p. 85, note d; p. 97, note g; cf. Duchet 1971, p. 330.

[15] Home 1968, vol. I, pp. 11, 14 f.; cf. Ferguson 1986, pp. 97–108; Robertson 1841, p. 79; d'Holbach 1960, pp. 69 f.; Herder 1984, vol. III, pp. 107–111.

[16] Buffon 2008, p. 136.

[17] Rousseau 1978, p. 108; Ferguson 1986, p. 42; Kant 1965, vol. XI, p. 35.

[18] D'Holbach 1960, pp. 67–72.

that the earth could burn out and disappear.[19] Thus, he considers the life history of humans on their home planet to be temporally limited. The dominance of humans is by no means permanent: "Man, who seems to be the masterpiece of creation," is not exempt from the "destruction of the world edifice." And he adds quite soberly that this destruction would not even be "a true loss to nature to be lamented." Explicitly, this is not done against, but within, the anthropology of the Enlightenment.

In a similar way, Herder arrives at the conclusion that human nature is by no means as unique as earlier philosophers had assumed. He applies this assessment especially to its physical and psychological constitution. In *On the Origin of Language* (1772), he regards humans as a being with "deficiencies," because they lack the protective fur and instinct of animals: "Considered as a naked, instinctless animal, man is the most wretched of beings."[20] He then interprets tools and language as "substitutes" for missing natural endowments. Culture is seen as compensation for an original deficit.

That not only language, but also *the making and use of tools* distinguishes humans from animals, belongs to the topos of the European Enlightenment. A representative example is the French *Encyclopédie* with its plates, which document the contemporary instruments of workshops and manufactories. In the above-cited article "Man," the proof of the distance between animal and human consists in the "superiority of his means."[21] In Helvétius one finds the original remark that the human "mind is not concerned with the need, but with the means to satisfy it. It is not difficult to eat, but to prepare the meal."[22] Ferguson even goes so far as to say that instruments not only serve to satisfy needs, but also contribute to the development of new human needs: "His means adapt to his ends [...] If his skill increases at every stage of his progress, then his desire must also expand in the process."[23] Kant too grants in his *Anthropology* a horizon-expanding function to the means: "The possession of the means to arbitrary ends indeed extends much further than the inclination directed at a single desire and its satisfaction."[24] Behind this stands the groundbreaking discovery that tools open up more possibilities for action than were anticipated at their creation. The triumphal march of

---

[19] Kant 1968, vol. I, p. 318.—In the *Conflict of the Faculties* Kant repeats his conjecture "that the epoch of man could, under certain circumstances, soon come to an end"; ibid., vol. VII, p. 89.

[20] Herder 1984, vol. II, pp. 266, 270; vol. III, pp. 60–69, 107 f.; cf. Godel 2007, pp. 214 f.

[21] Encyclopédie 1972, p. 675.

[22] Helvétius 1973, p. 95; cf. pp. 365 f.

[23] Ferguson 1986, p. 318; cf. Robertson 1841, pp. 105 f.; Condorcet 1976, pp. 205, 207.

[24] Kant 1965, vol. XII, p. 605; cf. Rohbeck 1993, pp. 80–97; idem 2000, pp. 118–137.

the tool thus has two sides: originally, it serves to compensate for natural weaknesses. Then, it provides humans with options that they would not have been capable of by nature.

Despite the significant differences among the authors of the Enlightenment, a common underlying tendency is nevertheless discernible: to substantially relativize the position of the human being in the world. By regarding the human as a rather contingent result of natural history, differing from animals only by degree, constituting merely an episode in the entire history of the earth, and exposing himself to the natural effects of his own artifacts, he loses his former special status in the cosmos. In the anthropology of the eighteenth century, the human being returns to nature, discovering his dependence on both external and internal nature.

When it is demanded today that humans should abandon their anthropocentric perspective, it should be noted that precisely this shift in perspective already took place during the European Enlightenment, that is, at the beginnings of modernity. But this does not mean a farewell to the human being, but rather a transformed position of the human, who becomes aware of his belonging to nature and his responsibility for nature. This change therefore leads to no posthumanism, but rather takes place in the tradition of Enlightenment anthropology and thus within the framework of European humanism. Such a new perspective on the relationship between human and nature will occupy us further in the final section: in the engagement with the current thesis of the Anthropocene.

Body and soul.—When the human is identified with the animal, the problem arises of the existence of a spiritual soul separate from the body, just as, conversely, the possibility is considered that the material body is capable of developing higher faculties. At this point, the divergence among the representatives of the Enlightenment, already observed in the critique of religion, repeats itself. Again, the spectrum ranges from radical materialism to rather skeptical views.

Above all, d'Holbach is among the early materialists, who mocked Cartesian spiritualism. For him, the mind is not separate from the body, but "spiritual substance and material body form a unity." Accordingly, the human is a "material being" capable of feeling and thinking.[25] D'Holbach is surpassed only by La Mettrie, who described himself as a materialist. However, he by no means understood the human as a mechanical apparatus, but as a living organism. As a physician, he conducted physiological

---

[25] *Letters to Eugénie*, in: d'Holbach n.d., pp. 356–358; idem 1960, pp. 67 f., 82.

investigations of the sense organs and nerves, to which he attributed sensitive faculties, and he also traced thinking back to the "fibers of the brain."[26] From these internal causes, he derived memory, feeling, and imagination.

Evidently, La Mettrie attracted the most criticism. In this context, Diderot does not make things easy for himself and shows himself torn between ideal freedom and material determination.[27] Helvétius is equally undecided, ultimately giving preference to the mind independent of the body. Condillac, who remained a clergyman until his death, rejects the identification of body and soul. And although Hume denies the "immortality of the soul," he is not willing to endorse its materiality. The same applies to Herder, although he, perhaps more than anyone else, emphasizes the proximity of humans to animals.[28] For a pioneer of German Idealism such as Kant, any form of materialism was not even worth considering.

Despite the indicated reservations, materialism evidently exerted a great fascination in the second half of the eighteenth century. For the materialist theory had two advantages: On the one hand, it was compatible with the new natural sciences of biology and medicine. On the other hand, it avoided metaphysical presuppositions intended to bridge the gulf between body and mind.[29] Such speculations were no longer tenable at all from the second half of the eighteenth century, even if the materialist variant did not offer a generally acceptable theory. Thus, Kant ultimately declared this problem insoluble.[30] In the end, this topic has by no means lost its relevance to this day.

Pleasure and pain.—A common denominator of the European Enlightenment is the anthropological basic assumption that humans strive for earthly *happiness*. Above all, Helvétius points out that this is not to be understood as unrestrained egoism, but as a civilizing of self-love,

---

[26] La Mettrie 2015, pp. 27, 33, 53, 55, 77.

[27] Diderot 1961, vol. I, pp. 93 f.; see Stenger 2013, pp. 583–814; Gumbrecht 2020, pp. 58, 197 f., 220 f.

[28] Helvétius 1973, p. 81; idem 1976, pp. 67–69; Condillac 2006, pp. 66 f.; Hume 1984, p. 87; Herder 1984, vol. III, p. 152.

[29] For example, Leibniz had devised a "pre-established harmony," according to which body and soul have been, so to speak, synchronized since the beginnings of divine creation. And Malebranche had conceived a theory of so-called occasional causes (occasionalism), according to which God constantly intervenes as a mediator between the two substances—a daring construction that, surprisingly, persisted among Christians well into the eighteenth century. An alternative was offered by Spinoza's monism, which later found success in *German Idealism*. Leibniz 1965, p. 241.

[30] In the doctrine of the insoluble antinomies of the *Critique of Pure Reason*, in: Kant 1965, vol. IV, pp. 399–439.

conceived both individually and socially.³¹ This goal forms the leitmotif in the *Meditations on Happiness* (1763) by Pietro Verri. From there, it is only a small step to utilitarian ethics.³²

Since physical motives take precedence, sensual *pleasure* functions as the corresponding driving force. Yet the point of this anthropology is that this feeling is constructed as a dual relation, namely as the opposition of *pleasure and displeasure*. At bottom, pleasure consists in the *avoidance of displeasure*; in other words: in the *aversion to pain*.³³ This also applies to human needs, which consist in states of lack. Whoever wants to eat is driven by hunger, which expresses the absence of food. It also applies to feelings of pain that are socially and culturally mediated, such as grief and shame. Fundamentally, the motives of human action are determined negatively.

This kind of negativity is placed at the center of above all by Verri and Beccaria in their anthropology. In his *Discourse on the Nature of Pleasure and Pain* (1773), Verri goes so far as to reinterpret the usually negatively connoted pain as a "positive feeling."³⁴ Accordingly, pleasure consists solely in the cessation of "pena" (pain), which remains constantly present. Since pains always exceed pleasure, he considers perfect happiness to be impossible. In this view, Kant follows him, who demonstrably received Verri's writings. He too distinguishes between a pleasant pleasure and an unpleasant pain: "Thus, pain must precede every pleasure; pain is always the first. [...] Pain is the spur to activity."³⁵ Like Verri, Kant revalues pain, which is negatively experienced, by assigning it a positive meaning.

In this pessimistic turn toward a *theory of pain*, a tendency of Enlightenment anthropology, already noted above, is confirmed. There can be no talk here of an alleged optimism of the Enlightenment, in which humanity rises above nature. Instead, a new sense of dependence on nature emerges, first on the external nature of other living beings, then on the internal nature of physically conditioned emotions. With the presence of bodily pain, the naturalness of the human being becomes conscious. In this case, one could even speak of a *negative anthropology*. In the twentieth century, such an anthropology was brought to bear against Arnold Gehlen and has recently been revived. I will return to this at the end.

---

[31] Helvétius 1976, pp. 11, 95; idem 1973, p. 131; likewise d'Holbach 1960, p. 229; Hume 1962, p. 170; Ferguson 1986, p. 137; see chap. 7.
[32] Verri 1996, p. 47; Beccaria 1966, p. 48.
[33] Helvétius 1973, p. 299; ibid. 1976, p. 95; Hume 1973, Book II, p. 62.
[34] Verri 1972, pp. 19 f., 36 f., 40; ibid. 1996, pp. 4 f.; cf. Rother 2005, pp. 66–79.
[35] Kant 1965, vol. XII, pp. 550 f.

The Nature of Woman

Was there a *feminist Enlightenment?* This question can only be answered in a highly controversial manner.[36] First of all, it is almost self-evident that women too benefited from the European Enlightenment. If all human beings are considered fundamentally equal, this must also apply to the relation between the sexes. This is especially true for human reason, from which women must not be excluded. But since the mid-eighteenth century, a contrary tendency has become apparent, which again restricts the abilities of women. The reasons are practical: in order to reduce the high mortality of mother and child, the processes of pregnancy and birth were studied, whereby the physical and emotional difference between the sexes increasingly came into play. In the relevant discourses, this was then justified by constructing a corresponding "nature of woman." This is not a reaction of the Counter-Enlightenment or simply male misogyny, but a dilemma of the newly emerging bourgeois society. But let us begin with the "feminist" side.

Egalité.—In the school of thought of *Rationalism*, the postulated equality of the sexes referred above all to intellectual capacities. In *On the Equality of the Two Sexes* (1673), the Cartesian Poulain de la Barre formulated: "Reason has no sex."[37] Marquise de Lambert referred to him, and in her *Advices from a Mother to her Daughter* (1703) lamented the inadequate education of girls and demanded more education for them, including knowledge of the sciences. In this tradition of the *Querelle des femmes*, not a few women participated in the intellectual debates of the Enlightenment. There were learned women such as Émilie du Châtelet, who translated Newton's *Principia Mathematica* into French and conducted physical experiments herself . Françoise de Graffigny wrote the aforementioned critical novel about colonial history, which became a bestseller and with which Turgot engaged.[38] Other women, such as Madame Helvétius, hosted salons in which they engaged in witty conversation with the *philosophes*.

Likewise, by the end of the century there were numerous Enlightenment thinkers who advocated for equal education for girls and women. Thus, Diderot criticizes the inadequate education of the female *sex* in his essay *On Women* (1772). In *Advice to His Daughter* (1794), Condorcet sees the

---

[36] Karremann, Stiening 2020, pp. 8 f.; here I follow Steinbrügge 2020, pp. 225–226; cf. Steinbrügge 1987, p. 11; Godineau 1996, pp. 321–358; Kersting 2010, pp. 101–121.
[37] Quoted in Steinbrügge 1987, p. 21; cf. Geier 2012, pp. 312 f.
[38] Graffigny 1999; Steinbrügge 2020, pp. 232–241.

path to a happy life in manual and intellectual work, which brings pleasure and protects against dependence in times of need. The aim should be to achieve a sense of personal security, respect, and dignity. Verri also wrote a treatise to his daughter, in which he laments the imbalance between the sexes and demands that women should not be reduced to their role as wives, but should be provided with education and sociability.[39] The first German treatise on the equality of women comes from Theodor Gottlieb von Hippel, who in *On the Civil Improvement of Women* (1792) criticizes patriarchal marriage. Kant, who was friends with Hippel in Königsberg, also grants women the "step to maturity," but then rather emphasizes the differences.[40]

As in the rest of Europe, in eighteenth-century Spain the female sex was also a central theme of reflection and discussion. Benito Jerónimo Feijoo initiates this with his *Defense of Women* (1726), in which he follows the example of the Frenchman Poulain de la Barre. He limits the difference between the sexes to the physical and maintains the idea of genderless reason: "And so those women who say that the soul is neither male nor female may remain firm in this: for they are right."[41] To explain why equality of abilities has not produced corresponding competencies, Feijoo draws attention to the central importance of education, whose lack he holds responsible for the fact that, despite their naturally equal capacities, women have distinguished themselves less intellectually than men. Feijoo's *Defense* was followed by numerous relevant texts throughout the century.

In the *anthropology* of the later Enlightenment, in which the physical characteristics of human beings came to the fore, not only was the male body discovered, but above all the physical particularity of women was examined and revalued. It was only the new medical research that made women the subject of a realistic discourse. In this way, they were freed from the life-denying prejudices of the Catholic Church and other pejorative connotations of femininity. In particular, reproduction lost its religious taboo and thus its stigma of sinfulness. This was sorely needed, for until the end of the eighteenth century and long after, childbirth was a deadly danger for women, which contemporary medicine no longer regarded as blind fate, but as a challenge to be mastered.

---

[39] Condorcet 1968, vol. I, pp. 611–623; Verri: *Manoscritto per Teresa* (1777), cited in Rother 2005, pp. 101 f.
[40] Kant 1965, vol. IV, pp. 53 f.; cf. Honegger 1991, pp. 78 f.; Geier 2012, pp. 307 f.
[41] Quoted in Monica Bolufer in: Rohbeck, Rother 2016, pp. 160–163.

Paradigmatic is the article "Woman" (femme anthropologie) in the French *Encyclopédie*.[42] In it, the author Jaucourt continues the anthropological discourse of the Enlightenment by describing the human being as a natural being who, like animals, reproduces in a natural way. He subordinates the cohabitation of man and woman solely to this purpose. Since marriage is also primarily intended for the procreation and upbringing of children, he no longer considers the prevailing patriarchy there to be legitimate. For this reason, he advocates a natural law justification of the marital community, which grants both partners equal rights.

The new attention to women is also reflected terminologically. Since in French the term "homme" means both *human being* and *man*, the above-cited article "Human Being" tacitly refers to the male human. This seems so self-evident that no separate entry for "man" is considered necessary. Yet, specifically for women, there are several articles in the *Encyclopédie*. This results in a linguistic asymmetry that is not further reflected upon. Nevertheless, the articles on the female sex can be interpreted as a revaluation. They show that the issue of gender has always involved, not least, linguistic problems.

Difference.—But it was precisely the new anthropology since the mid-eighteenth century that also had *negative flip sides* for the female sex, which again call into question the initial impression of a "feminist Enlightenment." Whereas in the rationalist tradition reason was considered gender-neutral and thus equally distributed between men and women, with natural history and medicine the physiological differences between the sexes could no longer be ignored. Exemplary here is the physician Pierre Roussel, who counts himself among the "medical philosophers." He sees the difference between the sexes as a universal principle that shapes the entire physical and psychological constitution of human beings. Because of the disposition of their nerves, women are able to perceive and feel differently than men. While they possess greater sensitivity and emotionality, their reason is so limited that they are incapable of abstract thought. This assessment is reinforced by the sensualism of the Enlightenment, which makes human cognition dependent on the bodily sense organs.[43] In this way, a particular female anthropology is now ascribed to women.

---

[42] Encyclopédie 1756, vol. VI, p. 468; see also the articles "Female" (femelle), "Marriage," "Husband," and "Child"; Steinbrügge 1987, pp. 31–52.—Likewise the article "Economy," in which Rousseau characterizes the patriarchal family; Encyclopédie 1972, pp. 336 f.

[43] Steinbrügge 1987, pp. 47 f.; Honegger 1991, pp. 143 f.; see also chap. 6.

Behind this lies a specific socio-political strategy. In order to increase the birth rate, women were encouraged to focus on their functions as wives and mothers and to withdraw from public life. As the process of industrialization began to separate gainful employment from family life, a gender-specific division of labor emerged. In the political economy of the French physiocrats as well as in English national economics, the shortage of labor was lamented. This increased the moral pressure on women to contribute to national prosperity by caring for offspring. The social utility of women now consisted in their biological particularity, to bear and raise children.

A special place is occupied here by Rousseau, who decisively shaped the relevant discourses. In this context, it is important to recall a circumstance that was already crucial in the conception of his *civil religion*. In contrast to the other Enlightenment thinkers, Rousseau, in his *Second Discourse*, is a vehement critic of bourgeois society, which he sees as shaped by self-interest and competition. For him, human reason is not only guided by selfish interests; rather, it is itself the intellectual origin of egoism: "It is reason that produces selfishness."[44] When he then seeks moral compensation, he finds a welcome agent in the female sex. While the man must prevail in capitalist competition, the tender wife is to form a protective haven within the sheltered family.

The consequences can be found in the novel *Émile, or On Education* (1762), where Rousseau goes significantly further than contemporary physicians and economists. In the fifth and final chapter, he calls for a separate education for girls, which should devote itself less to the cultivation of reason than to the fostering of a sensitive morality.[45] For anthropological legitimation, he constructs a female nature to which he denies the capacity for independent thought, associating it with the danger of selfishness. Instead, he characterizes girls and women by the specifically "feminine" qualities of empathy, gentleness, and obedience. In contrast to the writings of egalitarian Enlightenment, *Émile* remains to this day part of the canon of educational literature. What once arose from a medical and social emergency and is quite understandable has, since the nineteenth century and well into the twentieth, become an ideology of different gender characters.

---

[44] Rousseau 1978, p. 175.—This line of thought points to the *critique of instrumental reason* by Max Horkheimer 1985, pp. 30–32.

[45] Rousseau 1976, pp. 719–954; see Steinbrügge 1987, pp. 115–119; ibid. 2020, p. 242 f.; Opitz 2002, p. 109; Kersting 2010, pp. 106–110.

A prominent victim was Olympe de Gouges, who—like Condorcet—became a victim of the French Revolution. In response to the "Declaration of the Rights of Man" of the French National Assembly of 1789, she issued her own *Declaration of the Rights of Woman and of the Female Citizen* (1791). In the first article it states: "Woman is born free and remains equal to man in all rights."[46] The English writer, translator, and philosopher Mary Wollstonecraft traveled to Paris specifically to participate in the Revolution, though she did not meet Gouges in person. Shortly thereafter, she wrote a *Vindication of the Rights of Woman* (1792).[47] In our context, it is revealing that Wollstonecraft was one of the few who explicitly criticized Rousseau's conception of female education.

History of the Female Sex.—As has been shown, the discourses on the nature of woman take place under specific social conditions. Thus, the shift from the rationalist position of equality to a specifically female anthropology was owed to the newly developing bourgeois society. This connection is addressed in the philosophy of history, which also emerged around the middle of the eighteenth century.

First, Montesquieu in his *Spirit of Law* offers a social-historical explanation for the "position of women in the various forms of government."[48] Thus, he laments the role of women in monarchies, where at court they must rely on vanity and flattery. In despotic states, women are objects of luxury and are locked up by rulers like slaves. By contrast, women in republics are legally free, but bound by custom. This sounds as if Montesquieu ultimately wanted to grant women even more freedom. What is important here is that he makes the situation of women dependent on the political regimes, by which he ultimately means social formations. In the end, he even considers women to be legitimate and capable of leading a state government with "mildness and moderation," as the examples in England, Russia, and India show.[49]

This mode of explanation receives a philosophical-historical turn in *The Origin of the Distinction of Ranks, or An Inquiry into the Circumstances which Give Rise to Influence and Authority in the Different Members of Society* (1771/1778) by the Scottish philosopher John Millar, in which the position

---

[46] Gouges 2018, p. 24; cf. Opitz 2002, pp. 150–153.
[47] Wollstonecraft 1989, p. 43; specifically on women pp. 53 f.; Honegger 1991, pp. 93 f.
[48] Montesquieu 1951, vol. I, pp. 146 f.; cf. vol. II, p. 125.
[49] Ibid., vol. I, p. 155.

of women in society forms a central theme. At the outset he writes: "Of all our passions, those which lead the sexes to each other are probably most strongly determined by the circumstances in which they are placed."[50] In what follows, he assigns the position of women to the historically successive modes of production. At the "primitive" stage of hunters and gatherers, who lead a precarious and uncertain life, women depend on the rule of the warlike man. In the "pastoral age" and especially with "agriculture," where food is secured and there is more leisure, customs become refined and so does the interaction between the sexes. Especially with the development of "crafts and trades," the situation of women improves, as they no longer function merely as servants but rise to become equal partners of men. Millar still describes this situation of women in the style of Rousseau: "They are wholly absorbed in feelings of loving care for the members of their own family circle and thus have a special opportunity to ennoble all their heartfelt emotions and nurture tender bonds, so that one can say the purpose of their education is that they may become perfect in all domestic virtues." [51] Yet with the further development toward "luxury," he goes clearly beyond Rousseau. Now he allows women to participate in social and intellectual life and to enjoy the same rights as men.

In a single draft, Millar unites the two contradictory sides of feminist Enlightenment. He describes both the Rousseauian family idyll, in which the woman remains confined to the private household, and the emancipatory perspective, through which the woman enters the public sphere and the world of education. The resolution of this contradiction consists in the philosophy-of-history construction. In the style of the Enlightenment, this reads like a history of progress, but specifically as a history in which women in particular make "progress" in their social status. The crucial insight here is the fundamental realization that such emancipation of the female sex is not only morally required, but also has certain preconditions in the technical-economic and political civilization, which have arisen historically and are to be further developed. I consider it an advantage of the European Enlightenment to have theoretically reflected on such conditions and processes. This reflection can be taken up in the current gender debate.

---

[50] Millar 1985, p. 58; on the philosophy of history see chap. 9.
[51] Ibid., p. 115.

Gender, Identity, Anthropocene

The anthropology of the second half of the 18th century contains aspects that have received little attention and are highly topical. As we have seen, the human being loses his privileged position on earth and comes to understand himself in dependence on nature. He himself is regarded as a living organism, capable of feeling, thinking, and acting. From today's perspective, such an anthropology has significant consequences. This concerns the physiological constitution of the human being, from which the question of the difference between the sexes arises. This, in turn, is connected to the highly topical issue of identity. And this concerns the theory of the Anthropocene, in which the relationship of the human being to his inner and outer nature is reconsidered.

Gender.—Obviously, the prejudice held by some Enlightenment thinkers that women had a different nervous system than men, which supposedly made them more sensitive and less capable of thought, has not been confirmed in contemporary medicine. The fact that such findings are now outdated once again shows how biased physicians like Roussel were in order to assert not only the difference but also the inferiority of the female sex. Yet, despite the successful and generally recognized correction in the meantime, the polarization of gender relations originating from the Enlightenment has persisted up to contemporary feminism and. As mentioned, the positions of *equality* and *difference* still stand in opposition to each other. This raises the question of how compelling this dualism is in the present day.

Simone de Beauvoir is regarded, with her well-known work *The Second Sex* (1949), as a representative of so-called *egalitarian feminism*.[52] By placing herself as a philosopher in the tradition of Descartes, she, like Poulain de la Barre, assumes a gender-neutral reason. However, from this kind of equality it does not follow that there are no bodily differences between the sexes. Beauvoir does indeed address the particularities of the female body. In the chapter on the mother, she describes in detail the physical changes during pregnancy, childbirth, and breastfeeding. Like the Enlightenment thinkers, she also points to the medical advances to which the reduction in child and maternal mortality is owed. But then Beauvoir gives her argument an original twist: the biological characteristics of women may be undeniable, "but in

---

[52] De Beauvoir 2000, p. 10; in this passage on Beauvoir and Irigaray I follow Steinbrügge 2010, pp. 200–210.

themselves they have no significance"[53]—that is to say, they have no social or cultural relevance whatsoever. The differences between the sexes do not justify the legal, social, and political inequality between men and women. For the actual oppression of women is the result of the prevailing power relations. On this basis, Beauvoir calls on women to fight for their equality in society.

Among the most important representatives of *difference feminism* is the French psychoanalyst and cultural theorist Luce Irigaray with her dissertation *Speculum of the Other Woman* (1974), which has found particular resonance among academic circles.[54] In the tradition of postmodernism, she criticizes the modern and Enlightenment idea of a universal reason, which she equates with the patriarchal reason of men. She opposes this male reason with a genuinely female mode of thinking, which is said to be determined by the biological constitution of women. In this way, she seeks to find a feminine "counter-language" or "women's writing" in order to enable women to achieve a "positive sexual identity."

Such a differentiation of the sexes points back to the debates of the 18th century, when the physician Roussel wanted to ascribe less reason to women and when the philosopher Rousseau conceived a more emotion-oriented education for girls. But whereas at that time such exclusion could still be defended with gynecological and population-policy arguments, this discrimination against women only became the prevailing ideology in the 19th and 20th centuries, against which the women's movement and feminism in various forms then fought back. Yet Irigaray's position of difference should not be misunderstood. Although the construction of a specifically female rationality is hardly comprehensible, it must be acknowledged that Irigaray, too, advocates for the equality of women. Even though she distrusts male-dominated power structures, she demands equal participation of women in science, society, and politics.

A comparison of the two authors, Beauvoir and Irigaray, has shown that both feminist models contain elements of both *equality* and *difference*. From this I draw the conclusion to continue the egalitarian side of the Enlightenment. This concerns the insistence on the fundamentally equal intellectual capacities of all human beings. And it refers to the demand for equality of women in relation to men. Here it must be admitted that

---

[53] De Beauvoir 2000, p. 59.

[54] Irigaray 1980, pp. 22 f., 76 f.; for what follows, pp. 450 f.; on the problem of a discursive construction of gender, see chap. 6.

formal equality before the law has already been achieved in Western societies, which includes, for example, women's right to vote and their right to education. But the aspect of *difference* comes into play again when one examines the *factual equality* of women. In order to increase this, special measures are needed to improve their real opportunities. These include special support for women, more parental leave, and binding quota regulations.

Other feminists such as Nancy Fraser warn against a certain kind of equality policy, which they accuse of playing the women's movement into the hands of *capitalism*.[55] The efforts of women to participate in the labor market ultimately lead to an increase in wage labor hours per household, while wages decrease and employment becomes more precarious. The rush of women into the executive suites of companies has indeed brought success to a few women, but the basic services have been offloaded onto poor migrant women. From the perspective of companies, women have by no means been integrated into the labor market for emancipatory reasons, but merely to increase economic growth.

In an indirect way, this problem again points to Rousseau, whose image of women was motivated by social criticism. For his ultimate intention was to keep the female sex out of the society of competition. Women were not to throw themselves into commerce and industry, but rather to maintain practical and emotional distance from the business world. Rousseau even linked this to the hope that the family morality of women, mediated through men, could exert a moderating influence on the capitalist-shaped society.[56] Of course, this has proven to be illusory. But today it may perhaps serve as a reminder that feminist movements should not exhaust themselves in adapting to male-dominated capitalism, but should keep the fundamental problem of social justice in view. Recently, a feminist foreign policy has become topical.

Identity.—The criticism by Nancy Fraser goes in yet another direction. She accuses the proponents of difference feminism of having neglected the social question by placing the *cultural identity* of the female sex at the center.[57] The struggle against economic injustices, she argues, has been replaced by the pursuit of symbolic recognition. Old Marxism has been replaced by cultural politics, materialism by a new symbolism. Because the

---

[55] Fraser 1994, pp. 222 f.; Fraser, Jaeggi 2020, p. 275; for criticism of capitalism see chap. 8.
[56] Rousseau 1976, pp. 112 f., 726.—This model originates from David Hume, who in his moral philosophy transfers sympathy within a family to the population of a society or even to all humanity; Hume 1962, p. 13; see chap. 7.
[57] Fraser 1994, pp. 9 f.; cf. Frick 2020, pp. 47 f.

left stood powerless in the face of global capitalism, especially academically educated feminists have focused on symbolic orders such as gender-inclusive language. Unintentionally, they have thereby entered into an alliance with the prevailing conditions. Fraser calls the paradoxical result "progressive neoliberalism."

The irony of history now consists in the fact that conservative authors are now presenting a similar critique. While the feminist Fraser adopts a Marxist standpoint, the political right turns the same accusation against "leftist" feminism. The general accusation is *identity politics*.[58] What is meant is that a social movement defends its own "identity," which consists merely of subjective sensitivities and grievances of supposed victims. In the extreme variant, this term means that a person may only represent the position of a particular group if they themselves belong to it. According to the criticism, legitimate social interests have been replaced by an elitist symbolic politics that is essentially charged. By imposing the corresponding language regulations on the social majority, this strategy, it is argued, leads to a dictatorship of opinion, which ultimately targets the "old white man." The conclusion is: Such identity politics contradicts the universalist values of the Enlightenment.

It can be objected, however, that it was precisely during the era of the Enlightenment that the "identity" of certain social groups was recognized and defended. This includes slaves, which will be discussed in more detail in chapter nine. And this concerns women in particular, who have been discussed at length in this chapter. Since the *Querelle des femme*, authors such as the Marquise de Lambert and later Olympe de Gouges or Mary Wollstonecraft have done nothing other than practice identity politics. It is true that in the Enlightenment all people are formally considered equal. But they also recognized that the equality of women had not yet been realized. Authors such as Montesquieu and Millar examined the historical conditions under which the realization of social equality is even possible. So when equal rights and opportunities for such a group of people were demanded in society as a whole, these were universal and at the same time material claims. In this sense, the much-maligned identity politics has existed since the eighteenth century.

In the present day, identity politics consists in the legitimate attempt of disadvantaged groups to make themselves heard in order to achieve both

---

[58] Gabriel, M. 2020, pp. 188–200.—This also applies to other social movements such as those against homophobia and racism; cf. Boehm 2022, p. 17.

real and symbolic equality. The objection that identity-political debates displace the problem of social justice is not plausible. In reality, both aspects belong together. The struggle against existing inequality in society has always been the commitment of a particular group to social equality in society. This applies to the gender debates from the modern era and the Enlightenment up to the French Revolution, as well as to the subsequent women's movement up to contemporary feminism. But it also applies to the labor movement, in which workers defined and organized themselves as a disadvantaged social group or "class," and did not shy away from using corresponding symbols. By campaigning for a shorter working day, higher wages, and co-determination in the workplace, they strive for greater social equality. The group identity cultivated in this process is unproblematic as long as it does not exclude other groups and seeks institutional equality in society as a whole. The participation of many different groups even carries the potential to advance society as a whole.

Anthropocene. – This new concept expresses the ambivalent position of the human being. On the one hand, the human stands out from nature, which he seeks to dominate with his technical means. On the other hand, for about two hundred and fifty years, he has altered nature to such an extent that he is destroying his own natural foundations. This constitutes the ecological significance of the Anthropocene. In addition, this concept concerns artificial intelligence, which calls into question the uniqueness of the human being. After the old industrialization replaced muscle power and manual labor, it now appears as if the computer could take over the functions of the human brain. Added to this is modern neuroscience, which claims to explain human feeling and thinking in physiological terms. From a philosophical perspective, the problem of materialism is virulent here.

In contemporary *computer technology*, a process is repeating itself that could already be observed in the transition from the 17th to the 18th century. Whereas the human being was initially regarded as a rational being, later his material needs, motives, and emotions were emphasized. A similar change is currently taking place in the relationship between human and computer. As long as artificial intelligence was on the rise, it could appear as the sole norm for rationality. The entire individual and social life was to be rationalized according to the model of algorithms. In this, I see a modern form of rationalism.

But in the meantime, a sobering has set in. To the extent that computers become capable of ever greater achievements, the question arises as to how the human being can still be distinguished from this artifact at all. For a long time, human emotions served as such a criterion. But even here, it is becoming apparent that a computer is able to recognize and simulate human empathy.[59] Such a robot can, for example, be used in care work to respond to the conditions of patients. The last bastion consists in the fact that there still remains an essential boundary between "simulating" and "having" feelings, a boundary that probably can never be crossed. In this, I see the sensitive animality of Enlightenment anthropology confirmed.

Likewise, modern *brain research* corroborates the physiological approach of some Enlightenment thinkers, who already considered the possibility of intelligible matter. The results of such research are undisputed, so that a correspondingly materialist approach is also inescapable. However, the problem does not lie in materialism, but in the *naturalism* derived from it. This leads to all psychic phenomena being explained biologically and psychology being reduced to neuroscience. Then, empathy exists only in a neural network. Such a reduction becomes even more problematic when even social and cultural processes are primarily justified by neural findings, as is the case, for example, in neurosociology. In this way, the independent and sometimes self-dynamic mode of operation of social systems is ignored.

When a "new materialism" is proclaimed in the theory of the Anthropocene, this refers rather to the *external nature* of the human being. In this context, it means turning against the intellectual arrogance of the human and instead recalling his dependence on the natural environment and thus on material nature. If I have characterized the philosophy of the Enlightenment by its turning away from the exaltation of reason and its emphasis on the human being's connection to his inner and outer nature in the lifeworld, then already this kind of materialism acquires an ecological connotation, to which one can refer today.

At this point, the discourse on the Anthropocene needs to be supplemented. It is not only about the capacity to act, but in this case about the moral obligation to do so. In *posthumanism*, the impression arises that, after having devastated the earth, the human being could simply make himself scarce. This is reminiscent of the above-mentioned French Enlightenment thinker d'Holbach, who described the human being as an "ephemeral creature" that soon disappears from the face of the earth. If this is not to happen in the 21st century through an ecological catastrophe in which all humanity destroys itself, it remains the ethical responsibility of the human being to avert total evil. For, as already in Enlightenment anthropology, the concept of the Anthropocene—which, after all, also contains the Greek word

---

[59] Misselhorn 2021, pp. 134 f.; cf. Precht 2020, pp. 24–39; Harari 2018, pp. 87–129.

anthropos—means that no one other than the human being holds his fate in his own hands. Only, in view of the current crises, this monopoly on action must be newly defined. In the next chapter, I will take the Lisbon earthquake of 1755 as an occasion to address the ecological discourses of the Enlightenment and to transfer them to the present.

5

Nature and Civilization

At present, we are still suffering from the impact of the Covid-19 pandemic, which for a long time seemed to push the previously prominent climate change into the background. Both crises concern the relationship between humanity and nature across the entire globe. Yet, while climate change advances slowly and insidiously, the virus struck us quite suddenly. In both cases, we are dealing with natural disasters that threaten people and their societies. At the same time, however, these events reveal the pre-existing difficulties with modern civilization.

In the following, I intend to relate the Enlightenment of the 18th century to the current crises of the 21st century. A first step in this direction consists in recalling the experience of the *Lisbon earthquake* in 1755. Particularly insightful in this context are the reflections of certain philosophers such as Voltaire, Rousseau and Kant. For they resisted the sermons of the priests at the time, who interpreted the disaster as divine punishment, and insisted that it was a natural event that could be explained by scientific methods. Moreover, these authors recognized that, although the earthquake was not caused by humans, it was able to wreak such havoc under artificially created conditions. They interpreted the physical evil at the same time as a social problem, which they sought to solve in different ways. In doing so, they also displayed early forms of ecological awareness.

If one relates the Lisbon catastrophe and the corresponding reactions, in a second step, to our present, an instructive parallel emerges. Even today, Enlightenment means resisting religious myths and conspiracy legends, in this case, the deniers of climate change and the coronavirus pandemic.

© The Author(s), under exclusive license to Springer-Verlag GmbH, DE, part of Springer Nature 2025
J. Rohbeck, *Modern Enlightenment*, https://doi.org/10.1007/978-3-662-71637-3_5

Thus, Enlightenment also means restoring the *truth-claim of the sciences* to its rightful place. Without climate research, we would have no knowledge of the environmental damage that has been affecting us for about half a century. And without virology and epidemiology, we would not even be able to attribute the fact of so many illnesses to the virus.

Furthermore, it is important to ensure that these natural disasters are *also* perceived and treated as crises of modern societies. The environmental crisis is a direct consequence of humanity's predatory exploitation of nature. But even the pandemic, whose origin was not caused by humans, could not have spread so widely without the process of globalization. Here, philosophy has the task of avoiding false abstractions, i.e., not reducing the disasters to natural factors, but seeing them in their cultural context. This also applies to politics, which, although it must take advice from scientists, must also make its own ethically grounded goals transparent and assert them in relation to the experts.

At this point, we must consider what concrete conclusions should be drawn from the climate and coronavirus crises. A well-known topos consists in viewing the current crisis as an "opportunity" for change. As Rousseau already did, who advocated a departure from bourgeois society, some contemporaries are calling for a radical break with prevailing capitalism. Similarly to Kant, who supported a moderate reconstruction of the city of Lisbon, other observers propose more or less far-reaching reforms. Still others believe they have already detected tendencies toward the desired social renewals.

Learning from Catastrophes?

Before I apply the experiences of the Enlightenment thinkers with the Lisbon earthquake to the current crises, I would first like to briefly characterize these crises and the resulting consequences. To this end, I will begin with a structural comparison between climate change and the Covid-19 pandemic. This concerns the temporal and spatial structure, the causal relationships, as well as the visibility of the resulting damage.

Climate change and the coronavirus pandemic have different *temporalities*.[1] The looming climate catastrophe was only recognized in the course of

---

[1] Gesang 2011, p. 29; Horn 2014, p. 110; Birnbacher 2016, p. 9; Gabriel, M. 2020, p. 10; Reckwitz 2020, p. 312.

the 20th century. It became apparent that this process extends over a longer period, having begun with industrialization in the 18th century. It unfolds with temporal delays, especially since no one yet knows exactly when and how it will end.—In contrast, the pandemic has only recently emerged. It represents an acute danger, because in a relatively short time, numerous illnesses and deaths are to be lamented. The enormous speed corresponds quite closely to the velocities of advanced transport technology, especially air travel. As a result, public life slowed down, as the mobility of people and goods was, to a significant extent, interrupted.

Both climate change and the pandemic encompass the global *space*.[2] The environmental crisis is not limited to certain countries and regions, but extends over the entire Earth. Effects are evident that were caused in distant places. Likewise, the virus has spread worldwide, revealing paradoxical tendencies. While the pandemic takes on global dimensions, the responses often remain regional, as individual states take national measures. Thus, the plague acts as a counter-movement to accelerated globalization.

There are significant differences in the *perceptibility* of the two catastrophes. Even though the virus itself is not visible, its acute and dramatic consequences can be experienced directly. When people fall ill, certain symptoms appear. Even if they feel healthy, an infection can be detected by a test. In everyday life, masks are present everywhere and at all times; they have become omnipresent symbols of the catastrophe. Added to this are the media presence of case numbers, images of deserted cities, and the scenarios in hospital intensive care units. For every woman and man, the consequences are directly or indirectly tangible: for the sick, the bereaved, businesspeople, employees, schoolchildren, students, and families.

By contrast, climate change is at first less perceptible. The data transmitted by science remains rather abstract for the majority of the population. The change in the Earth's atmosphere can only be measured by specialists. Nor is the rise in global temperatures noticed by everyone. The scientific fact that an increase in the average temperature by two degrees compared to 1990 marks a tipping point, leading to an ecological state that may no longer be reversible, eludes immediate perception. Not even the decline of natural species is directly observable. Nevertheless, certain phenomena are already obvious to many people, such as hot summers, drought, forest fires, storms, and melting glaciers.

---

[2] Osterhammel 2020, p. 256, 259.

Despite their global reach, it must not be overlooked that the inhabitants of the Earth are by no means affected by the catastrophes in the same way. The negative effects of climate change are more apparent in the South, in poor countries. The people living there suffer from rising heat, drought, and famine, which leads to local wars and attempts at emigration. Some wealthy countries in the North even benefit from global warming, as more agriculture becomes possible there.

In contrast, it appears as if the Covid-19 pandemic can affect all people equally. Any person, whether rich or poor, ordinary citizen or statesman, can be infected by the virus, become seriously ill, or even die from it. This is evidenced by prominent cases and hotspots in affluent regions such as Northern Italy. It is even documented that, at first, wealthy citizens living in metropolises and flying around the world became infected. So are we all in the same boat? Is the virus a democratic "leveler" among people?[3]

However, this is only true to a limited extent. Like climate change, the pandemic also has different effects on rich and poor countries.[4] With some delay, the virus has also reached Africa, Asia and Latin America. It can spread more rapidly because the people living there are less healthy and suffer from poor sanitary conditions. Added to this is the lack of protective masks and vaccines, which are in part withheld from these countries. The same applies to the poor in rich countries, as can especially be observed in the USA, where people of color living in unhealthy neighborhoods or even slums fall ill and die at disproportionately high rates. This asymmetrical situation brings social inequality and racial discrimination to the fore and even exacerbates the disadvantage of non-white segments of the population.

The *causal chains* of the two crises are also different. Even though it is scientifically difficult to prove,[5] there is broad consensus that climate change is caused by modern civilization. In this respect, this ecological crisis is man-made. The most important cause is the emission of greenhouse gases through the burning of fossil fuels. Ever since it became known, there has been talk of the limits of economic growth. Some even speak of an *ecocide*.

In contrast, the pandemic was explicitly *not* triggered by humans. The suspicion that the virus was artificially created in a Chinese laboratory has

---

[3] Žižek 2020, p. 17, 33, 42.
[4] Rohland 2020, pp. 46 f.; Knoblauch, Löw 2020, pp. 108 f.; Stichweh 2020, p. 221; Block 2020, p. 167.
[5] Gesang 2011, p. 18; Birnbacher 2016, p. 9; Ostheimer 2020, p. 179.—Apparently, there are also indications that the emergence and spread of Corona are connected to the climate crisis. Adloff 2020, pp. 147 f.; Rohland 2020, p. 45.

not been confirmed. For the individual, the virus is an exogenous shock that has struck them as something alien and hostile. Yet at the same time, it would be mistaken to reduce the pandemic to a mere natural disaster. For it has only become possible under the conditions of present-day civilization, which in turn is created by humans. Thus, the active behavior of those affected contributes to the virus being able to spread across the entire globe. This is an unintended and undesirable side effect of human action, mediated by the latest technologies.[6] This includes travel and the population density in urban centers.[7]

If this interrelation between nature and society holds, the aforementioned catastrophes not only reveal the weaknesses of modern society, they even exacerbate the existing problems.[8] In the course of the pandemic, new limits of globalization have become apparent, so that there is already talk of de-globalization. This strikes at the core of modernity, which was once understood as the overcoming of boundaries of space and time. For not only is global space being restricted, the horizon of the future of modern societies has also shrunk dramatically. In place of boundless economic growth and endless economic progress, there is now social stagnation or even regression.

There is agreement that the pandemic—prior to the war in Ukraine—marks a first *historical turning point*. But how should this caesura in history be assessed?

Some feel their fundamental critique of modernity has been confirmed and repeat the old thesis of the "end of history" or of *Posthistoire*.[9] Behind this lies the view that the virus has made the failure of modernity visible. In place of the belief that the world can be ever better calculated and controlled, there is now the experience of the unavailability of nature and society. The old megalomania is being replaced by the experience of contingency. In order to cope with this kind of contingency, all that remains is to simplify the social. Whereas previously differentiated social subsystems were assumed, now the whole of society is being fixed on a single and absolutely valid "disease system."[10]

---

[6] Shklar 1992, pp. 8, 89, with reference to the Lisbon earthquake pp. 9 f., 90 f.; Knoblauch, Löw 2020, pp. 89 f., 102; Vielmetter 2021; pp. 34–42.
[7] Stichweh 2020, p. 221; Reckwitz 2020, p. 242; Mukerji, Mannino 2020, p. 12.
[8] Gabriel, M. 2020, pp. 10, 282; Münkler 2020, p. 106; Knoblauch, Löw 2020, pp. 108 f.; Block 2020, p. 9; Adloff 2020, p. 145; Mau 2021, p. 23.
[9] Adloff 2020, p. 149; Stichweh 2020, p. 231; on *Posthistorie* and the future perspective see chap. 9.
[10] Stichweh 2020, pp. 198 f., 229, 232, 236.

Yet some observers see the current crisis as an opportunity for embarking on a new future. In this context, they counter postmodernity with a "new Enlightenment."[11] They take the pandemic as a positive occasion to free themselves from the capitalist compulsion to grow and to develop innovative visions. These future designs differ again in their radicalism and pragmatism. They range from the demand for a "global emancipatory project," a "moral progress," a consistent "economic democracy," to a "new communism."[12]

On closer inspection, these proposals also amount to more or less radical reforms. Their realism consists in identifying potentials in the crises that enable technical, economic, and social changes. As a rule, these are alternative developments that can already be observed within the current crisis. As with the earthquake of 1755, this includes a reform of urban planning to improve hygiene in the slums. The point, then, is to continue and intensify these tendencies that have already been initiated.

These reactions to the current crises will be further elaborated in the final section and explored in greater depth in the subsequent chapters. But first, we turn to an event that took place around the middle of the 18th century and triggered a wide range of commentary throughout Europe. The comparison with this earlier catastrophe is intended to make it possible to translate the reactions of the Enlighteners into the present day.

The Lisbon Earthquake

On the morning of November 1, 1755, a massive earthquake struck Lisbon. The three shocks lasted barely ten minutes, with only brief pauses. The first made the buildings tremble, the second destroyed 15,000 structures, including numerous churches, monasteries, and palaces. A third completed the devastation, after which a suffocating cloud of dust darkened the sky. The candles in the churches and the open fires in the houses led to devastating blazes.

According to eyewitness reports, the tremor tore open fissures several meters wide in the ground and reduced the city center to rubble and ashes. The survivors fled to the harbor and saw there how the sea had receded, exposing a seabed covered with shipwrecks and lost goods. A few minutes

---

[11] Frick 2020, p. 7; Böhme 2021, pp. 11 f.
[12] Gabriel, M. 2020, pp. 212, 281, 286, 308; Reckwitz 2020, p. 318; Žižek 2020, p. 39; cf. Block 2020, p. 155; see chap. 8 and 9.

later, a tidal wave swept over the entire city. Of the approximately 275,000 inhabitants at the time, between 70,000 and 100,000 perished.[13]

So many people fell victim to the debris in part because the Catholic feast of All Saints was being celebrated that day. Added to this was the curiosity about a session of the Inquisition with subsequent burnings of heretics. Thus, the faithful had crowded into the churches, where they were then killed en masse by the collapsing vaults. At another time, people would not have been so endangered in their homes.

The disaster was a *global event* because it was registered in many places around the world almost simultaneously. When the ground shook in Lisbon at 9:30 a.m. local time, the tremors were felt shortly afterward in Madrid. The tidal waves reached not only southern France and North Africa, but also the north in England, Scotland, Ireland, Norway, Sweden, and Finland. They even crossed the Atlantic and struck the West Indies, the Azores, and the Cape Verde Islands. Even wells and lakes cut off from the sea were set in motion, as far as the Mark Brandenburg, as Theodor Fontane reported.

Moreover, this catastrophe was a *media event throughout Europe*, because the news spread very quickly.[14] More than three thousand articles appeared about it within a year. There had already been severe earthquakes before, for example in Messina and Palermo in Sicily, but the Lisbon quake received special attention because the city was then one of the richest and most flourishing commercial metropolises and maintained close ties with Madrid, Paris, London, Amsterdam, Hamburg, and Venice. An essential prerequisite for the dissemination in numerous reports and commentaries was the already developed European market for newspapers, magazines, and books.

The destruction of Lisbon very soon had *practical consequences*. The Marquês de Pombal, who served King Joseph I as First Minister of Portugal from 1756, managed to overcome the ensuing chaos relatively quickly. He also initiated a precise survey through questionnaires in the parishes. He then took care of the reconstruction of the city, where now larger squares, wider streets, and lower houses were built. Finally, Pombal succeeded in persuading the Catholic Patriarch to forbid sermons of punishment and prophecies of new catastrophes.

---

[13] The earthquake reached an estimated magnitude of about 8.5 to 9 on the moment magnitude scale.—Günther 2016, pp. 13–23.

[14] Jürgen Wilke: *The Lisbon Earthquake as a Media Event*. In: Lauer, Unger 2014, pp. 75–95; Matthias Georgi: *The Lisbon Earthquake in English Journalism*. In: Lauer, Unger 2014, pp. 96–109.

Ecological Consequences

The Lisbon earthquake triggered a heated debate throughout Europe, especially among theologians and philosophers. How can an omnipotent and benevolent God allow such a terrible disaster?

The first answer came from the Catholic priests. In their penitential sermons, of which about 2,500 were counted in the European countries, they interpreted the inferno as God's punishment for a sinful port city. Here, the vengeful God of the Old Testament had revealed himself. However, even at the time, this was not very convincing, since it was precisely the devout churchgoers who were affected, while the actual sinners, who at that time frequented the huts of prostitutes on the outskirts of the city, were hardly harmed.

In response, the Protestant preachers used the earthquake as an occasion not only to denounce the immense wealth and pernicious luxury of Lisbon, but above all the Catholic superstition with its Inquisition court. In particular, the English Protestants published several dozen pamphlets in which they branded the disaster as a specifically "Catholic catastrophe."

Critique of theodicy.—Then the philosophers spoke up, above all the already famous Voltaire. He not only mocked the clerical sermons, but also criticized contemporary theology and philosophy. Thus, he saw in the fiasco a refutation of the view that God had created the world solely for the benefit of humankind. He adopted the standpoint of modern natural science and spoke of a purely physical event. For him, it was nothing more and nothing less than a natural disaster, a natural accident without any higher meaning.

Immediately after the event, Voltaire composed his *Poem on the Lisbon Disaster* with the subtitle *Examination of the Axiom "All is well"*,[15] which appeared in twenty editions within the first year, 1756. In this way, he contributed significantly to the spread of the news and stylized the incident as a world event. "The axiom *All is well*," he writes in the preface to his *Poem*, "seems somewhat strange to those who are witnesses of this catastrophe. Everything is arranged, everything is ordered, no doubt, by Providence, but it is only too evident that by no means everything is arranged for our present well-being."

The formula "All is well" refers to the English poet-philosopher Alexander Pope, who in his *Essay on Man* (1733) had described the world as a divine

---

[15] In: Breidert 1994, pp. 58–73; the following quotation p. 58.

order.[16] Since human beings are not capable of grasping the whole as something good, they see only the imperfections in the parts of creation. Voltaire does protect this dictum from "abuse," as if the terrible event had ultimately contributed to the general good of humanity.[17] But ultimately, despite all the tributes—which are more to the poet—he distances himself from the idea that the world as a whole is "good."

Voltaire, however, criticizes the German philosopher Georg Wilhelm Leibniz much more sharply, as was already evident in the third chapter. In a letter he wrote immediately after receiving the news from Lisbon, he states: "There you see, sir, how cruel nature is. It will be difficult to guess how the laws of motion can cause such terrible devastation in the *best of all possible worlds*. [...] What a sad game of chance is the game of human life! What will the preachers say, especially if the palace of the Inquisition still stands?"[18] With the phrase "best of all possible worlds," Voltaire alludes to Leibniz's *Theodicy* (1710), which he considers incompatible with the Lisbon earthquake.[19]

Leibniz is also the primary target of the tale *Candide, or the Optimism* (1759), which appeared four years later.[20] In it, Voltaire confronts Leibniz's doctrine with the harsh experiences of the recently survived apocalypse in Portugal and the just-beginning Seven Years' War in the rest of Europe. While Leibniz had conceded in his *Theodicy* that the world in which humans live is by no means perfect, Voltaire, both in his poem and in his tale, imputes the propagation of a perfect world. Whereas Leibniz meant the best of all *possible* worlds, Voltaire twists this formula into the *best* of all possible worlds. The case of Lisbon provides a welcome opportunity for this polemic.

Critique of civilization.—It was Jean-Jacques Rousseau who was not satisfied with such a solution. In his *Letter on Providence* to Voltaire, he defends the "optimism" of Pope and Leibniz and accuses the addressee of

---

[16] Pope 1997; cf. in this context Saul 1992, pp. 54 f.; Hellwig 2014, pp. 217 f.

[17] In contrast, Voltaire sets his empathy with the victims of the earthquake; *Poem* in: Breidert 1994, pp. 58 f., 63–65.—Thus, Voltaire justifies neither a "metaphysical optimism" nor a traditional Christianity, as Harald Weinrich claims; Weinrich 1971, p. 67.—Likewise, chapters XXI and XXII on Pope in Voltaire's *Lettres philosophiques* (1734) and the article "Bien, tout est bien" in his *Dictionnaire philosophique* (1764).

[18] Letter of November 24, 1755 to Théodore Tronchin; quoted in Günther 2016, p. 33.

[19] See in this context Weinrich 1971, p. 66; Marquard 2014, p. 207; Concha Roldán, in: Wagner, Asmuth, Roldán, 2017, pp. 9–24.

[20] Voltaire 1948, vol. I, pp. 179–297; on the Lisbon earthquake pp. 191 f.

exaggerating the misery present in the world.[21] In doing so, Rousseau does not limit himself to theological arguments, but gives his discourse a surprisingly social-critical turn. To lament the "evils on earth" is, in fact, something only those who, like Voltaire, "live in the midst of abundance" can afford. In contrast, Rousseau describes himself as a "poor man" who has no choice but to "find everything good": "You enjoy, but I hope, and hope beautifies everything."[22] This is no longer theology, but, in the best sense, ideology critique, because here the social basis and function of a position are taken into account.

But this critique is only a side issue in Rousseau's *Letter*, which comments on Voltaire's *Poem*. The core argument consists in linking the Lisbon earthquake with the critique of modern civilization. Against Voltaire, Rousseau argues that this catastrophe can by no means be reduced to a "physical evil." For "it was not nature [that] built 20,000 houses there with six or seven stories," but rather this city, built much too densely and high, was "our own work."[23] Had people not built such a metropolis in the first place and lived in lighter buildings, the destruction would have been much less. And if the greedy inhabitants had not tried to save their property, they would have fled to the countryside earlier and escaped death. It was not God who punished humans, but humans who harmed themselves through a misguided civilization. In this light, the collapse is not a natural disaster at all, but a consequence of human-made culture. Natural *events* become natural *disasters* only through human agency.

With this civilization-critical interpretation, Rousseau simultaneously gives his argumentation a *philosophy of history* dimension. For he situates this event within the historical process of all humanity. Consequently, the wealthy commercial center of Lisbon stands at the end of a long development achieved through technical, economic, and cultural progress. Yet the drama demonstrates that this progress has led astray. This world *is* by no means good any longer, but it *was* once good, when humans were still in the so-called state of nature. As Rousseau explains in his *Discourse on the Origin of Inequality*, which appeared shortly before, the revision does not consist in a "return to nature," but rather in a return to an agrarian social formation

---

[21] In: Breidert 1994, pp. 79–93, here p. 80.—In the following theological passages, Rousseau already outlines the conception of his later "civil religion," here still called the "catechism of the citizen"; ibid., p. 92.

[22] Ibid., p. 93.—At this point it should be added that Voltaire himself later added the prospect of "hope" at the end of his *poem*. In: Breidert 1994, pp. 72 f.

[23] Ibid., p. 81; cf. Steinbrügge 2020, pp. 125 f.

with a rural way of life.[24] Only under this condition is there reason to hope that the human world could become "good" again in the future.

In this *discourse* Rousseau even alludes to *ecological problems*. Already at the outset, he condemns the negative consequences that consist in the scarcity of natural resources and a deterioration of the climate. For, in the middle of the 18th century, the forests in Europe had been cleared to such an extent that a shortage of wood began to make itself felt, which then led to mining. Thus, Diderot in the article "Wood" (bois) of his *Encyclopédie* lamented the already noticeable shortage of wood.[25] Moreover, Rousseau laments the damage to air and soil. Accordingly, the forest influences "rainfall" and is thus able to store "vapors." Yet the dryness caused by deforestation also affects the soil, which becomes sandy and desolate. If, finally, "the earth is civilized," the farmland is threatened with exhaustion.[26] What is striking is this: Rousseau's actual topic is the emergence of social inequality. But because he sees this "origin" in the human being's estrangement from his inner and outer nature, the natural conditions are also mentioned.

But back to the Lisbon earthquake: The young Immanuel Kant also engaged with this catastrophe. In his *History and Natural Description of the Remarkable Events of the Earthquake, which at the End of the Year 1755 Shook a Great Part of the Earth* (1756), he deals extensively with the scientific aspects.[27] He traces the "tremors of the earth" back to constant "laws of nature" and considers the analysis of such terrible "accidents" to be instructive. But Kant does not content himself with the geology that was just emerging at the time.

Like Voltaire, he turns against the "culpable presumption" of interpreting such fates as divine punishment for the misdeeds committed in the devastated city. And like Rousseau, he holds the people living in Lisbon responsible for their own tragedy: "It was necessary that earthquakes should sometimes occur on the earth's surface, but it was not necessary that we should build splendid dwellings upon it. The inhabitants of Peru live in

---

[24] Rousseau 1978, p. 219; on the earthquake p. 117.—In this discourse, Rousseau generalizes his view that the first humans were brought onto the path of civilization by accidental natural disasters. Ibid., p. 75; cf. chap. 8.

[25] "If one considers the astonishing consumption of wood in carpentry and joinery and in other trades, as well as in the fires of forges, foundries, glassworks, and fireplaces, one easily sees how important the establishment, care, and preservation of forests must have been at all times and among all peoples, both for the public and for private individuals." Encyclopédie 1972, pp. 167 f.

[26] Rousseau 1978, p. 85, note d.—See also Montesquieu's remarks on climate and soil in chap. 7; likewise in chap. 8 the political economy of the Physiocrats.

[27] Kant 1968, vol. I, pp. 430–461.

houses that are only built to a small height, and the rest is made of reeds. Man must learn to adapt himself to nature, but he wants nature to adapt itself to him. [...] Man is not born to build eternal dwellings on this stage of vanity."[28] This formulation contains the beginnings of an ecology to which one can still refer today.

Finally, Kant even sees a certain "benefit of earthquakes," which consists in drawing practical consequences from misery. He regards the quake as a "sign" that calls upon people to take preventive measures in the future.[29] In this way, he anticipates the concept of the "sign of history," the theory of which he would develop much later in his philosophy of history. At this point, he calls upon people to develop their civilization not against, but in harmony with nature. Although Kant is inspired by Rousseau's critique of civilization, here he contents himself with pragmatic advice that had already been implemented by the Portuguese minister Pombal: to build structures so safely that they neither suffer nor cause great damage when they collapse.

Shock of the Enlightenment?—In the extensive literature on the contemporary reception of the Lisbon earthquake, one sometimes gets the impression that the catastrophe not only shook this city, but also brought down the edifice of European Enlightenment thought. Thus, a corresponding documentary bears the title "The Shock of the Perfect World," by which the teachings of Pope and Leibniz are meant. Or it is claimed that the disaster cured Voltaire of the Leibnizian theodicy. Overall, the calamity is regarded as a "turning point in European intellectual history," at which "the optimism of the Enlightenment turns into pessimism."[30] Such an interpretation virtually turns the relationship between religion and Enlightenment on its head. If one were to identify the Enlightenment with theodicy, the earthquake could indeed have dealt the death blow to the Enlightenment. Against this, it can

---

[28] Ibid., pp. 456, 459 f.; cf. p. 431.—At the time of the earthquake and the reactions to it, the debate on theodicy at the Berlin Academy of Sciences reached its peak. In the spring of 1755, the prize question was posed on Pope's dictum "All is good." The winner was a critic, which was probably very much in the spirit of the then director Pierre Louis Moreau de Maupertuis.

[29] Kant 1968, vol. I, p. 461.—Cf. Steffen Dietzsch: *Thinking and Acting in Catastrophe. Pombal and Kant as Masters of Crisis*. In: Lauer, Unger 2014, pp. 258–274; see chap. 9.

[30] Breidert 1994, pp. 15 f.; Lauer, Unger 2014, p. 13; Hellwig 2014, p. 216; Günther 2016, p. 12; Weinrich 1971, pp. 64, 71.—Theodor W. Adorno claims: "The Lisbon earthquake was enough to cure Voltaire of the Leibnizian theodicy." *Negative Dialectics*, Frankfurt a. M. 1966, p. 354.

be objected that only theodicy was affected, while an Enlightenment long since emancipated from it was confirmed. In this sense, the event in Lisbon can even be interpreted as the *beginning of modernity*.

The authors already cited support these interpretations. As shown, Rousseau continued to defend his religiously motivated optimistic basic attitude even after the earthquake. And he had already published his critique of civilization in the two *Discourses* of 1750 and 1755. Nor did Voltaire revise his benevolent and at the same time distanced response to Pope. Already in 1748 he wrote the tale *Memnon*, in which he mocked the theodicy of Leibniz—just as he would later do in *Candide*—through an absurd story. In the end, he describes the globe as a "madhouse" and thus rather as the "worst of all worlds."[31] Here it is quite evident that the catastrophe did not cause any philosophical about-face. On the contrary, both authors felt confirmed in their original views.

With their secular and scientific consideration of the earthquake, Voltaire, Rousseau, and Kant demonstrated their genuinely Enlightenment attitude. It can even be stated that the position of the Enlightenment was actually strengthened by the experience and processing of this debacle. Thus, the Enlightenment of the eighteenth century was not at its end, but rather underwent a decisive boost, through which it acquired a new and specific profile. This new Enlightenment overcame the speculative metaphysics of a Leibniz, whose theodicy rather belonged to the philosophy of the modern era, and instead established the aforementioned new sciences, which consistently oriented themselves toward experience.

In summary, it must be stated that the Enlightenment did not fail because of the Lisbon earthquake; on the contrary, it was able to intellectually cope with and practically overcome the resulting damage. Several indications for this perspective can be identified. First, the incident served to search for exclusively earthly causes and thus to continue the process of secularization. More important, however, was the conclusion that it is possible to reverse certain negative developments of human civilization and thereby avoid such catastrophes in the future. This decisive response to the crisis now needs to be updated.

---

[31] In: Voltaire 1948, p. 133; cf. Hellwig 2014, p. 220.

Dealing with Climate and Pandemic

Rarely before has science been so important and central. This is especially true for the current pandemic, in which, in religious contexts, a divine intention is still invoked.[32] Meanwhile, other and not a few opponents of the sciences have emerged, such as climate and Covid deniers. For a long time, we believed we were living in a knowledge society, but it is precisely this formation that is increasingly being called into question today. Against this background, contemporary science is under extreme pressure to legitimate itself. What medical doctors, virologists, and statisticians research and communicate decides over life and death, even if they do not always agree among themselves. Those who ignore this endanger and destroy countless human lives, as was especially observable in Brazil. What is needed is a new Enlightenment with epistemic authority.

Science and Politics.—However, its defense is becoming increasingly difficult, because individual scientists must not proceed in an authoritarian manner. On the one hand, this is due to the fact that both the Earth's climate and the spread and effects of the Covid-19 virus are extremely complex systems that harbor many uncertainties. The unforeseen outbreak of the pandemic in particular makes it clear how uncertain our knowledge is about the current state and further course. Reliable forecasts about infection rates and disease progressions are lacking.[33] On the other hand, this leads to scientists often disagreeing and disputing their methods and results. Some newspaper articles read like an introduction to the philosophy of science, in order to convey to the public that science has always essentially consisted of controversial discourses, without thereby degenerating into mere opinion. Ultimately, there are certain evidences about which there is broad consensus.

In view of this precarious situation, science must be defended against the accusation that it is elevating itself to an absolute authority. In particular, virologists and epidemiologists are currently accused of dominating public discourse and putting governments in a straitjacket. In this way, politics is said to become dependent on experts, who, with their para-state institutions, consulting firms, and think tanks, form their own and increasingly

---

[32] See the volume *Jenseits von Corona*, which contains a chapter "Religion—Church—Philosophy." In it, there is (no longer) talk of a "punishment from God"; rather, the "lack of interpretive competence" and thus the "silence" of the churches is lamented. Striet 2020, pp. 159 f., 163; cf. Kortmann, Schulze 2020, pp. 137–174.

[33] Münkler 2020, pp. 103, 105; cf. Adloff 2020, pp. 145 f.; Gabriel, M. 2020, p. 284; Block 2020, p. 155; Mukerji, Mannino 2020, pp. 23 f.; Keil, Jaster 2021, p. 12; Vielmetter 2021, p. 67.

independent centers of power. There is already talk of an "expertocracy," and now even of a "virocracy."[34] It is especially against the supposed power of experts that populists direct their criticism. In this critique, I see the expression of a deeper conflict.

On the one hand, politicians have no choice but to follow the recommendations of scientists. They owe this to their own claim to deal rationally with the pandemic. It is also the essence of a democracy to trust, especially in times of crisis, in the power of publicly funded, generally accessible, and discursively negotiated knowledge. Thus, talk of the "death of expertise" appears not only vastly exaggerated, but even reckless.[35] Such talk plays into the hands of the currently resurgent conspiracy believers and so-called "lateral thinkers", with whom we will deal more closely in the next chapter. For these reasons, the primacy of scientific validity must be upheld.

On the other hand, this kind of orientation toward the sciences carries the risk that political decisions lose their own specific legitimacy. For it creates the false impression that there is a direct path from scientific evidence to the right policy. Political conflicts appear as pure matters of fact, supposedly without alternatives. This, in turn, means that the respective goals that should guide political action are not even negotiated. As a result, certain normative claims such as values and worldviews fall out of view.[36] Governments then limit themselves to handling appropriate means for unreflected ends, that is, to technical administrative acts. Within political systems, this technocratic tendency corresponds to a shift of power to the executive. Here, those who speak of a "post-democratic turn" feel vindicated.[37]

To resolve this dilemma, it is necessary to regain what is specifically political. Although a crisis like the Covid-19 pandemic requires a strong executive, this by no means justifies an authoritarian style of government. On the contrary, this crisis can also be understood as an incentive to renew *democracy*. Thus, it should be demanded that parliaments be involved earlier and more intensively in government decisions. Moreover, the crisis can serve as

---

[34] Willke 2016, p. 16; Reckwitz 2020, p. 244; Bogner 2021, pp. 13, 21 f., 16, 119, for the following pp. 18 f., 97.

[35] Nichols 2017, pp. 1–12.—Gil Eyal 2019, pp. 138 f., considers the talk of the crisis of experts to be exaggerated; cf. the critique of *post-truth* by Lee McIntire 2018, p. 1.

[36] Bogner 2021, pp. 47 f., 77 f.; Münkler 2020, p. 107; cf. Willke 2016, p. 126; Mukerji, Mannino 2020, pp. 77 f.; Keil, Jaster 2021, pp. 8 f.

[37] Bogner 2021, pp. 38 f.; Stichweh 2020, pp. 230 f.; cf. Crouch 2008, pp. 10 f.; Blühdorn 2013, p. 114; Nassehi 2021, pp. 18 f., 25; see also chap. 7.

an occasion to curb the dependence of governments on expert committees. This includes making the selection, tasks, and powers of experts transparent and subject to political control, in other words, to democratize expertise itself. If it is decided democratically which knowledge is requested and implemented politically, something like "epistemic justice" arises.[38] What is required, then, is scientific reason, democratic decision-making, and social sensitivity.

Ultimately, it is necessary to determine the *goals* that should guide political action in a democratic manner. Because this can only occur in pluralistic societies through public discourse, the corresponding controversy must be conducted argumentatively and fairly. Especially in the Corona crisis, a whole series of goal conflicts arise. If one follows only epidemiological statistics, certain figures appear as benchmarks that function as imperatives for restrictions. In doing so, it is overlooked that the assumed value of prevention collides with other norms of society: with certain freedoms of individuals or with their claims to health, work, prosperity, education, and quality of life. The social differences between population groups and generations are also relevant here. In the context of ethics, the issue is the proportionality of the measures to be taken. Against the abstraction of an absolutized benchmark, the concrete context of the diverging norms and values must be set.

Given the fact that the Corona pandemic has taken on global dimensions, the tendency to want to solve the problem within individual nation-states must be counteracted. This is especially true in the worldwide distribution of vaccines, where an ominous competition has arisen between states and regions. Here too, the social divide between poor and rich countries plays a decisive role. In the ethical context, the issue here is *global justice*, which will be discussed in detail later. This raises the fundamental problem of the extent to which people are obliged to care for the well-being of fellow human beings living far away. The question of the scope of moral responsibility is a central topic in climate ethics and has become more acute with the pandemic.

If one now asks about the *concrete alternatives* that arise from the pandemic, one is again dependent on the connection between the climate crisis and the Corona crisis. The demands for an ecological transformation have existed for more than fifty years. But while the corresponding reforms have so far progressed only very slowly, the current catastrophe raises the question of whether and to what extent these long-demanded renewals can be realized

---

[38] Kortmann, Schulze 2020, p. 111; Vielmetter 2021, p. 137; cf. Fricker 2007.

at this moment. In fact, there are some tentative signs of this in business and politics, both in individual nation-states and within the framework of the European Union. As much as people long for a "normal" life, there is consensus that after the "exit" from the pandemic, the old normality must not return. Just as after the Lisbon earthquake, our cities too must be renovated to prevent the spread of epidemics.

In addition to the expansion of the healthcare system, necessary reforms include the promotion of public welfare. Following the experiences with the procurement of masks, measures against corruption in politics are being intensified; there is even a call for a general ban on lobbying by members of parliament. Particularly important is the restructuring of the energy sector that is already underway. Reinforced by the current shortages in the supply of gas and oil, the expansion of renewable energies must be massively accelerated. Added to this is the necessary transformation of the transport sector, with the banning of domestic flights and fewer international flights, the planned ban on combustion engines and their replacement by electric cars, the expansion of bicycle paths as well as public transport by rail and bus. Finally, industrial livestock farming, which in Brazil, for example, led to deforestation and probably also contributed to the pandemic, has come under criticism.

Concluding comparison.—In conclusion, I would like to summarize some parallels that emerge from comparing the current crisis with the era of the Enlightenment and that allow for a transformation of certain features. In doing so, I focus—as throughout the book—on the specificity of science and philosophy in the second half of the eighteenth century.

First, the example of the Lisbon earthquake has shown that the *limits of modern civilization* had already been recognized before that point. By demanding the adaptation of culture to nature, very early *ecological* considerations already come into play. This is represented not only by Rousseau, but also by other authors, who thereby do not represent the position of the Counter-Enlightenment, but rather contribute to the self-reflection of the Enlightenment . Kant as well shows traces of civilizational critique, although he does not advocate a departure from bourgeois society. As during the Enlightenment period, the current crisis can be used as an opportunity for changes in technology, economy, and society.

Second, the Enlightenment *recognition of the sciences* must be transformed into the present day. Here, the distinction from the early modern period is essential. While Descartes still believed he could deduce the movement of mechanical bodies with mathematical certainty, with the advent of inductive methods the uncertainty of human knowledge became a central issue.

It is no coincidence that with empiricism the epistemological skepticism of Hume emerged. Predictions for the future in the philosophy of history of Condorcet have only a probabilistic value. In this way, an awareness of social and historical contingencies arises. Instead of fantasies of omnipotence, the more realistic attitudes of Hume, Kant, and many other philosophers take their place.

Third, a parallel can be drawn from *rationalism* of the modern period to contemporary expertise, which, especially in the Corona crisis, runs the risk of absolutizing scientific reason. Against this, the later Enlightenment already made it clear that science should be "useful," in the sense that it should serve, not least, the goals and purposes of human beings. And these purposes are based not only on rational calculation, but also on interests, motives, and emotions. In this way, science is subordinated to individual, social, and political practice. These topics will occupy us in the following chapter.

6

Knowledge and Ability

In his book *Postmetaphysical Thinking,* Jürgen Habermas rightly states: "The horizon of modernityis shifting.[1] He refers to the 19th and 20th centuries and diagnosesthe following four motives: 1. the turn from metaphysical speculation to empirical science,2. the transition from consciousness to language philosophy, 3. the primacy of the humanlifeworld, and 4. the reversal of the relationship between theory and practice.

But even in this prominent case, a classic dilemma repeats itself: The thought motives from which modernity is supposed to distinguish itself all originate from rationalist philosophy of the modern era. The epoch of European Enlightenment is either equated with rationalism or simply overlooked. Against this widespread misunderstanding, I want to prove that exactly these transformations mentioned by Habermas have already taken place in the second half of the 18th century. With this, I try to substantiate my guiding thesis that the Enlightenment itself has shaped and reflected certain moments of modernity.

I want to demonstrate this here in three areas: first, in a theory of knowledge based on *experience* epistemology, which emphasizes the dependence of human reason on external impressions; second, in a novel *language philosophy*, which shows how linguistic signssignificantly shape and expand human knowledge; and third, in the transformation of religious criticism into a general theory of individual and societal *prejudices*, in which unconscious motives of human judgment and action also come to light. In all these cases,

---

[1] Habermas 1988, pp. 11–17; idem. 1994, pp. 15–60; cf. Wellmer 1985, pp. 77–85.

a detachment from metaphysics takes place much earlier than commonly assumed.

In the theory of human *knowledge,* there is no absolute opposition between rationalism and empiricism, because rational thought and action should still take place. But no thoughts are now admitted that are not based on perception and experience. In addition, a metamorphosis takes place within human understanding. For it is not content to process the given sensory data, but already operates in the field of perceptions, which thus become intelligent themselves. And through inner sensations, feelings arise, which develop a specifically emotional intelligence.

Language has been a topic earlier, since antiquity it was considered a characteristic of human reason. But the anthropologists of the 18th century do not limit language to the mere expression of thoughts, but already attribute a constitutive function to it in the process of thinking. Using linguistic signs, people form concepts, link facts and draw logical conclusions, to which cognitive competence alone would not be capable. Only this reversal of perspective leads to the emergence of an independent language philosophy.

Recently, the paradigm of knowledge based on experience has fallen into a deep crisis. For not a few people, the truthhas no value anymore. We speak of an era *after the truth*(post-truth), of *news beyond facts* (fake-news) or of *alternative facts.* This puts the entire system of a liberal democracy at risk. What helps against this? The answer is: Enlightenment! In our context, however, this does not only mean the claim of reason to autonomous thinking, because this is also claimed by the current "lateral thinkers. Nor is the recently established *New Realism* (realistic turn) sufficient, which is supposed to guarantee the empirically secured knowledge of facts. Rather, it is necessary to analyze and destroy the cognitive, linguistic, emotional, and social mechanisms of truth denial and conspiracy. As shown in the previous chapter, it ultimately comes down to the relationship between knowledge, society, and politics.

Post-factual Age?

The Denial of Truth was not invented in recent years, it has a long history. The modern sciences like Physics, Medicine and Natural History were only able to assert themselves against the resistance of the *Catholic Church.* Even in the 18th century, it was in Italy and Spain not possible to openly profess to Newton mechanics. The last remnants of such hostility towards science can still be observed today among the Evangelicals, who reject the theory of evolution and want to have it banned. The attenuated form is found in a religiously motivated resentment against the natural sciences, which are denied the ability to provide a veritable equivalent for religious belief.[2]

From a completely different direction come various relativizations of truth claims, which have established themselves under the label *Poststructuralism* and *Postmodernism* since the sixties of the last century. These positions are more or less explicitly directed against the European Enlightenment.

It was initially Michel Foucault who established a connection between *knowledge and power*. He breaks with the idea of knowledge as a "reflection" of reality, but analyzes how subtle power relations manifest themselves in everyday and scientific discourses. In *Madness and Civilisation* (1961), he shows how since the 17th century the newly emerged medicine and psychiatry have declared "madness", which had previously been tolerated, to be a "disease" and thus "non-reason".[3] In this way, modern and enlightened rationality has exercised an excluding and repressive function. Even though Foucault in his Kant-oriented writing *What is Enlightenment?* takes a rather neutral stance by resisting the alleged "blackmail" that "one must be for or against the Enlightenment",[4] he sees the tendency, which can still be felt today, that an increase in abilities has led to more power relations, already laid out in the 18th century.

As Jean-François Lyotard suggests in *The Differend* (1987), the discourses of the various sciences do not fit together; they neither merge into each other nor can they be mediated.[5] The communication between the fragmented disciplines is disturbed or even interrupted. Therefore, there are also no transitions from the discourse of the individual sciences to that of philosophy, which seeks orientation knowledge. From science there is no way to humane knowledge. For this reason, Lyotard is suspicious of "scientific knowledge" and replaces it with the *narrative,* which does not require any deeper legitimization. From the theoretical assumption that the real world cannot be represented reasonably, he draws the practical consequence that a politics should be considered outdated that makes its decisions on the basis of a supposed "reality".

---

[2] Lübbe 1986, p. 27, 60 f.; Frick 2020, p. 32 f.; see Chap. 3.
[3] Frankfurt a. M. 1969, pp. 7 f., 99.
[4] Foucault 1990, p. 46; for the following p. 50 f.
[5] Munich 1987, p. 12.

While Lyotard had already declared history to be a "grand narrative", Hayden White in *Metahistory* (1973) considers *narration* as constitutive for historiography. Accusing the philosophy of history of the Enlightenment of naive "realism", he separates historiography from historical research and only deals with the "literary form" of representation.[6] With this, he rejects the idea that historical facts can be narratively reproduced as a "fiction of the representation of the factual".[7] Objections have been raised primarily by historians who have researched the victims of genocides. They demand criteria according to which the narrative must not contradict the historical sources. It is therefore not surprising that White has revised the claim that historical and fictional representation are fundamentally indistinguishable in a later defense.

Among the influential philosophers in North America is Richard Rorty, who asks in several writings whether the world in which we live is an *objective or constructed reality*, and considers this question unanswerable. Therefore, he advocates abandoning the, in his view, contingent concepts of truth, reality, and objectivity. He also considers the concept of reason, derived from the modern age and the Enlightenment, to be a fetish that has become superfluous. The idea that the mind is a "mirror" of reality contains a claim to truth that can no longer be fulfilled today. In its place, Rorty puts human language: "Since truth is a property of sentences, since the existence of sentences depends on vocabularies, and since vocabularies are made by humans, the same applies to truths.[8] In particular, the linguistically composed metaphors have no fixed meaning and can only be understood by chance.

In our context, the question arises, both philosophically and politically exciting, whether this kind of discourse theory has influenced the current positions of a "post-factual" age. This is indeed the case. For it is by no means sufficient to doubt certain facts. To form a stable ideology from this requires theoretical confirmation. Thus, Armin Nassehi ironically notes: "You need grand theory to conceal the independence of the real from the rational!"[9] Therefore, it is not to be dismissed out of hand that the currents of poststructuralism and postmodernism have contributed to the current situation. They have spread the myth that reality consists only of various and

---

[6] White 1991, pp. 20, 23; idem 1990, pp. 9, 12 f.; see the section on the philosophy of history in Chap. 9.
[7] White 1986, p. 145; for the following p. 101.
[8] Richard Rorty: *The Mirror of Nature*, Frankfurt a. M. 1987, p. 49.
[9] Nassehi 2021, p. 33; cf. Harari 2018, pp. 358–360.

ultimately equivalent narratives. And they have spread a mistrust according to which a claim to power hides behind every assertion. Foucault emphasized that scientific theories can exert social and political power, the right-wing radicalssharpen this theorem to the point that one can dominate social and political public with any statements. They thus read social and discourse theory like an instruction manual for their own purposes.

In fact, it can be concretely demonstrated that some representatives of the new right have received and applied certain authors of poststructuralism. Thus, the successful right-wing radical website operator Mike Czernowitz admitted in the American magazine *The New Yorker:* "You see, I read postmodern theory at uni. If everything is a narrative, we need alternatives to the prevailing narratives." Trump's chief strategist Steve Bannon has repeatedly referred to Foucault, as has his predecessor and founder of the right-wing radical *Breitbart News,* Andrew Breitbart, who stated: "In the 21st century, the media is everything. The liberals win because they control the narrative. The media controls the narrative. Narrative is everything. I am at war to win the American narrative."[10]

Under the influence of Steve Bennon, for example, future President Donald Trump claimed that candidate Barack Obama was not born in the USA and therefore did not have the right to run for office. During the election campaign, the lie was spread that Hillary Clinton was running a child pornography ring. After his election, Trump boasted that more people had attended his inauguration than ever before, even though the film footage clearly contradicted this. During his term of office, fact-checkers at the *Washington Post* registered twenty false statements per day. He did not acknowledge his later defeat to Joe Biden and spoke of election fraud. After the internet platforms blocked his account due to constant misinformation and his own people declared the era of *post-truth,* it is all the more perverse that he has now founded his own channel with the name "Truth Social".

Already under the Bush administration, the deliberately used lies included the false claim that Saddam Hussein possessed weapons of mass destruction, which led to the painful and unsuccessful Iraq Warand ultimately to the "Islamic State". In the election advertising for Britain's exit from the European Union, it was pretended that the United Kingdom paid 350 million Euros per week to the European Union.Although there has been scientific consensus on global warming since at least the late 1990s, climate changewas doubted or even denied by large parts of the population. The

---

[10] Quoted from Neiman 2017, p. 53; cf. McIntire 2018, pp. 124–126.

same applies to the Covid-19 pandemic that broke out in 2020, which leads deniers to refuse vaccination and wearing masks.

Most recently, the brutal war of annihilation against Ukraine was accompanied by brazen lies from Russian dictator Vladimir Putin. First, he deceived his interlocutors about his apparently long-established intention to wage war in endless negotiations. Then he lied about the motives of his "military operation", claiming he wanted to fight alleged Nazis. Finally, he claimed that the horrific atrocities against civilians were staged by the Ukrainian army. In Russia, too, there is a counterpart to Bannon and Breitbart, namely the neo-fascist Alexander Dugin, who claims: "Postmodernism shows that every truth is a matter of belief.[11]

To avoid being misunderstood, I do not at all suggest that the authors of poststructuralism quoted above intended in any way the current perversion into far-right ideologies. It would also be unfair to hold them directly responsible for it.[12] Foucault and Lyotard were known to be left-wing intellectuals who were disappointed with dogmatic Marxism. Hayden White initially opposed the rather conservative historicism. Rorty also held a left-liberal position.

When considering the scientific achievements of these authors, it is undeniable that the consideration of language, discourse and narrationen-riched political and historical research. The problem lies in the absolutization, which has been reinforced by a one-sided reception. Even if it is true that facts are interpreted in a discursive way, it should not be concluded from this that these facts are created by discourses in the first place. The current misuse of these theories should be understood as a warning not to push the principle of discursivity to the extreme. The appropriate counter-measure is to return to the supposedly despised reference to reality of the Enlightenment in the sciences.

In its extreme form, such a consequence also applies to the so-called lateral thinkers *Querdenker*. They too could refer to a philosophical tradition in which self-determined thinking, which defends itself against the prevailing opinion, is elevated to the primary principle. Kant demanded in his famous writing *What is Enlightenment?* that people become mature by learning to "think for themselves".[13] This maxim has become such a common theme

---

[11] Quoted from Slavoj Žižek, in: DER SPIEGEL, 26.3.2022, p. 49.

[12] This is exactly the accusation against the critics of postmodernism recently raised by Daniel-Pascal Zorn 2022, p. 9.

[13] Kant 1965, Vol. XI, p. 54; cf. Frick 2020, p. 32 f.

that it has found its way into recent popular philosophy and philosophy education. And now, ironically, the right-wing radicals claim autonomy from the societal and state elite by "thinking laterally". This example illustrates the ambivalence of a merely abstract and formally conceived principle of *independent thinking,* which can be used both productively and destructively. It follows that not every independent thought is enlightened. The "light of reason" needs to be supplemented by illuminating a reality that has remained in the dark or even been obscured. Enlightenment therefore means that reason is bound to certain facts. In view of the current situation of "post-factual" thinking, this aspect should also be considered in a transformation of enlightenment.

The term *post-truth* was declared the word of the year 2016 in the *Oxford English Dictionary* and defined as "objective facts having less influence on public opinion than emotions and personal beliefs". In German, the term "postfactual" is preferred.[14] With this motto, the general standard for truth fades, so that the boundaries between objective and alternative facts, science and belief disappear and are politically manipulated. The word "truth" shifts to "truthiness", which is not necessarily based on facts, but means a "belief in truth" that refers to prejudices and feelings. What is new about *post-truth* is that the relevant politicians do not even try to give their lies the appearance of plausibility. In addition, not only has our knowledge about reality changed, but reality itself. When powerful politicians deny certain facts, it has significant practical consequences. If Trump and Bolsenaro ignore the effects of climate change or the pandemic, the long-term consequences are devastating.

In this case too, the *critique of the Postfactual* can connect to the *philosophy of enlightenment.* This includes an understanding of science that relies not on rationalistic speculations, but on empirical facts, as first developed in the theory of knowledge of empiricism. Likewise, the Enlightenment thinkers showed in the transition to sensualism how closely human knowledge is linked with emotions. Furthermore, the language philosophy that began in the 18th century can serve to deal critically with linguistic clichés. Last but not least, it has already been shown in the Enlightenment's critique of religion that the claim to truth is not a purely theoretical question, but a problem of practical behavior, which is linked with social interests and political power struggles.

---

[14] Neiman 2017, p. 13; McIntyre 2018, p. 5; Fuller 2018, p. 17; cf. Bogner 2021, p. 15 f.; Kumkar 2022, p. 19 f.

Sensual Knowledge

The *criterion for truth* changed during the transition from the modern era to the Enlightenment. While in Rationalism human thought was primarily the basis, in Empiricismthe observable facts provide the first guarantee for truthful knowledge. These positions are closely related to the contemporary *sciences*. Thus, René Descartesoriented himself towards Galileo's kinematics, who tried to derive the movements of physical bodies from mathematical principles. In contrast, John Locke refers to the physics of Isaac Newton, who took the reverse step by inferring the hidden forces from the observable movements.

Reality and Experience.—This exact method was adopted in the 18th century by Hume, who made the exploration of invisible forces a central problem. In the French *Encyclopedia,* an "experimental philosophy" was proposed, with the help of which the laws of nature could be explored and thus useful knowledge could be generated . Even Kant posed the question "How is pure natural science possible?" in his *Critique of Pure Reason* to philosophically justify Newtonian physics.[15] This connection between science and epistemology is important to me, so that it becomes clear in our context that the theoretical philosophy of the Enlightenment was essentially about the legitimization of scientific knowledge. The cheap accusation of scientism has proven to be untenable from today's perspective.

The corresponding philosophical conceptions of *Rationalism* and *Empiricism*initially represent a shift in emphasis. For even Descartes analyzed empirical facts, just as Locke tried to explain these facts rationally. The latter in particular shows how the old dualism of experience and reason still persists. First, sensory data are collected, which are then linked to concepts and explanations.[16] This gap between sensory perception and thinking is still noticeable in Kant, who reduces "sensuality" to mere "receptivity".[17] While the sensory organs passively receive the "impressions" of objects, the cognizing subject only becomes active with the processing by the understanding. Throughout the entire European Enlightenment, a *realistic attitude* prevails,

---

[15] Newton 1963; Locke 1962, Vol. I, p. 404 f.; Hume 1973, Book I, p. 94; ibid. 1964, p. 4; Article "Experimental", in: Encyclopedia 1972, pp. 546–551; Kant 1965, Vol. III, p. 59.—Adler, Godel 2010, pp. 9–19 refer to the "forms of non-knowledge of the Enlightenment".

[16] Locke 1962, Vol. I, p. 268.

[17] *Critique of Pure Reason,* Kant 1965, Vol. III, p. 69; *Anthropology from a Pragmatic Point of View,* Vol. XII, pp. 424–426.

which presupposes the independent existence of the perceived objects.[18] Although Kant is one of the founders of *German Idealism,* he defines "truth [as] the adequacy of concepts to the cognition of the object".[19]

Convergence of the senses.—The specificity of the European Enlightenment in the second half of the 18th century now consists in the fact that the emphasis shifts decisively further towards perception and experience. The physical basis is conceived in an *Anthropology,* as shown in the fourth chapter, in which the sensory organs of man are thematized and declared the starting point of all knowledge. Thus, Hume in his *Treatise on Human Nature* more consistently than before bases all human knowledge exclusively on "sensory impressions" (impressions), which he describes and compares with each other. Similarly, Condillac in his *Essay on the Origin of Human Knowledge* sees the source of knowledge solely in external perceptions and internal sensations. Later, Helvétius characterizes in his works *On Mind* and *On Man* the five senses in relation to the bodily organs hand, ear, eye, nose, and tongue.

In the article "Existence" of the *Encyclopedia,* Turgot draws the original conclusion that it is precisely the independence of the different impressions that suggests the existence of an external reference point.[20] If, for example, the hand moves towards a visible object and if touching and seeing then combine through experience and lead to the recognition of this object, this process presupposes a common bond that could only be based in things existing independently of the cognizing subject. Turgot also derives self-consciousness from the perceptions of one's own body; more precisely: from the combination of the different types of perception of one's own body in relation to other things.

Even Kant, who pays little attention to sensory perception in his *Critique of Pure Reason,* revisits this fundamental aspect of human knowledge in his much later written *Anthropology from a Pragmatic Point of View,* where he

---

[18] This is directed against the idealism of George Berkeley, who in his *Principles of Human Knowledge* (1721) treated perception as a purely mental act: "The being (esse) of such things is being perceived (percipi)." Berkeley 1964, p. 26; explicitly against Hume 1973, Vol. I, p. 30.—See also the *Lettres sur le système de Berkeley* by Turgot 1919, Vol. I, p. 185; the same 1990, p. 168.—Helvétius describes the "ability to receive various impressions as they are made by external objects on us". Helvétius 1973, p. 81; the same 1976, p. 77; d'Holbach 1960, p. 82; Condillac 2006, p. 69; Beccaria 1990, Vol. II, pp. 73 f.

[19] *Anthropology,* Kant 1965, Vol. XII, p. 506.—Such a clear commitment to epistemological realism is missing in the *Critique of Pure Reason.*

[20] Article "Existence (Metaphysics)", in: Turgot 1919, Vol. I, pp. 518–520; the same 1990, pp. 203, 207 f.

discusses and compares touch, hearing, sight, and smell individually.[21] Perception and experience are not only understood as necessary prerequisites for human knowledge, but as independent sources of knowledge.

On this basis, a completely new theorem has emerged. Because the faculty of understanding is extended into the sphere of sensory perception, cognitive achievements can already be attributed to human senses. Here, one can speak of a *sensory knowledge*.

This innovation is explained by Diderot in his *Letter on the Blind* (1749), starting from a specific case in which a person born blind regains sight.[22] This experiment aims to investigate whether the formerly blind person immediately sees what he previously only knew and could represent through touch. Can he distinguish a cube from a sphere by mere observation after a successful eye operation? Although Diderot expresses skepticism, his answer is that the formerly blind person must learn to see by experimentally connecting touch and sight. In this way, the relationship between the different senses is discussed for the first time. And this relating turns out to be a cognitive task. It consists in developing a specific "attention" within sensuality that allows the comparison and combination of incoming sensory stimuli. In Diderot's words: "The thinking instrument becomes capable of sensation", just as sensations are able to "think".

Sense and Understanding.—The step of the theory of knowledgeof the Enlightenment towards Empiricismcan also be observed in reverse. In this case, it is the human understanding that takes on sensory qualities. This involves inner perception, through which certain feelings arise. As noted, Hume has developed a systematic theory of *affects* in the middle part of his *Treatise,* with which he tries to justify his subsequent moral philosophy, which will occupy us more closely in the following chapter. But at this point, we are interested in the preceding influence of affect theory on the theory of human knowledge. Apparently, the first book "On Understanding" was conceived in anticipation of the yet to be elaborated book "On the Affects".

---

[21] Kant 1965, Vol. XII, pp. 447–451; cf. Hume 1973, Book I, pp. 8–17; idem. 1964, pp. 17–23; Condillac 2006, pp. 60–69; Helvétius 1973, pp. 81, 262–264; idem. 1976, pp. 67, 105.—The psychological aspect is emphasized by Ernst Cassirer 1932, pp. 123, 131; Panajotis Kondylis 1981, p. 286, speaks of an "anti-intellectual mainstream".

[22] Diderot 1961, Vol. I, p. 518.—See also Condillac's thought experiment, in which a statue receptive to sensory impressions is successively given the sensations of the various senses that a human is capable of. Condillac 1983, pp. 1–20.—Also Voltaire 1948, Vol. 2, p. 9 f.

In his theory of knowledge, Hume makes it clear that the understanding is also influenced by certain feelings. Following Newton, he expresses fundamental skepticism about whether the physical forces that manifest in observable movements could ever be directly recognized. Instead, he only accepts the "habit" by which people infer similar cases from experiences made so far. Thus, he traces the knowledge of a causal relationship back to a habitual connection. Because the sun has risen regularly so far, people assume that this will also happen the next day. In another example, the practical motivation of life becomes even clearer: Whoever has experienced that the bread eaten nourishes him, will expect the same at the next meal.

In our context, it is crucial that Hume sees the knowledge-guiding power of habit as rooted in a "psychic compulsion" or a felt "inclination", even in a spontaneous "intuition", an "original instinct" or "natural impulse".[23] The famous dictum is: "Reason is and ought to be the slave of the passions and can never pretend to any other office than to serve and obey them.[24] Hume thus conceives of the activity of the mind as ultimately an emotional act.

The lesser-known Scottish philosopher Thomas Reid went even further down this sensualist path. In his *Inquiry into the human mind* (1764), he only accepts knowledge that comes from *sensory perception*. He distinguishes between the five senses of smell, taste, hearing, touch, and sight, and elaborates their different characteristics. While objects are only indirectly inferred when smelling and tasting, people perceive certain qualities with the sense of touch such as heat and cold, hardness and softness, roughness and smoothness, shape and movement. Like Diderotbefore him, Reid also discusses the question of which properties of things—apart from colors—a blind person can recognize and how he can combine sensory perceptions.

Furthermore, Reid considers human perception as a distinct kind of *reflection*. Although he insists that people perceive the things themselves and not their mental representations, this does not mean for him that perception is a direct and simple act. The medium through which one sees, hears, or smells something, such as light rays, air vibrations, or exhalations, plays an important role. Moreover, perceptions are in a complex relationship with sensations, which Reid calls "suggestion".[25] For example, when a person hears noises on the street, these "suggest" to him a passing carriage. In this way,

---

[23] Hume 1973, Book I, pp. 94, 201, 210 f., 223 f., 226 f., 240.

[24] Hume 1973, Book II, p. 153; cf. Rousseau 1978, p. 135.—If one applies the standard "crisis of the absolute", one might already call Hume "postmodern". Zorn 2022, p. 78.

[25] Reid 1967, Vol. I, p. 111; for the following see p. 194.

the sounds function as "signs" of a carriage, "things are made known to us by signs". These considerations point to the elementary role of language, which will be the topic of the next section.

Like Kant later, Reid also tries to ground his theory of knowledge even more deeply. For he asks about the intellectual *prerequisites* under which human perception is possible at all. Reid counts the assumption that the perceived objects actually exist and that this perception corresponds to a self or ego in the sense of a conscious subject as the first principle.[26] He explicitly does not derive the second principle from reason, but bases it on a "Glaube" (belief) that he sees as inherent in human "nature". It is tempting to interpret these basic convictions as *intuitions,* which come close to Hume's affections. This once again confirms the Enlightenment's attempt to locate cognitive processes within sensory knowledge and to ground them anthropologically.

If we summarize the contribution of Enlightenment epistemology to the justification of truth, several characteristics can be distinguished. *Firstly,* it is no longer reason alone that guarantees true knowledge, but this is based on perceptible facts. A further step is to empirically justify the categories of thinking as well. This intensifies the realisminherent in empiricism. *Secondly,* sensory perceptions are considered in such a way that a sensualistic system emerges, within which the senses mutually complement and support each other. I call this ability *sensitive intelligence. Thirdly,* it becomes apparent that the human mind is also guided by inner perception, which manifests itself in affections. I see this as the beginnings of an *emotional intelligence.*

Ultimately, the consequence is to link perception and thinking with motives of action. This already became apparent in the call to connect human knowledge with practical use. This contains the view that every human knowledge is guided by certain interests and is thus embedded in life practice. This insight is directed against the rationalistic illusion of an "objective" truth and serves—as will be shown at the end of this chapter—the critical analysis of prejudices.

Language Signs

In epistemology, however, not only was empiricism continued and developed into sensualism. In addition, a completely new *philosophy of language* has emerged, which brought to light the sign-mediated dimension of human

---

[26] Ibid., pp. 452–461; for the following see pp. 108, 130, 185.

knowledge. While the rationalistic school of Port-Royal saw language as an obstacle to pure thinking, following Locke, especially Condillac worked out the importance of linguistic signs in the process of knowledge. In his *attempt,* he combined a sensualistic theory of knowledge with a new theory of human language.[27]

Thinking through language.—Historically, it is about the history of the origin of language, to which Condillac dedicates the final chapter on the "origin of language". As we saw, the anthropology of the Enlightenment integrated humans into natural history, within which animals have evolved into humans. This process now essentially also includes the history of language. Accordingly, humans and animals initially form a "natural" language, consisting of cries and gestures, and develop sounds and written symbols from it, with the help of which they can represent objects of the outside world.[28]

Systematically, Condillac succeeds in distinguishing the individual functions precisely. First, language is a *representative of ideas,* in that the perceptions gained through perception are expressed by means of linguistic signs. He calls this "transformed sensory perceptions". Once these are recognized, the corresponding ideas can be invoked. In this way, language forms the basis for human memory: "As soon as a person begins to connect ideas with self-chosen signs, the development of memory can be observed in him.[29] As the signs multiply, which are remembered by memory, the idea detaches from the immediate perception and gains relative independence from the perceived things. This in turn forms the prerequisite for thoughtful reflections.

It is to Condillac's credit that he introduced the aspect of human language into the discourse of the later Enlightenment in Europe. The Italian philosopher Cesare Beccariaexplicitly refers to the French pioneer in his *Ricerche intorno alla natura dello stile* (1770).[30] He too sees human ideas, which

---

[27] Locke 1962, Vol. II, third book; Condillac 2006, second part; cf. Trabant 2006, pp. 170–177.

[28] Condillac 2006, pp. 173–179.—This theory is continued by other authors of the European Enlightenment. This includes Rousseau, who devotes himself to the development of language in his *Discourse on Inequality.* Rousseau 1978, pp. 141–161; idem. 1976, pp. 172.—Cf. Turgot 1990, pp. 193 f., 208; idem. *Réflexions sur les langues,* Turgot 1919, Vol. I, p. 346.—Also Herder, who explicitly refers to Condillac, emphasizes that the origins of language should already be sought in the transition from animal to human. Herder 1984, Vol. II, pp. 253–257, 296; idem. Vol. III, pp. 126 f.—See also the prize question of the Berlin Academy of 1771 on the origin of language; according to Trabant 2006, pp. 220 f.

[29] Condillac 2006, p. 92; cf. Ricken 1984, pp. 94, 121.

[30] Beccaria 1990, Vol. II, pp. 83–91; see Rother 2005, pp. 82–86; idem in: Rohbeck, Rother 2011, pp. 306–309.

originate solely from sensation, represented by "words" which in turn serve to evoke the original ideas. In this context, Beccaria identifies a mutual conditioning of ideas and words: "For easier comprehension of ideas we need words, and to understand words we depend on ideas.[31] Words are even capable of amplifying the original ideas and evoking additional sensations. For example, if the word "sail" is used instead of "ship", the associated movement is expressed. This suggests that the function of language goes beyond mere representation.

Even Kant mentions the importance of language for gaining knowledge.[32] While in the early *Critique* linguistic signs do not appear at all, this changes in the late *Anthropology*, where Condillac and Beccaria are apparently received. However, although Kant assigns more importance to sensory perception there, he does not relate semantics to perception and experience, but solely to human thinking: "All language is a designation of thoughts." In this context, he introduces the concept of the symbol; he speaks of a "capacity for designation" that uses "symbols" and leads to a "symbolic knowledge". Consequently, he refers to symbols as "means of understanding". In this way, Kant transfers the use of linguistic signs to the intellectual abilities of humans. However, a reflection on the function of language in the transition from perception to thinking is missing. What is needed is a philosophy of language that does not merely presuppose understanding, but is capable of explaining its emergence through signs.

Signs as means of cognition.—This is precisely the innovative achievement of Condillac, which his recipients have apparently overlooked. He is concerned with the *mediation* between ideas and thoughts with the help of linguistic signs. If one follows this conception, the ciphers are capable of linking ideas in such a way that cognitive insights emerge: "Ideas connect with signs and only through this are they, as I will prove, also interconnected.[33] In this way, he allows thinking and speaking to emerge from a gradual process of interaction between sensory impressions and signs. With the help of linguistic signs, sensory impressions can develop into stages of

---

[31] Beccaria 1990, Vol. II, p. 188, for the following p. 88.

[32] Kant 1965, Vol. XII, pp. 497–502; for the following p. 500.

[33] Condillac 2006, p. 59.—See also above Thomas Reid on the function of signs in perception; cf. Ricken 1984, p. 182.—In the philosophy of history, writing is considered an essential prerequisite for historical consciousness: Turgot 1990, pp. 91 f., 144, 170; Condorcet 1976, pp. 62, 123 f.—The intercultural aspect of writing is emphasized by Françoise de Graffigny in *Letters from a Peruvian Woman* (1747), where she compares the cords and knots of the Incas with the European alphabet. Graffigny 1999, pp. 80–82.

thinking. For only through signs can thought contents be fixed and combined with each other.

An interesting addition to this is Condillac's sketch of a *theory of mathematics*.[34] In this too, he makes it clear that mathematical insights are not possible without signs. In this case, the written signs represent those numbers and their relations that would not have been invented by reason without these aids. In his succinct words: "However, it should be noted that the method of invention is always one step ahead of the inventors.[35] In the spirit of contemporary philosophy of history, these are *advancements* of the human mind.

In a similar way, Antoine-Yves Goguet had already examined the *use of symbols in mathematics* in his extensive cultural history of antiquity. He shows in detail how people learn to count and calculate through the use of tangible representatives—first through the fingers of the hand—and through this practical handling arrive at theoretical results such as the invention of zero as a blank space on a counting board. Finally, linguistic fixations of numbers can be derived from the handling of counting stones. These steps are not even consciously anticipated. On the contrary, the use of aids opens up more possibilities than were foreseeable: "Nature has provided us with arithmetic instruments," he concludes, "whose use is of greater scope than was initially believed.[36] The semantic means extend further than the intended purposes.

If we generalize these discoveries in the fields of language and mathematics, a common tendency can be recognized. Here, a fundamentally new understanding of human reason is gained. It is the *externalizations* or—if you will—materializations of reason that now make the difference. They no longer limit themselves to the traditional function of expression, but conversely exert a retroactive influence on human thinking. This means that the tangible representatives and linguistic symbols act as *means of knowledge,* on which cognitive structures can be read that were not anticipatable by pure reason. By generating such a surplus, the symbols reveal the hidden obstinacy of writing. This kind of *contingency* will occupy us again in the context of the philosophy of history.

Critique of language.—We have already learned from the criticism of religion of the Enlightenment that the philosophy of languagecan fulfill a

---

[34] Condillac 2006, pp. 98, 134.
[35] *La langue des calculs,* Condillac 1798, Vol. XXIII, pp. 9, 221.
[36] Goguet 1758, Vol. I, pp. 203–208, here p. 204; cf. Rohbeck 1987, pp. 162–165.

critical function. There it was criticized that the concept of God, for example, was an empty word, to which no perception and experience corresponded, so that theological debates exhausted themselves in a meaningless dispute about words. In the new context, this objection can be generalized into a *critique of prejudices*. The label "misuse of words" now means that linguistic signs generally detach themselves from their sensually perceptible origins and thus from the things to be represented, multiply and become independent. As Condillac explains, this applies to metaphysical concepts such as "being", "essence" or "substance", which often become a source of errors for Hume. This even applies to ethical concepts such as "virtue" and "vice".[37]

In his introduction to the *Encyclopedia,* d'Alemberteven denounces the misuse of words as the greatest obstacle to human knowledge and evil of mankind, which the work he edited is intended to counteract.[38] And his co-editor Diderot adds a social-critical dimension to the critique of language in his article "Lowliness, Abjection" (bassesse, abjection). He complains that the word "lowliness", which actually has a neutral meaning, is associated in French with the low origin and dignity of a socially weak person. From this observation he concludes: "Let us note here how language alone instills prejudices in us.[39] Such words can be used to insult the less fortunate.

Rousseauuses language criticism in the mentioned *discourse*for his radical critique of bourgeois society. With increasing civilization, language is no longer an expression of natural feelings, but becomes a tool of oppression for the powerful. Thus, language already contributes to the creation of social inequality in the dialogue between the poor and the rich.[40] Words such as "public welfare", "citizen" or "fatherland" serve to obscure class differences. Expressions like justice and obedience are verbal instruments of deception and subtle violence.

Particularly revealing are the suggestions of some Enlightenment thinkers on how to avoid the misuse of language is. Authors like d'Holbach and Helvétiuspropose to define the meaning of words through "clear definitions".[41] But Condillac goes a crucial step further. He prefers a method that

---

[37] Condillac 2006, p. 448, cf. p. 150.—Also Helvétius 1976, pp. 78 f.; Turgot 1990, pp. 145, 195 f.; Hume 1962, pp. 166 f.

[38] D'Alembert 1989, pp. 16, 36, 94; Helvétius 1976, pp. 114–120; cf. Ricken 1984, p. 202.

[39] Encyclopedia 1972, p. 132.

[40] Rousseau 1978, pp. 227–229, 233.

[41] D'Holbach n.d., p. 257; idem 1960, pp. 273, 278, 283; Helvétius 1973, p. 96; idem 1976, p. 126.

I have already referred to in relation to religion as *ideology critique*. This is not satisfied with proving that certain concepts are not clear; rather, it seeks the causes of the errors associated with these concepts. Instead of mere word definitions, Condillac attempts to analyze the original relationship between the words and the ideas they represent in order to trace the process of semantic shift. The aim is to reverse the resulting misinterpretations in order to avoid them in the future. Ultimately, it should become apparent how the different use of language depends on individual and societal interests. This type of language criticism can now be applied to the current situation, in which generally accepted knowledge is denied through verbal prejudices.

Value of Truth

Recently, the claim to truthhas come under threat. As initially outlined, the highly questionable attitude of *post-truth* has established itself in the USA and Europe, according to which *fake news* has replaced established facts. When powerful politicians adopt this, not only the theoretical attitude towards reality changes, but also the practical handling of reality. This shift has been observable for some time in climate policy and most recently in the dramatic effects of the Covid-19 pandemic. From a philosophical perspective, it is particularly tragic that the fundamental relativization of the truth value goes back to poststructuralist and postmodern theories, in which any realismis denounced as naive and the linguistically or narratively mediated discourse is absolutized.

Realism.—Now, a *New Realism* has emerged in recent years, which is gaining profile in international debates. In his eponymous anthology, Markus Gabriel rejects the assertion of an allegedly post-factual agein which alternative facts are circulating. Instead, he strives for a "new realistic philosophy" that refers to the Enlightenment but at the same time aims to overcome its "old realism".[42] *Realistic* is this philosophy because it holds the view that people can recognize reality as it actually exists. *New* is this realism because it does not mean a consciousness-independent external world. This results in the thesis that there is not only a single reality as a singular object, but many realities, which also include human thinking.

I see a very special approach to the era of Enlightenment in Gabriel's book *The Meaning of Thinking*, in which he addresses the sensual level of

---

[42] Gabriel, M. 2014, pp. 8 f.

human cognition.[43] He understands human thinking as a sense organ, which stands equally alongside the other five senses. While the ear perceives sounds, the "sense of thought" receives so-called fields of meaning, which consist of certain arrangements of objects and thoughts. For example, in the field of meaning science, all contents are arranged in their own structure. Thinking no longer opposes sensual perception, but is part of it. If Gabriel claims for himself that with his proposal he leaves behind the entire philosophical tradition since Plato, I would like to remind that the empiricists of the Enlightenment have already taken this step by equipping sensory perception itself with intelligence.

However, fundamental differences cannot be overlooked. Insofar as Gabriel declares thinking to be the sixth sense, he does not mean another type of perception, but a meaning-making in the model of hermeneutics, as an interpretation of a certain thought structure. He uses the concept of meaning only in a transferred sense, without linking thinking with experience.

An objection to this kind of realism, in my view, is that it blurs the fundamental difference between consciousness and reality. While it is true that a perceiving and thinking human being belongs to reality, just like the chair he is looking at, it must also be conceded that without this interpretive observation, there would be no such chair for the observer. But it cannot be denied that this object exists even without observation. In Gabriel's words, both observer and chair are "real", but this does not negate the gap between these different kinds of realities. In my view, this is a case of label fraud, as this realism ultimately rests on the reality of thinking.

One might consider the *realism* of the Enlightenment to be outdated or naive, but if one does not polemically equate it with "image", which was demonstrably not the case already in the 18th century, it still holds true today, in my opinion. As the experience with Hayden White quoted above demonstrates, the realistic standpoint has long since prevailed in the historical sciences, which consists in the fact that historiographic statements must not contradict the sources, which represent the historical reality.[44] The corresponding solution thus consists in applying the newer explicative, discursive and narrative methods and at the same time acknowledging the resistance of the historical material.

---

[43] Ibid. 2018, pp. 87–89.
[44] Kocka 1984, pp. 395 f.—A "veto right" of the sources is also claimed by Koselleck 1979, p. 206.

Finally, the *New Realism* also deserves credit for having distanced itself from post-factual impositions. However, it lacks the emotional and motivational dimensions and thus the potentials for a critique of truth deniers and lateral thinkers. Here we should benefit from the Enlightenment thinkers. They understood already 250 years ago that insights from perception to causal explanation are also guided by certain motives for action, emotions and language patterns. As their critique of religious and everyday prejudices has shown, it is not only possible to doubt the truth of a statement, but also to explore the individual and societal reasons for the emergence of errors. Such a form of critique of prejudices, which will later be called *ideology critique*, is now also available in the confrontation with post-factual ideologies.

Critique of Ideology.—The corresponding mechanism can be described with the term *confirmation bias,* which refers to the "inclination" (bias) to seek, select, and interpret information in a way that confirms one's own expectations.[45] Through the *bias effect,* only those perceptions and experiences are allowed that correspond with the prejudices previously intuitively and unconsciously formed. Thus, certain individuals who are subject to such a confirmation error perceive correlations that do not exist at all or not to the perceived extent. For example, if two facts are observed together, it is claimed that they are regularly connected, so that a causal relationship between the occurrence of the first and second event is assumed. For example, if a migrant commits a crime, it is unjustifiably concluded that "all migrants" are criminals and should be deported.

The use of *language* plays a decisive role in this. Thus, certain terms serve as simplifying interpretation patterns with which the world is divided into good and evil. For example, if a government takes state measures against the Covid-19 pandemicto protect the population, this is referred to as "deprivation of freedom" and "servitude". Also relevant are the words "Merkel dictatorship", "elite", "high finance" or "world Jewry", which in specific situations at the so-called regulars' table or during political meetings evoke the corresponding associations and defensive reactions.[46] Such emotional and verbal

---

[45] The term originates from cognitive psychology: Hamilton, D. et al. 1994, pp. 291–321; Werth, Mayer 2008, pp. 419–429; Kotzur 2018, p. 12.—Similar effects include: In the *status quo bias,* the existing is preferred over the new. In the *boomerang effect,* one's own views solidify when new facts contradict them. The *Barnum effect* enhances acceptance in the case of imprecise observations. In the *myside bias,* proposals from the other side are worse than those from one's own. *Stereotyping* leads to faster and unconscious labeling to distinguish. In *cryptomnesia,* memories are confused with imaginations.

[46] Butter 2018, p. 21, cf. pp. 22 f.

dispositions are then so pronounced that they classify new data in the context of their own worldview.

In this context belong the so-called *conspiracy myths*. These narratives claim that a group operating in secret, namely the conspirators, is trying to control or destroy an institution, a country, or even the whole world for base motives and by means of a secret plan. In this way, the insurmountable contrast between the *own group*, consisting of "good" conspiracy believers, and the *foreign group*, perceived as a threat in the form of the "evil" political "elite", is created. In extreme form, the state is even suspected of implanting microchips in the population during vaccination in order to enslave them. If a member of the foreign group shows negative behavior, this confirms the original assignment, just as good deeds can no longer change it. Conversely, it is equally irrelevant whether a person of the own group behaves positively or negatively. Corresponding value judgments stabilize and consolidate through *interaction* in social media.[47] The group dynamic processes ultimately contribute to solidifying the *division of society* into supporters and opponents.

Experience has shown that rational and fact-based arguments that are brought against this are only to a small extent able to shake such ideologies. It is far from sufficient to prove that the "alternative facts" are in truth "false" representations. However, from the European Enlightenment one can learn that certain prejudices perform an emotional and social function. Exactly this type of critique of ideology is confirmed in modern social psychology. The therapy that follows from this is to explore the deep structure of prejudices and to get to the bottom of the societal causes. If the "elites" of a society are constantly attacked, those addressed should consider how they can change their behavior towards the less privileged. Because habitual respect is not enough for this, social reforms are needed that sustainably improve the economic and social situation of the poor and needy.

The relationship between knowledge and society refers to the, from my point of view, problematic concept of the *knowledge society*.[48] Originally, this referred to the expanding sector of information processing, which is more relevant than ever due to the ongoing increasing digitization. As we have seen in the fifth chapter about current catastrophes, scientific knowledge about climate change and the Covid-19 pandemic has taken on a higher rank.

---

[47] Kumkar 2022, pp. 27 f., 159 f., 262 f.
[48] Beck 1986, p. 15; Wingens 1998, p. 173 f.; critically on this Rohbeck 2000, p. 216 f.; Negt 2001, p. 186 f.—More detailed in Chap. 8.

This knowledge is now as indispensable as it is controversial and must be continually reasserted against today's deniers of truth. Nevertheless, I consider it one-sided to declare *one* aspect of societal life as the entirety of the commonwealth and thus to absolutize it. Apparently, people no longer dare to refer to this formation as bourgeois society or as capitalism. This means that the recognition and enforcement of knowledge depends on economic and societal interests. This requires morally justified goals as well as political power, which we will now turn to.

7

Morality and Politics

It may seem strange that this book does not include a chapter on the theory of the state. However, this is due to the peculiarities of European Enlightenment in the second half of the 18th century, which left behind the "great" state theories of the 17th century. As is well known, Thomas Hobbes published his *Leviathan* in 1651, with which he tried to pacify the English Civil War (Civil War 1642–1649). He saw the solution in a strong state, which should create the torn community by means of a contract.[1] Because he missed social cohesion, he transferred absolute power to the head of state. John Locke also understood his *Two Treatises of Government* (1689) as an attempt to solve the second government crisis in England (Glorious Revolution 1688/89), which ended peacefully and led to a constitutional monarchy.[2] Because he, unlike Hobbes, already recognized approaches to a civil society, he proposed a state constitution in which the parliament had the task of recognizing and protecting this new social formation.

This liberal form of government has, as is well known, been preserved in Great Britain to this day. In France, which suffered under an absolutist regime until the Revolution of 1789, it already fascinated many Enlightenment thinkers of the 18th century. The young Voltaire spent a good two years (1726–1728) in London, where he was enthusiastic about the parliamentary system and the relatively great intellectual freedom. Shortly afterwards, Montesquieu also traveled via Germany and Holland

---

[1] Hobbes 1966, pp. 136–144.
[2] Locke 1967, pp. 264 f., 256.

to London, where he was even elected a member of the Royal Society in 1730. Conversely, Hume was invited to Paris, Reims, and La Flèche, where he lived from 1734 to 1737 and completed his *Treatise on Human Nature* (1739/40). It is worth remembering these contacts within the European Enlightenment to explain why no significantly new state theories emerged in the 18th century, neither in England nor in France and the rest of Europe.

On the one hand, there was the impression that nothing new could be added to the political philosophy of Locke. British authors like Hume, Ferguson and Millar criticized the model of the social contract as unrealistic, as such agreements could not be historically proven. Therefore, they largely avoided the topic and focused on morality, law, and history.[3] French authors like Voltaire, Diderot, Helvétius and d'Holbach primarily devoted themselves to anthropology, history, morality, education, and religion. Montesquieu described in his *Spirit of Law* (1748) the "Constitution of England" as a historical phenomenon, highlighting the separation of powers.[4] And Kant, in his late work *Metaphysics of Morals* (1797), very briefly and unoriginally subordinated the theory of the state to the aspects of "Public Law" and "Constitutional Law", briefly touching on the separation of powers.[5] Although Herder, unlike Kant, favored the nation-state, he preferred cultural and historical philosophy. Finally, the Swiss philosopher Isaac Iselin in *Political Attempt on Deliberation* (1761) no longer presented a systematic state theory, but merely a pragmatic guide for good politics in legislation and government up to the training of a good statesman.[6]

Secondly, behind this apparent disinterest in a theoretical foundation of the state order, a specific socio-political attitude was hidden. Because people in England could be satisfied with the parliamentary form of government, there was no motivation for a new design of the state. And because people on the mainland had come to terms with French and German absolutism, they preferred to avoid this topic. Moreover, it was far too risky to rebel against it: Voltaire spent eleven months in the Bastille and was only released on the condition that he fled to England. Diderot was imprisoned in the fortress of Vincennes, where Rousseauvisited him several times. In addition, there was strict censorship, which was also enforced by the Catholic Church.

---

[3] In Hume's *Treatise*, there is only a small section on the state: Hume 1973, Book III, pp. 283–288; likewise in the *Principles of Morality*: Hume 1962, pp. 45–52; also the *Essays* IV–IX, in: Hume 1963.
[4] Montesquieu 1951, Vol. I, eleventh book, 6th chapter, pp. 214–229.
[5] Kant 1965, Vol. VIII, pp. 429–437; on the separation of powers pp. 431 f.
[6] Iselin 2014, Vol. I, pp. 499–587.

As noted, criticismof clerical absolutism in Italy and Spain could cost one's life.

The only exception was Rousseau, whose radical social criticism has already been discussed in the context of philosophy of religion. In his *Discourse on Inequality* (1755), he subjected bourgeois society to a devastating critique, which, in his view, no longer allowed for any reform. He saw the consequence in a new foundation of society and state. In his work *The Social Contract* (1762), he designed a state that should guarantee the social and political equalityof all citizens.[7] In it, he indeed demanded direct democracy, preferably in small countries like the cantons of Switzerland. But because he allowed no interest groups, only a homogeneous "general will" of the "people" to be represented by a "ruler", this theory of the state—like the corresponding "civil religion"— ultimately bears totalitarian traits. Thus, this design falls short of the liberal concept of a Locke, as society is no longer appreciated as an independent sphere.

Rousseau's proposal found no approval in the enlightened public, neither in France nor in other European countries. The reason for this was less the danger of an autocratic ruler than the fear of a too powerful popular will. The American founding fathers even took precautions to limit the power of the people, by having not the eligible citizens directly, but so-called electors determine the president. Not even during the French Revolution was grassroots democracy realized.[8] Only in Switzerland, whose constitutions Rousseau originally oriented himself on, is this form of government still present today. For these reasons, I will not further pursue Rousseau's political philosophy, while his critical social philosophy will occupy us in the following chapter.

Behind this is the general observation that theoretical interest has shifted from the state to society. It should be noted that at this time there was no separate term available for the new object "society". Thus, the expression *Civil Society* had both a political and social meaning.[9] Nevertheless, society as a matter of fact emerged as an independent sphere around the middle of the century. This refers to the beginnings of industrialization, which were

---

[7] Rousseau 1978, pp. 59–208, esp. pp. 72–75; idem 1977, pp. 72–75; idem 1972, pp. 342 f., 349.

[8] At the beginning of the Revolution, the mathematician and philosopher Condorcet, who was a supporter of the moderate Girondists, pointed out a problem of majority voting, which leads to irrational preferences with several parties and alternatives, because ultimately the order of the votes decides. Condorcet: *Essai sur l'applicacion de l'analyse à la probabilité des voix* (1785).—On this paradox and recent studies of *collective choice* see Nida-Rümelin 2020, pp. 84 f., 87–105.

[9] As is well known, Hegel was the first to coin the term "civil society" as an independent sphere beyond the state: Hegel 1969, vol. 7, p. 307.

reflected in the new science of Political Economy. There, the dynamics of economic processes were recognized and assessed quite controversially, so that from today's perspective one can already speak of the *contingency* of social systems.

In the following, I would like to make the not simple attempt to prove that there have been *social science* reflections in the European Enlightenment. Analogous to the liberal economy, it is recognized for the first time that results also occur in the sphere of social interaction and communication that are not directly intended by any individual and rather come about naturally. In this case, too, *contingent processes* are decisive, which significantly curtail the rationalistic idea of an autonomous subject. Not only Freud discovered the unconscious, but also the Enlightenment and thus at the same time modern social philosophy. With this, I repeat my general thesis that a modernity shaped by the experience of contingency has emerged within the Enlightenment.

I consider the *moral philosophy* as the *first* such discipline, which replaced the old state theory since 1750 and formed the center of practical philosophy. This was based on the Enlightenment anthropology, in which moral judgments, even insights, were rooted in human emotions, so that I have diagnosed the discovery of an *emotional intelligence*. In this context, the social dimension of moral justification came to the fore, according to which moral feelings not only belong to the "nature" of man and are "innate" as it were, but develop, spread and stabilize within a community. In this case, morality is the result of communicative processes, so that I will now speak of a specifically *social intelligence*. Viewed from the outside, such social processes can be described as "customs and habits", i.e., life habits, of the peoples. Again, Humeis one of the groundbreaking authors of the Enlightenment in this respect.

The *second* manifestation of the social is associated with the name Montesquieu, who is counted among the founders of the just emerging *sociology*.[10] In the mentioned main work, he related the forms of government, social structures and values of the peoples to natural circumstances such as climate and soil conditions. In this way, he wanted to explain under which natural, societal and cultural conditions certain forms of government are

---

[10] So already Émile Durkheim in: *Montesquieu et Rousseau, précurseurs de la sociologie* (1892).— Although Niklas Luhmann calls his project *Sociological Enlightenment*, Montesquieu does not appear in it at all. Luhmann even asserts a fundamental "difference" between the Enlightenment of the 18th century and modern sociology, even a "break with tradition with the Enlightenment". Luhmann 1970, p. 66 f.

possible or which factors influence the formation and stability of certain state constitutions. In this way, Montesquieu reversed the relationship of state and society. Accordingly, the state no longer generates the community, but depends on the given conditions. It is not created in a spontaneous act, but develops in a contingent event.

If these results are transformed into today's present, a highly ambivalent situation arises. *On the one hand*, we owe the beginnings of modern social sciences to the Enlightenment. This not only allows us to formulate moral and political norms, but also to describe and explain the factual conditions in society and politics. *On the other hand*, it must be admitted that the representatives of the Enlightenment were not convinced democrats in today's sense. Although they praised the English constitution, which was progressive at the time. But they could not bring themselves to a representative democracy, which is standard today. Only in the course of the French Revolution did democratic ideas, including the right to vote for womenmentioned above, emerge.

Nevertheless, I consider it possible to apply certain theorems of the European Enlightenment from the second half of the 18th century to the problem situation of current democracies. This includes, first and foremost, the principle of *separation of powers*, which Montesquieu conceived in its still valid form with the innovative addition of the judiciary. In view of the spreading populism, I consider this principle to be particularly relevant. Then, the *moral philosophy* contains updatable potentials, because the cohesion of society presents itself as a communicative process that is fundamental for the formation and preservation of law and politics. Not least, the interaction of emotions plays an important role. This is something that recent political philosophy can return to, the *consensus* and *cooperation*in society declares as an essential prerequisite for modern democracies.

Post-democratic Turn?

At the beginning of the 21st century, democracy has fallen into a *crisis*. After the Second World War, the aim was still to overcome fascism and associate democracy with reconstruction and economic upswing. Especially after the collapse of the Eastern Bloc, democracy was at the peak of its development. From the fall of the Berlin Wall to the turn of the millennium, the number of countries where reasonably free elections took place worldwide rose to almost two hundred, at least half of which could be considered functioning democratic states. But in recent years, the number of democratically constituted nations has been declining in almost all regions of the world.[11] This is compounded by the low voter turnout in some countries like France and Spain. Above all, socially disadvantaged citizens no longer feel represented by the parliaments.

At the same time, many authoritarian states, led by China and Russia, have become more aggressive. Some countries that had given the impression of successful liberal democracies in the nineties, such as Hungary, Poland, Thailand, Turkey, and Italy, are sliding back towards authoritarianism or even open dictatorship. Even more surprising and perhaps more significant was the electoral victory that populism won in 2016 in one of the oldest liberal democracies in the world: in the USA, where Donald Trump became president. Even though this era is over for now, the dangers are far from over. Putin has since tightened his dictatorship.

But also in Western Europe, a new right-wing *populism* is spreading. This not only propagates xenophobia and racism, attacks the free press, and questions the jurisdiction and the state's monopoly on violence, but also casts doubt on the democratic constitution as a whole. In France, the far-right *Front National*, now under the name *Rassemblement National*, is steadily gaining strength, and its presidency was narrowly prevented in the last election. Right-wing radical parties have also established themselves in other European countries, such as the post-fascist party *Fratelli d'Italia* and the nationalist *Alternative for Germany*. In this way, the triumphant advance of democracy has come to a halt for the time being.

This creeping erosion has been termed by Colin Crouch as a *post-democratic turn*.[12] Like the other postisms we have already encountered, the term *post-democracy* also signifies the supposed "end of democracy". After democracy allegedly failed to fulfill its progressive promise of freedom and justice, it has, so to speak, outlived itself. It is perishing from the paradox that there are exaggerated expectations and at the same time these hopes are disappointed. The decline in politicians' ability to act and the growing dissatisfaction of the population with politics is lamented. The accusation is that real politics takes place behind closed doors. This puts the future viability of democracy into question. Thus, another end-time narrative is added to the numerous "post-histories".

---

[11] According to the criteria of Freedom House, only 77 out of about 200 states qualify as democracies today.—Crouch 2008, pp. 7–20; cf. Blühdorn 2013, p. 10; Nida-Rümelin 2020, pp. 7–28; Heidenreich 2022, p. 23.

[12] Crouch 2008, p. 10; cf. Blühdorn 2013, pp. 9, 114, 116; Bogner 2021, p. 39.

What causes are cited for the decline of democracy?

The sociologist Andreas Reckwitz sees a *first* reason in a *crisis of late modernity*, which is characterized by a post-industrial capitalism and a growing service sector. In the face of these societal upheavals, a cultural struggle has erupted between the winners and losers of modernization. On one side, a new urban, academically educated middle class has risen, while on the other side, the old class of the working class is threatened with decline.[13] This is accompanied by a new form of particularization and individualization, through which traditional ties to unions and parties have been lost. Similarly, the general public is breaking up into diverse communities and various collective identities. In this way, the state as a whole is losing its ability to govern the community in a democratic and socially compatible way.

A *second* reason is seen by Arnim Nassehi in the "overburdening of society", which triggers a "discomfort" with democracy.[14] By speaking of an "overburdening of society with itself" or "self-overburdening", he seeks the cause *within modern society*. As a result of its plurality, complexity, differentiation, and decentralization, it is unable to cope with overarching tasks. Its strength lies in solving isolated and specific problems, but it fails in solving collective challenges. It is not possible to focus all social and political forces on the realization of a common goal. Nassehi summarizes this observation in a paradox: "This society has almost all knowledge, almost all resources, most means and also the opportunity to solve the great problems of the world […] And yet it seems that exactly this is not possible, although it is obviously possible."

Long-known examples include dealing with climate change, the social impoverishment of many people, and the glaring injustice in the world. More recently, the Corona crisis has been added, which has particularly starkly highlighted the lack of coordination of necessary measures. Often, according to Nassehi, it has not been possible to translate medical evidence into political action. This is due, on the one hand, to competing programs that are not capable of gaining a majority, and on the other hand, to institutional barriers such as separation of powers and federalism. In democracy, decisions cannot be enforced with the necessary power. In this way, modern society fails itself. Nassehi cannot resist the temptation to point out the advantage of authoritarian systems like in China in dealing with crises.

---

[13] Reckwitz in: Reckwitz, Rosa 2021, pp. 108–122; idem 2019, pp. 135–201; cf. Beck 1986, p. 14 f.; Crouch 2008, pp. 71–76; Blühdorn 2013, p. 120; Negt 2010, pp. 163–171; Grau 2022, pp. 103, 107.
[14] Nassehi 2021, p. 16; for the following pp. 63, 169, 19, 309–316.

In our context, it is interesting that Nassehi considers the *Enlightenment* to be an unsuitable means to overcome the mentioned crises of society. According to his own interpretation, his theory is "a frontal attack on the enlightened, academic-professional self-understanding of those who think that people just need to be adequately explained how to behave".[15] The fallacy of the Enlightenment, therefore, lies in the assumption that theoretical insight already contains the practical decision. Consequently, it is necessary to break with the paradigm of the Enlightenment. Against this, it can be argued that rational explanation is indeed necessary to initiate societal changes at all. Furthermore, nobody really claims that reasonable arguments alone would suffice to politically realize certain goals. Finally, this truncated view does not even apply to the epoch of the Enlightenment. Once again, the Enlightenment is equated with an idealized rationalism and it is overlooked that the practical side of human reason was emphasized especially in the 18th century.

A *third* reason for the post-democratic turn is seen by Ingolfur Blühdorn in the fact that current politics are merely "simulated". Just as Jean Baudrillard has proclaimed the age of *simulation*, Blühdorn asserts the existence of a "simulative democracy".[16] This consists of the mere appearance of the sovereignty of the people or only the vague feeling of freedom and participation. Free elections still take place, so the suspicion goes, but these are manipulated by professional PR experts as a media spectacle. Symbolic signs become a substitute for practical politics. Political action degenerates into aesthetic performance and theatrical staging. Spaces for action for individuals and collectives turn into self-deceptions. Citizens retreat into the private sphere, while politicians build up beautified facades. Thus, post-democracy leaves only boredom, frustration, and disillusionment.

A *fourth* reason for the current crisis of democracy is identified by Julian Nida-Rümelin in the process of *globalization*.[17] According to this, the global order restricts the possibilities for action of democracies organized at the national level. As we have seen in the second chapter, this problem already arises in Europe, where the further development of the European Union is viewed with suspicion from a national perspective. Some critics accuse the EU of a lack of democracy because neither the citizens elect the executive in

---

[15] Ibid., pp. 328 f.; cf. pp. 332, 337. This polemic is specifically directed against the books by Göpel (2020) and Schneidewind (2018).

[16] Blühdorn 2013, pp. 12, 116, 177 f.; cf. Crouch 2008, p. 42.

[17] Nida-Rümelin 2020, pp. 13 f., 22; cf. Streeck 2021, pp. 115, 122; see Höffe 1999, pp. 13 f.

Brussels nor the elected parliament in Strasbourg is allowed to pass laws. The populist opponents of the EU even want to return to the old nation-states in order to save the sovereignty of their governments, with the democratic aspect receding into the background. They tolerate at most a cooperation between strong national executives.

Behind the criticism that democracy suffers under globalization, lies the *fifth* and in my opinion most important reason, that this process is significantly involved in the formation and establishment of the global market.[18] If one follows Wolfgang Streeck, it is the *global capitalism* with its inter- and transnational corporations, which massively restrict the scope of action of nation-states and thus contribute to the erosion of democracy with social consequences. After the Second World War, a "democratic capitalism" seemed possible because an expanding economy was able to guarantee modest social benefits. But when economic growth stagnated in the 1980s and neoliberalism took hold in Western countries, the democratically legitimized welfare state was scrapped. The economic loss of control by nation-states was accompanied by a new tension between capitalist economy and democratic politics.[19] Conversely, declining prosperity threatens the acceptance of democratic institutions. This contradiction is most acute in those states that primarily depend on the export of fossil energies. This is traditionally the case in the Arab Emirates, but also in Russia, where an authoritarian regime rules. Countries like Russia have failed to promote industrialization and have preferred the export of oil and gas. The connection between energy export and dictatorship is evident because there are few, state-dominated companies that are in the hands of oligarchs. Most recently, this connection has been negatively confirmed as democratic states try to weaken the Russian empire through import bans. These sanctions in turn lead to shortages in the energy supply, with which the governments are overwhelmed are.

However, all these diagnoses include the theoretical and practical punchline that none of the authors mentioned are willing to accept this depressing state. Even the term post-democracyis to be understood more as a wake-up call to open up a future perspective for democracy despite everything. Even the view of the overwhelmed society leads to cautious proposals on how this crisis could at least be mitigated. Even with the talk of simulative democracy,

---

[18] Streeck 2021, pp. 21, 261–274; cf. Crouch 2008, p. 42; Blühdorn 2013, p. 9; Schneidewind 2018, p. 85; Nida-Rümelin 2020, pp. 31, 195; Fraser, Jaeggi 2020, p. 227.

[19] From this diagnosis, Streeck draws the highly problematic conclusion to rehabilitate traditional nations and thus return to the level of individual state politics. Streeck 2021, pp. 13 f., 27–29, 39 f., 56–59.—See already Streeck's sharp criticism of the politics of the European Union in Chap. 2.

an attempt is made to turn the aspect of creative performance contained therein into a positive. Above all, the criticism of capitalist globalization is a plea to regain political control over the autonomous economy. Before I get to these proposals, I will first reconstruct the social science tools provided by the Enlightenment.

Emotional and Social Intelligence

Around the middle of the 18th century, the *moral philosophy* moves into the center of practical philosophy. Especially in this discipline, the national and regional differences are significant. The moral sentiment of Hutcheson and Hume is primarily a direction of thought of the *Scottish Enlightenment*. In *France*, the new principle of moral feeling was largely adopted and integrated into various writings on anthropology, social philosophy, and philosophy of history. In *Italy*, there was a legal and social philosophy in which individual and social happiness was declared the predominant goal. In contrast, in *Germany*, rationalist ethics prevailed, so that no moral sentiment arose there. Quite programmatically, Kant then rejected sensualist moral philosophy and built his ethics on reason.[20] Although there was not *the* ethics of the European Enlightenment in this case either, the moral feeling can be considered a new paradigm.

We have already become acquainted with the theoretical prerequisites in the preceding chapters. *Firstly*, morality is founded *beyond religion*. This does not mean, as shown, that the Christian faith would no longer be granted any social function. But the new moral rules are now no longer considered commands decreed by God. *Secondly*, the Enlightenment thinkers base their moral philosophy on the newly developed *anthropology*. According to this, humans are by nature social beings and thus also sociable beings. The biological nature also anchors the needs and emotions of humans. This now applies in particular to the "moral feeling", the existence of which is to be demonstrated alongside egoism in human nature. *Thirdly*, this proof can only be provided with the help of the *empirical method*. This applies to both

---

[20] In the *Groundwork of the Metaphysics of Morals* (1785), Kant excludes the "natural dispositions" of man as a basis for morality from the outset: both the individual "pursuit of happiness" and "sympathy". Kant 1965, Vol. VII, pp. 18, 20, 23 f.—Only in the *Critique of Judgment* (1790) does he invoke "the general feeling of participation". Ibid., Vol. X, p. 464.—And in the *Anthropology* (1798), he mentions the "union of well-being with virtue" and thus a "civilized happiness", without even considering the possibility of a moral feeling. Ibid., Vol. XII, p. 616.

the external perception of the actions of other people and the internal sensation of one's own emotions, for which the new term *moral sense* stands.

Feeling and Understanding.—Hume before Kant presented the most innovative and influential *moral philosophy* of the Enlightenment. It has both an *emotional* basis, which is supported anthropologically, and a *social* dimension, which contains sociological approaches. This ethics I would now like to analyze in more detail as an example: first on the basis of the *Enquiry Concerning the Principles of Morals* (1751) and then in the earlier draft *Treatise of Human Nature* (1739/40).

Firstly, Hume opposes the rationalist ethics of the 17th century, which is oriented towards an allegedly God-given natural law.[21] Following Hutcheson, he bases human morality solely on "feeling" (sense, sentiment), which is inherent in human nature and can be directly perceived by humans within themselves: "The concept of morality includes a feeling common to all humans."[22] He distinguishes between "self-love", which he acknowledges, and a "moral sense", which is related to "benevolence" towards other people.[23] This also includes "sympathy", which consists in the ability to put oneself in the position of other people in order to empathize with their feelings or to let them share in one's own feelings.[24]

However, Hume has to admit that feelings can also be mistaken. A drastic example of misguided benevolence is spontaneous pity for a beggar, because the resulting alms promote laziness and harm industry.[25] In contrast, Hume demands not to lose sight of the "public utility", the "interests of people" or the "happiness" of the community, by which he understands economic prosperity and legally secured private property. At this point, he lets the previously excluded *reason* back in through the back door, assigning it the task of analysing the social situation and thereby correcting the moral feeling. Thus, he answers the initial "question of whether morality should be derived from

---

[21] Specifically against Samuel Clarke's *A demonstration of the being and attributes of God* (1705/06); Clarke 1998.—However, Lord Shaftesbury had already opposed this with his *Inquiry concerning Virtue, or Merit* (1711) and introduced the concept of the *moral sense*. Shaftesbury 2012.—Against this background, Hume mentions a "controversy" at the beginning of his *investigation* and takes sides for Shaftesbury. Hume 1962, pp. 4 f.

[22] Hume 1962, p. 120; cf. ibid., pp. 5, 7, 9, 135–146; cf. Hume 1973, Book III, pp. 198, 212.—The theory of the *moral sense* was first developed in 1725 by Francis Hutcheson, whom Hume greatly appreciated. Hutcheson 1986, p. 87.

[23] With this, Hume opposes Bernard Mandeville, who in his *Fable of the Bees* (1705) posited that it is not "virtue" but "vice" that advances civil society. Mandeville 1968, pp. 80 f., 87; Hume 1962, p. 3.

[24] Hume 1962, pp. 11–18; idem 1973, pp. 96, 99, 103 f.; cf. Rohbeck 1978, pp. 117–131.

[25] Hume 1962, p. 16; for the following see p. 14 f.—With this judgement, Hume again agrees with Mandeville. Mandeville 1968, pp. 286–353.

reason or from feeling" with a final compromise that postulates the "interaction of reason and feeling."[26]

However, I do not want to be satisfied with this result, as I have already tried to show in the last chapter how the Scottish Enlightenment thinkers overcame the traditional separation between sensory perception and thinking. For here too, I see signs that Hume attributes *rational competencies to the feeling itself*. He speaks of a "sense of justice" that could be determined either rationally or emotionally. In the latter case, it follows that "one recognizes the property, the object of justice, as it were, by a simple, original instinct, not by argumentation or reflection".[27] Even if Hume relativizes this statement, numerous formulations follow that point in this direction. He repeatedly speaks of a "certain inclination towards the welfare of mankind" inherent in man and that the usefulness corresponds to a "natural inclination" by creating a "general, unchangeable standard" through the "exchange of feelings".[28] Ultimately, human happiness is determined in a purely emotional way: "It appears evident that the ultimate ends of human actions can never be explained by reason, but that they are exclusively determined by the feelings and inclinations of people, completely independent of intellectual abilities." While Aristotle still developed happiness argumentatively as an end in itself, Hume points to the emotional basis of the feeling of happiness. I refer to this ability of moral feeling as *emotional intelligence*.

Secondly, Hume tries to justify the moral sociophilosophically. While Hutcheson has characterized the *moral sense* as a merely innate ability of man, Hume transforms this natural disposition into a social process. The term *sympathy* already means the feeling of people *with* other people, just as one can feel sympathy with the sympathy of a person. In this way, sympathy becomes autoreflexive.

In the *Treatise*, it says: "People behave towards each other in their interior like mirrors. And not only in the sense that they mirror their emotional reactions to each other; but the radiations of the affects, feelings, opinions are also repeatedly thrown back and forth." The image of two strings, one of which sets the other into simultaneous vibrations, is also famous: "If two strings are equally tensioned, the movement of one is communicated to the

---

[26] Hume 1962, pp. 4, 7; cf. 135, 145 f.
[27] Ibid., p. 40 f.; for the following see p. 53, 56, 61, 70, 72.
[28] Ibid., p. 56, 68–70, 72; the next quote p. 144.

other; in the same way, emotional movements easily pass from one person to another and generate corresponding movements in all human beings."[29]

The *investigation* is about the reciprocal transmission of social feelings such as "friendship and gratitude" or "affection and community spirit": "These characteristics seem, wherever they occur, to overflow onto every observer and to arouse the same feelings of benevolence and affection that they trigger in everyone around them."[30] Finally, they gain a "tacit validity" through habit. Starting from the family as the natural haven of morality, the moral feeling expands to society and finally targets all of humanity. In the end, individuals adopt a "general standpoint", which corresponds to the perspective of a real or fictional impartial "spectator" and is eventually internalized.[31] Again, it is crucial that Hume does not burden this task of objectifying generalization on a solitary reason. Rather, he lets the universally valid judgment emerge from the social process of mutual adoption of moral judgments. The *affectivecommunication* corresponds with the *reciprocalrecognition*. With this snowball system of emotions and judgments, Hume conceives a *social philosophy of morality*.

Interaction of interests.—Particularly interesting is now that Hume constructs the mutual interaction of people also *without* the moral feeling of sympathy. He replaces altruism with *enlightened egoism*. Like his predecessors Hobbes and Locke, he is well aware that in the bourgeois society there is great uncertainty, which intensifies if the state is to refrain from protecting private property. According to Hume, this danger can only be averted if every owner realizes that it is in his own interest to recognize the private property of other citizens: "So there is no affect capable of keeping the selfish inclination in check, except this inclination itself, if it is given a different direction."[32] If all citizens recognize that they can only realize their interests in the long term if they renounce their immediate advantages, they evoke corresponding behaviors in other individuals.

But how can such a system of recognition establish itself, especially since "at the beginning" no one knows whether the others have the same insight? Hume's answer is that people first act and deduce the common intention from the corresponding actions:

---

[29] Hume 1973, Book II, p. 98 f., 329.
[30] Hume 1962, p. 13; for the following ibid., p. 68, 117, 124, 137.
[31] Hume 1962, p. 72, 121, 124, 141; cf. 1973, Book III, p. 335.—This motif of the disinterested observer is increasingly found in the *Theory of Moral Sentiments* (1759) by Adam Smith 1977, p. 169 f.; see Honneth 2018, p. 92–95; 104–111.
[32] Hume 1973, Book III, p. 227–245, here p. 236.

"I see, it is in my interest to leave another in possession of his goods, *provided* that he behaves in the same way towards me. He, in turn, is aware of a similar interest in regulating his behavior. [...] And this can aptly be called an agreement or mutual consent. The intermediary of a promise is not necessary for this. The actions of each of us are conditioned by the actions of the other."[33]

This civil order is thus established through observation and imitation in practical execution. A common system of action arises through mimetic transmission, without this, as Hume explicitly emphasizes, being "intended by its creators". The social system stabilizes through "habituation", so that people eventually perceive an "artificially" formed society as "natural". Similar to the economic sphere, emotions are supposed to regulate themselves. With this system of natural recognition, Hume develops a social philosophy a social philosophy, in which the *contingency* of collective action appears. He thus demonstrates how the Scottish Enlightenment counts towards the beginnings of modern *sociology*.

In the *French Enlightenment*, there are no separate writings on moral philosophy, but there are passages on morality in anthropological and historical philosophical works. Here, "feeling" plays a dominant role, as it is part of the natural equipment of man. In *On Man* (1772) Helvétius avoids the postulation of a specifically moral feeling and focuses on "self-love" (amour de soi), which consists in the avoidance of pain and the search for pleasure.[34] The same applies to d'Holbach's *System of Nature* (1770), in which pleasure and pain are also the essential drives of man.[35] Needs and interests are then also considered as causes for all forms of sociability, from division of labor to state formation. Especially with him, the impression arises that he only recognizes selfish motives as natural, while the "moral feeling", which transcends purely egoistic interest, seems too idealistic to him. Both authors see in individual and social "happiness" (bonheur) and in the corresponding "benefit" the highest and last measure of morality. More than Hume, they prove to be precursors of utilitarianism.

Social genesis of egoism.—In contrast, Rousseau in his *Discourse on Inequality* presupposes an original "compassion", which he even extends to the whole "human race". But he combines this with the mentioned criticism of bourgeois society, in which, in his opinion, exactly this moral feeling

---

[33] Ibid., p. 233, the following quotes p. 270; cf. ibid. 1962, p. 159.
[34] Helvétius 1976, p. 179 f.; idem 1973, p. 299.
[35] D'Holbach 1960, p. 229 f.

has been lost. In the course of trade and industry only private interests have remained and even been intensified. The originality of Rousseau thus lies in the provocative assertion that the modern economic form has created selfish behaviors in the first place. To this end, he distinguishes between a naturally given "self-love" (amour de soi) and a socially produced "selfishness" (amour propre).[36] Here, even blatant egoism mutates into a sociological category.

However, Rousseau lacks a theory of mutual interaction, as we have come to know it from the Scots. I do not see this as a simple omission, but suspect behind it the motive to connote selfishness *negatively*. In the field of economy, it consists of selfish private interest, which causes social inequality. Social-psychologically, *amour propre* is also supposed to mean that a person makes themselves dependent on the appreciation of other people. Such a desire for recognition leads, according to Rousseau, to this person striving to appear better than they actually are, thus trying to merely pretend ethical and intellectual virtues. He writes: "Selfishness (amour propre) is only a relative, artificial feeling that has arisen in society. It tempts every individual to make more fuss about themselves than about anyone else. It gives people all the evils they do to each other."[37] The further consequence is then again that the individual ends up deceiving themselves about their own nature. The need for social recognition thus does not result in the stabilization of a community, but in the loss of self of the human being and in the destruction of society. The difference between Hume and Rousseau could not be more stark. But in both cases, these are specifically sociological insights.

From these positions, a bridge can be built to the representatives of the *Italian Enlightenment*, who are more oriented towards Hume. As we saw in the second chapter, reverse influences of the Italian authors on the rest of Europe can also be demonstrated. Not only the later Kant, but also Helvétius and d'Holbach have adopted the anthropological constants of pleasure and pain from Verri, who thereby founded the "feeling of self-love".[38] Even more interesting is how Verri defines the feeling of "compassion": Thus, compassion is the pain that leads to freeing the unfortunate from their misery. Like Hume, Verri does not consider moral feelings to be

---

[36] Rousseau 1978, pp. 169–171.—The late Kant comes to a similar result when he critically states that only the handling of money has brought forth "greed". Kant 1965, Vol. XII, p. 611.

[37] Rousseau 1978, p. 169, note o.—This network of deception and self-deception refers back to Mandeville 1968, p. 95.—See also Madame de Graffigny 1999, pp. 124, 141.—Cf. Neuhouser 2012, p. 50 f.; Honneth 2018, pp. 34–47.

[38] Verri 1972, pp. 19 f., 36 f., 40; idem 1996, pp. 4 f.; cf. Rother 2005, pp. 119–146; idem in: Rohbeck, Rother 2011, pp. 285–288.

innate, but the result of a civilizing process. With him, he agrees that individual and societal "happiness" is the highest good of all morality.

Finally, with Beccaria we can observe how moral philosophy is linked with *legal and political theory*. His goal is to unite morality and politics, so that politics becomes moralized and morality becomes politicized. A concrete example of this is the aforementioned work *Crimes and Punishments* (1764), in which he rejects torture and the death penalty and advocates for a "mild" punishment.[39] Here it is recognizable how a humane moral attitude can contribute to the reform of the legal system. And the justification to replace retribution with the principle of prevention testifies to a pragmatic standpoint that declares the *utility* of a state measure for society and state as the essential standard. Again, the *happiness* of the community is at the center of a morally inspired political philosophy.

Conditions of Political Rule

After examining the socio-philosophical implications of moral philosophy, I now turn to political philosophy and the newly developed *sociology* of Montesquieu. Like Hume, he abandons the construction of the social contract. Consequently, the founding of the state no longer appears as a one-time and free act of will, but as the historical result of social *contingency*. This also eliminates the normatively charged idea of natural law, because now the factually established law claims validity, i.e., the *positive law* of certain nation-states. No ideal state appears anymore, but several *forms of state in the plural* present themselves, in which the different modes of operation are of interest. The postulation of an ideal is replaced by the social scientific description following the model of empirical natural sciences.

Internal and external factors.—In his extensive work *The Spirit of Law*, Montesquieu understands "laws" (lois) as the factual "relations" between the manifold factors that determine the emergence and preservation of state structures. This is the program:

The forms of government must "correspond to the *nature* of the country, its cold, hot or temperate climate, the nature of the soil, its location and size, the way of life of the peoples, whether farmers, hunters or shepherds: they must correspond to the degree of freedom that is compatible with the

---

[39] Beccaria 1966, pp. 107, 110.

constitution; the religion of the inhabitants, their inclinations, their wealth, their number, their trade, their customs and traditions."[40]

In this context, Montesquieu distinguishes between three forms of government, which he initially associates with *internal factors*, consisting in the aforementioned "inclinations" and "customs" of the peoples. The topic is the relationship between social mentality and political system.

To the *Republic* or *Democracy* Montesquieu assigns the "virtue" that is supposed to curb greed and prevent the commonwealth from becoming private booty.[41] This corresponds with Hume's moral philosophy, according to which a liberal commonwealth only persists if the citizens restrain their egoisms and mutually respect their interests. However, Montesquieu does not consider a special moral feeling necessary; at most, he sees in the Protestant religion a favorable precondition for republics. It is important here that this consensus forms itself and does not require the exercise of power from outside. In this case, the democratically constituted society is relatively autonomous and self-regulating.

The *Monarchy* or *Aristocracy* Montesquieu associates less with virtue than with the driving force of "honor".[42] This is related to the fact that in this form of state the nobility has power, which in its hierarchical order strives for promotion and distinction. Here Montesquieu sees a parallel between monarchy and the Catholic Church. At least he suggests to the aristocracy to lead the people out of their insignificance and to approach democracy. The model here is the constitutional monarchy in England.

In contrast, Montesquieu attributes "fear" to *despotic states*, in which a single person rules according to their own arbitrariness.[43] This again corresponds with the state theory of Hobbes, who saw fear as the decisive motive for the social contract. Also in this case, the relationship is mutual: As the despot spreads fear and terror, so can the fear of the people, who cannot help themselves, be a cause of despotism.

Montesquieu primarily counts the *climatic* conditions among the *external factors*. He describes how "the character of the mind and the passions of the heart are different in different climates" and how corresponding forms of government and laws emerge from this.[44] While people in cold climates,

---

[40] Montesquieu 1951, Vol. I, p. 16.
[41] Ibid., pp. 19–24, 34–37; on Protestantism p. 165.
[42] Ibid., pp. 25–31, 37–42; on Catholicism p. 165.
[43] Ibid., pp. 31 f., 43 f.; see Hobbes 1966, p. 98.
[44] Montesquieu 1951, Vol. I, p. 310 f.

according to the author, possess more strength, balance, and courage, the inhabitants of warm countries are supposedly weak and passive. Apart from the problematic characterizations of foreign peoples, which we will still deal with, it is fundamentally important to note here that Montesquieu views human civilization as dependent on natural living conditions. The emphasis on climate, especially extreme heat in poor countries, has an ecological dimension from today's perspective.

One should not accuse this climate theory of determinism, because Montesquieu recognizes very well that under the same climatic conditions, different societal and state conditions can be found, just as under different climates, similar societal and state forms can emerge. This type of theory aims at the conditions of the possibility of cultural development.

This interpretation is also supported by the fact that Montesquieu uses other factors to explain certain societal and state forms. When he declares the *soil condition* to be an essential natural condition alongside the climate, he directly reaches "agriculture".[45] He makes the "number of inhabitants" dependent on its level: While pasture lands are sparsely populated because only a few people can be fed there, more people find employment in countries with grain cultivation.[46] In the "surplus" produced in the process, which goes beyond the "own needs" of the farmers, Montesquieu sees the prerequisite for the mechanically operated "craftsmanship", thus for the beginning of industrialization. From this groundbreaking discovery, which points to later political economy, he draws a development line to "trade", to which he also attributes a great influence on political conditions: "Trade is related to the constitution of the state." While luxury favors monarchy and despotism, simple supply meets the needs of republics, as do trading companies prefer the republican form of government. Overall, a very complex network of relationships is shown here to explain the natural and societal factors for the emergence and preservation of political formations.

Division of power.—Montesquieu is, however, known for his theory of the *separation of powers* in a state.[47] Following Locke, he defines "three types of powers" as "legislative", "executive" and "judicial" power. The legislative power of parliament, where the political "representatives" come into play, has remained the same. Montesquieu combines Locke's "executive" and "federative" power into the "executive power" (Executive), which is

---

[45] Ibid., p. 317 f.
[46] Ibid., Vol. II, p. 132–134; for the following p. 5 f.
[47] Ibid., Vol. I, p. 214–229; cf. Locke 1967, p. 298 f.

now responsible for both domestic and foreign policy. In addition, he adds another power, namely the "judicial" (judicative) power. In the struggle for the distribution of power in the state, he, who lived in Bordeaux, wanted to strengthen the independence of the courts in the French provinces in order to set limits to the central power in Paris.

With his theory of the separation of powers, Montesquieu has gone down in history books, especially with his innovation of the judiciary, which is supposed to exercise control over the other state institutions. This merit remains undisputed and is part of the indispensable and valuable legacy of the European Enlightenment.

Indeed, Montesquieu's position on the aforementioned forms of government is not so clearly transformable. While he condemns despotism and thus indirectly the absolute monarchy in France, he is not averse to a moderate aristocracy. And while he even harbors certain sympathies for the republic and democracy, he fears the simple "people", whose power he wants to limit, because he considers them too unenlightened.[48] Ultimately, it comes down to the constitutional monarchy following the English model. Most philosophers of the 18th century agree on this. However, what remains remarkable in Montesquieu, as in Hume, is the deeper insight that such a preference is not a spontaneous decision, but depends on certain societal and cultural prerequisites. In essence, the *socialconsensus* decides whether and how a community can succeed.

Democracy in Transition

If we consider the initially referred diagnoses of a *crisis of current democracies*, the question arises as to which theorems of the Enlightenment in the second half of the 18th century can be transformed into the beginnings of the 21st century.

Separation of powers.—A fundamental principle is the *separation of powers*, as Montesquieu conceived it with an emphasis on the judiciary. In the present day, this component is of utmost importance. In particular, the judicial power serves to defend representative democracy against right-wing populism. For even right-wing radicals insist on the "power of the people", who

---

[48] Montesquieu 1951, Vol. I, pp. 21–24; cf. Turgot 1990, p. 180 f.—Contradictory assessments can be found in recent literature: While Lilti considers the Enlightenment thinkers to be "politically conservative", Israel emphasizes the origins of modern democracy. Israel 2009, p. VII f.; Lilti 2019, p. 22; cf. Pečar, Tricore 2015, p. 110.

should directly elect their "leader". The result can be seen in Russia, Poland, or Turkey, where elected autocrats endanger the rule of law. To counter this misunderstanding, it is necessary to uphold the autonomy of the judiciary as a corrective. The judiciary has the task of controlling both the legislation of the parliament and its implementation by the government. In this respect, I consider Montesquieu's contribution to political theory to be extremely current.

Another issue that is connected with Montesquieu's opposition to absolutism is the problem of *center and periphery*. Even today, there is a demand for a decentralization of politics. This not only concerns the urgently needed strengthening of federal structures in France and the preservation of American and German federalism. A decentralized democracy also includes new forms of political decision-making and public manifestation.[49]

Direct Democracy.—It is worth considering whether the introduction of certain elements of a *direct democracy* à la Rousseau could contribute to the revitalization of modern democracies. The corresponding means is the so-called referendum or popular initiative, through which citizens are enabled to directly participate in legislation. Indeed, this institution is expressly provided not only in Switzerland, but also in Austria and in some German states. In view of the symptoms of crisis, there are increasing voices calling for the direct participation of citizens to be strengthened.[50] This is not only aimed at individual decisions on specific issues, but also at the general desire to let the mass of the population participate in political life and thus counteract the diagnosed fatigue with democracy.

To avoid the daunting example of Brexit, it is important to limit the referendum put to the vote to such legislative proposals that can be assessed locally, concretely, and tangibly by directly affected citizens. Examples of this are the construction of a bypass, the reopening of a decommissioned railway station, or the alleviation of housing shortages in a specific city. But caution is also needed here, for instance when angry citizens want to prevent the erection of wind turbines in their surroundings.

The fifth chapter on the pandemic and climate change has shown how scientific research is gaining more and more influence and threatens to overshadow political decisions. However, according to my explanations in the

---

[49] Crouch 2008, pp. 20–24; Schneidewind 2018, pp. 304–313; Redecker 2020, p. 15 f.; Fraser, Jaeggi 2020, pp. 238, 247, 252; Bogner 2021, p. 111.

[50] Proponents with different emphases are: Cheneval 2003, p. 11; Crouch 2008, p. 20; Negt 2010, p. 210; Nida-Rümelin 2020, p. 93; Reckwitz in: Reckwitz, Rosa 2021, p. 124; Streeck 2021, pp. 56–59; Böhme 2021, p. 128.

sixth chapter, it is to be welcomed that not conspiracy theories, but empirically tested facts determine the public debate and political opinion formation. Without an understanding of reality, no democracy is possible. To strengthen the effectiveness of political action, hybrid forms of expertise and politics are also conceivable here. Added to this are social movements such as trade unions, citizens' initiatives, protest actions, organizations for human rights, feminism and ecology. For example, they are indispensable for making a difference in climate protection.

Democracy and consensus.—The most important lesson from Hume's practical philosophy, which can be transferred to today's time, is the sociological insight that the stateis based on an already existing society. For the current democracy is not based solely on political voting rules, but is essentially founded by a *social consensus*.[51] This is a consensus of a higher order, which forms the normative framework for a reasonable handling of the unavoidable and indispensable issue-related dissent. Because such a consensus consists in the agreement of free and equal citizens, it has a peace-making and legitimizing function. The democratic state thus requires a civil society foundation. Democracy is not exhausted in formal procedures, but is a distinct way of life.

Such a consensus is also the result of *cooperation*, which is to be understood as an independent type of action.[52] Again, it applies that the democratic order does not generate cooperation through state coercion, but essentially presupposes it and then possibly intensifies it. Cooperation consists in the mutual interaction between people who represent their private interests, but are wise enough to realize that it is in their own interest to recognize the interests of other people. Success depends on whether those involved expect the other participants to be willing to cooperate as well. Similar to how Hume has based on the "habit", modern sociology speaks of *latency*,[53] which refers to a process that the participants get used to over time and that only becomes conscious to them retrospectively.

---

[51] Nida-Rümelin 2020, pp. 16 f., 132–140; cf. Höffe 1999, p. 40; Negt 2010, p. 207; Gabriel, M. 2020, p. 16; Reckwitz in: Reckwitz, Rosa 2021, p. 119; Heidenreich 2022, p. 97; following the Enlightenment with a communitarian turn Frick 2020, pp. 77, 80.
[52] Nida-Rümelin 2020, pp. 220–223; cf. Höffe 1999, p. 40; Honneth 2000, p. 282; Gabriel, M. 2020, p. 16.
[53] In *Sociological Enlightenment* by Luhmann 1970, pp. 68 f.; recently Nassehi 2021, pp. 228–337; cf. Redecker 2020, p. 147.

This finding corresponds to the principle of *recognition*, which also played a central role in Scottish moral philosophy.[54] While Rousseau started from an individual seeking societal acceptance and failing, Hume assumes a mutual interaction of several or even all people within a community and evaluates the result of the emotionally based interaction positively. In this last tradition, recognition today can mean that the citizens of a country draw their approval of a democracy from a societal communication process in which they always co-decide on its appropriateness and correct application and decide whether the jointly practiced norms can be approved. Social distinction and appreciation of one's own good behavior can then be internalized through their constant repetition and serve to control one's own actions, thereby creating a moral self-commitment. Here, a graduation is possible by extending the recognition beyond one's own federal state, to the nation and Europe, or to the entire world society.

This process is also based on *emotions*. In today's philosophy, a distinction is made between elementary feelings, which consist of sensations such as fatigue or pain, and emotional feelings, which are directed at something in the world. Feelings such as fear, anger, outrage, envy, grief, admiration, shame, or pride are therefore intentional states that represent certain facts.[55] In our case, the feeling of belonging can arise from social cooperation, which refers to certain fellow human beings, a regional group, or the national community.

The current experiences with anger, hatred, and violence make it clear how important humane handling of emotions is. Here, *morality* also comes into play. For in the populist hate tirades, the moral convictions of democratically minded citizens are often attacked, even the morality in toto is defamed as "hyper-morality". Against this, the aforementioned basic consensus has to assert itself, which ultimately is a community of values that shares normative convictions like freedom and equality of all people.[56] Even in this current case, one could speak of a moral-philosophical or ethical foundation of politics.

The social system with the hardest contingency is undoubtedly the *capitalism*. The late modern democracy stands or falls with the relationship

---

[54] From my point of view, it is interesting that Axel Honneth considers the theory of recognition from Hegel through Scottish moral philosophy to be in need of supplementation. Honneth 2018, pp. 182–235, esp. pp. 202–210; idem. 2000, pp. 171–179.

[55] Christoph Demmerling: *Feelings and Morals*. Bonn 2004, p. 14; Sabine Döring: *Philosophy of Feelings*. Berlin 2009, p. 9.

[56] Nida-Rümelin 2020. p. 139, 226; Gabriel, M. 2020, pp. 12, 33–38.

between economy and politics. After the neoliberal phase, the resulting problems of social inequality and ecological destruction have come more into consciousness, so that corresponding political measures are up for debate.[57] However, this presupposes that democratic states regain their influence on the so-called free markets. After a far too long phase of neoliberalism, the increased *regulation* of a capitalism that has gotten out of hand is necessary. At the moment, a revival of democracy primarily means building democratic institutions capable of enforcing the protection of the environment, the humanization of the working world, and the social provision of the mass of the population. Social movements and organizations can be helpful if they succeed in influencing governments. What is needed is a democratization of the economy or an economic democracy.

---

[57] Crouch 2008, p. 133; Negt 2010, p. 509; Streeck 2013, p. 90; idem. 2021, pp. 23, 44; Rapic 2020, p. 10.

8

Crisis of Capitalism

Recently, there has been renewed talk of *capitalism*. There is an increasing number of books that already feature the term in their titles.[1] Even in the liberal and conservative cultural sections, people are no longer hesitant to speak of capitalism—even when this economic system is to be defended against its critics. This was not the case for a long time. There were several reasons for this.

First, the concept of capitalism was taboo during the *Cold War*. People did not dare to utter the word. Anyone who did was suspected of sympathizing with communism. With the fall of the Berlin Wall, the situation changed abruptly. Now that socialism is finished, it is possible to adopt the terminology of the ideological opponent. A similar development can be seen with Marxism, which has been experiencing a renaissance for several years.[2] In business, this would be called a hostile takeover.

Second, academic discourses had distanced themselves from the problems of capitalism. In the tradition of *Critical Theory*, it was above all Jürgen Habermas who placed social communication at the center and pushed economic theory into the background. In poststructuralism, there was more interest in the symbolic forms of society, or even talk of "symbolic capital."[3]

---

[1] Streeck 2013; Zuboff 2018; Fraser, Jaeggi 2020; Rapic 2020.—In the main text, see: Schneidewind 2018, pp. 69 f.; Precht 2020, p. 41; Redecker 2020, pp. 9, 14 f.; Göpel 2020, p. 67; Streeck 2021, pp. 24–28; Nassehi 2021, pp. 62 f.; Reckwitz in: Reckwitz, Rosa 2021, pp. 102, 104.

[2] Johannes Rohbeck: *Marx*. Leipzig 2006, p. 10; Fraser, Jaeggi 2020, pp. 13 f., 162.—The term capitalism is particularly controversial in the German-speaking world.

[3] Jürgen Habermas: *Theorie des kommunikativen Handelns*. 2 vols., Frankfurt a. M. 1981; Pierre Bourdieu: *Zur Soziologie der symbolischen Formen*. Frankfurt a. M. 1974.

In this context, I refer to the observation described in Chapter Six, that hard facts in general have lost their significance. With the advent of new realism, this tendency has also been reversed.

Third, the *real situation* of capitalism has changed dramatically. As has been indicated several times, capitalism has entered a *crisis*. Up until the 1970s, it was still possible to speak of a "social market economy" that allowed a certain level of prosperity for the entire population. But when economic growth came to a halt and was to be revived by neoliberal measures, social acceptance noticeably declined. Especially in the wake of the 2008 financial crises, critical voices became louder, calling in particular for a replacement of financial capitalism and thus a general mutation of capitalism.

But anyone who wants to make capitalism a topic again today should not do so in the traditional way. Instead, it is important to take into account the transformations of this system. This also modifies the range of topics. Although questions of the distribution of social wealth—for example, in wage negotiations—still play an important role, especially since real wages have recently declined, new problems are being added: the destruction of the natural environment, the waste of natural resources, recent difficulties in energy supply, the structural transformation of industrial production, globalization with its migration flows, and social inequality between the genders. What is needed, then, is a complex concept of capitalism and thus a *critique of capitalism* that includes the physical, political, and cultural dimensions.

In our context, the specific question now arises as to how such a critique can relate to the *Age of Enlightenment*. I have already pointed out several times that it was precisely around the middle of the eighteenth century, in the course of the beginning industrialization, that the entirely new science of *political economy* emerged. With this, I expand my thesis that within the Enlightenment, in nuce, a modernity developed that, for the first time, discovered the contingency of economic systems. If, in the previous chapter, I already addressed the experience of contingency in social interaction, I now add that the economy constituted the core area of this insight, which was then transferred to the moral, legal, and political spheres. From today's perspective, this results in a rather contradictory assessment.

On the *one* hand, the Enlightenment economists not only identified the inherent dynamics of economic processes. As liberal thinkers, they were even convinced that politics would be well advised to let the cycles of goods, money, and capital operate "freely." This seems to contradict the current critique of neoliberalism.

On the *other* hand, it is completely unhistorical to claim the political economy of the eighteenth century as a precursor of the current laissez-faire ideology. Despite all professions of faith, the power of the state was maintained. Thus, not only philosophers but also economists advocated massive political interventions. Added to this is the central concept of *reproduction*, which contains both ecological and social policy potentials. For the Enlightenment thinkers hoped that the wealth created by agricultural and artisanal labor would be in harmony with nature and benefit as many inhabitants of the country as possible.

In the following, I will demonstrate in detail to what extent the economic theorists primarily characterized agriculture as a process that is both ecologically and socially sustainable. An explicit justification of unequal fortunes is found only in Turgot, the later finance minister of Louis XVI, who, by liberalizing grain prices, helped to trigger the French Revolution. But other Enlightenment thinkers advocated a clearly perceptible balancing of incomes. There was also a remarkably far-sighted prognosis of the negative effects of factory work and the impoverishment of the working class. At the other end of the scale is Rousseau, whose radical social critique is now to be elaborated. In this way, a whole range of positions opens up, to which one can still refer today.

Neoliberalism at an End

When the pros and cons of neoliberalism are discussed today, I would like to point out that economic liberalism is, by its very nature, a contradictory construct.

It does indeed promise to keep out of the economy and to let it run free. This concerns the market for goods and services, whose prices are supposed to regulate themselves automatically through supply and demand. The same applies to the labor market, where wages and hiring conditions are ideally negotiated autonomously. The form of capitalism is again characterized by the fact that, in principle, no limits are set to the use and accumulation of capital. Capital accumulation is, as it were, the driving force of this economic formation.[4] Where it is endangered, the system begins to falter.

---

[4] This initially "orthodox" characterization is oriented toward the main work *Capital* by Karl Marx. In: Marx Engels Werke (MEW), vols. 23–25; see Rohbeck: *Marx*, pp. 22–31; more recently Fraser, Jaeggi 2020, p. 32.

But in this idealized picture, it is often overlooked that the "free market" of goods, money, capital, and labor did not emerge naturally, but has always been the result of politics. This was already true in the eighteenth century, when international "free trade" had to be enforced by nation-states against the resistance of mercantilism.[5] The leap into the twentieth century shows that the liberal doctrine was deliberately promoted in the 1970s by politicians such as Margaret Thatcher in England and Ronald Reagan in the USA. And when authors at the beginning of the twenty-first century complain that modern democracies have been overrun by unleashed capitalism, it should be remembered that precisely this scenario was politically intended and implemented by democratic means only a few decades earlier. For these reasons, the usual opposition between economy and democracy obscures the fact that this relationship is also reversible, in that democratically legitimized governments have staged their own limitation or even endangerment.

So when the *end of neoliberalism* is now being called for, it should be recalled that state decisions and practices have stood behind it. This can be taken as an indication that this system can only be reversed with the help of political action. While the question marks in all the other subheadings of this book are meant to signal that I am attempting to theoretically overcome the "postist" terms mentioned therein, such as most recently "post-democracy," the above title "Neoliberalism at the End" has the opposite meaning. It expresses affirmation and a demand. Means and ways are being sought to transform the currently prevailing liberal system into a socially and ecologically sustainable economy.

This is also urgently necessary. For the self-regulating *capitalism* has not developed in the last two decades as the neoliberals had prophesied. Even in the traditional sphere of industrial production, economic performance stagnated. The capitalist mode of production tends to produce ever more goods than can be sold on the markets. This leads to a surplus of accumulated capital, which can only be compensated by increased growth.[6] When this pressure for expansion reaches its limits, the crisis of capitalism becomes apparent. One way out is to cross national borders and recruit new sales markets and cheap labor in the global arena.

---

[5] Karl Polanyi 1978, pp. 19 f., 192, 195, 330, points to this second side of economic liberalism; cf. Fraser, Jaeggi 2020, pp. 61, 113 f.

[6] Wallerstein 2013, p. 21; Streeck 2013, pp. 31 f.; idem 2021, pp. 62–68; Schneidewind 2018, pp. 411 f.; Rapic 2020, p. 11.—On globalization see Chap. 9.

The truly new sphere that is owed to neoliberalism is *finance capital*, which has become independent from industry. Today's economists speak of a decoupling of the financial sector from the real economy.[7] Since return expectations are measured by monetary value, they are, so to speak, blind to concrete economic activities. Since the turn of the millennium, this has led to an increasing virtualization of value creation. A global financial sector emerged without the real economy developing to the same extent. Because banks had granted too many loans, some of which were not covered, the resulting bubble burst in the financial crisis of 2008. The negative consequence for governments, which then had to intervene after all, was the chronic indebtedness of public finances.

The obvious dysfunction of capitalism is particularly evident in the worsening *social inequality*.[8] Since the 1990s, the workforce has no longer benefited from economic growth in the USA and Europe. Real wages in Germany have fallen significantly, especially in the last decade. In addition, there are widespread precarious working conditions in the form of fixed-term contracts, part-time and temporary work. There are still significant differences between the salaries of men and women; in 2020, this difference amounted to eighteen percent. When more women are now being hired, it is often with the intention of lowering wages overall.[9] So-called classism leads to multiple discrimination based on gender, origin, and culture. In Germany, the richest ten percent own 67% of total net wealth. Globally, one percent of the world's population owns half of the world's wealth.

Now, capitalism is at its core an economic system, but it does not have only economic effects. For this system extends to the whole of society. It produces *cultural effects* that affect the entire lifeworld of human beings. In this sense, one can speak of a capitalist shaped culture or even of capitalism as an overarching "form of life."[10] This appropriation consists in the fact that more and more areas of everyday human life are being colonized by capitalism. Some Enlightenment thinkers already had an inkling of this, as for example Rousseau declared "selfishness" (amour propre) to be a consequence

---

[7] Schneidewind 2018, p. 412; cf. Streeck 2013, pp. 9, 23, 29 f.; idem 2021, pp. 70–81.
[8] Piketty 2014, p. 237; Nida-Rümelin 2020, p. 53; Rapic 2020, p. 12; Böhme 2021, pp. 103–114.
[9] See the feminist critique of the adaptation of women to "progressive neoliberalism" in Chap. 4.
[10] Fraser, Jaeggi 2020, p. 10, 15; see already Polanyi 1978, p. 19; cf. Schneidewind 2018, p. 82; Göpel 2020, p. 68; Reckwitz in: Reckwitz, Rosa 2021, p. 80, 109; Böhme 2021, p. 19, 40 f.

of bourgeois society.[11] In the late-capitalist lifeworld, economic rationalization has consequences for how people interact with one another and for the psyche of individuals. The increasing pressure to perform leads to the acceleration of work and leisure and to discipline in family and professional life. Those affected develop different coping strategies, which impair people's well-being.

Currently, a *woke capitalism* is under discussion, which is particularly interesting in our context because it reverses the relationship between economy and society.[12] While it was just lamented that capitalism commercializes the whole of society, the issue now is that capitalist culture appropriates certain social and cultural phenomena. This is evident in the current corporate culture, which presents itself as more diverse and less hierarchical, thereby adopting elements of the anti-authoritarian and identitarian movement. This tendency is also visible in advertising, where luxury clothing brands appear with rainbow flags and heavy automobiles are driven by female *people of color*. It goes without saying that such behaviors and presentations primarily serve the image and are intended to increase profit by adapting to the new lifestyles and views of the middle classes.

How should one deal with this? Certainly, it would be too simplistic to dismiss these phenomena as mere hypocrisy and to condemn them morally. But at the same time, one should be wary of ascribing any leftward turn to "woke" capitalism. Nor should this trend be interpreted as a sign that conservative capitalists are the new "anti-capitalists."[13] For fundamental criticism of capitalism still refers to the by no means resolved problem of social justice.

In order to analyze the negative consequences of neoliberalism, it is finally necessary, alongside the social, to also consider the *ecological appropriation* of capitalism.[14] In this case, it should be noted that the capitalist economic system depends on preconditions that it did not itself create. Most fundamentally, this includes external nature. This condition was not an issue as long as it appeared simply given and inexhaustible. But since resources have

---

[11] Rousseau 1978, pp. 169–171; see ch. 7.—Karl Marx also recognized the cultural effect of capitalism, complaining that the bourgeoisie "has left remaining no other nexus between man and man than naked self-interest, than callous 'cash payment.'" MEW, vol. 4, p. 464 f.

[12] The term "woke capitalism" was coined in 2015 by Ross Douthat in the *New York Times*; according to Schneidewind 2018, p. 378.—Böhme 2021, p. 40 f., speaks of an "aesthetic economy."

[13] See Grau 2022, p. 14, 41.

[14] Birnbacher 2016, pp. 19–24; Schneidewind 2018, pp. 144–149; cf. Fraser, Jaeggi 2020, p. 58.—On ecology, see the last section in Chap. 8, as well as Chap. 10.

become scarce and the natural environment has been damaged over the past four decades, this ecological dimension has suddenly entered public consciousness. The climate catastrophe discussed in chapter five is initially characterized by the increase in the average temperature on Earth. With a temperature rise of two degrees relative to 1990, a tipping point is reached, after which further developments are no longer calculable and the consequences would be irreversible. The current trend is heading toward three to four degrees. One of the main causes is carbon dioxide, which is produced by burning coal, oil, and gas and released into the atmosphere. At this point, fossil capitalism undermines its own foundations.

Against the background of the obvious failure of neoliberalism, there has for some years been discussion about how the state could and should intervene more in the economy. For decades, economics was shaped by the bitter dispute between liberals and Keynesians, with the neoliberals ultimately gaining the upper hand and excommunicating the "Keynesian" minority faction, which was understood as "left." In the meantime, the Keynesians are experiencing a resurgence.[15] The instrument of economic management consists in a policy of government spending, which is accompanied by a positive reassessment of public debt. While in the Anglo-American countries the economic reversal is taking place through debt-financed expansive fiscal policy without much debate, in Germany the "debt brake" added to the Basic Law in 2009 and the "black zero" as a guideline for the federal budget stand in the way. However, even here, for some time now, if not a rethinking, then at least a reconsideration has been underway. Economists and politicians are now providing pragmatic contributions to a sustainable economic policy on topics such as government debt and an efficient fight against climate change. The current occasion is the economic embargo against Russia and the resulting energy crisis as well as the new military rearmament.

Foundations of Political Economy

Insofar as neoliberalism is subject to criticism today, its historical origins are often attributed to the Enlightenment. Above all, the Scot Adam Smith is regarded as the founding father of modern economics and thus as the originator of economic liberalism. The polarization "free market economy or

---

[15] See the subtitle: "Economics in the Late Neoliberalism" by Streeck 2021, pp. 81–84; cf. Nida-Rümelin 2020, p. 46 f.; Gabriel, M. 2020, pp. 247, 295, 305.

planned economy" seems to correspond to the personal alternative "Smith or Marx."[16] Regardless of whether this attribution applies to Marx, it must be denied in our context that Smith belonged to the early ideologues of laissez-faire capitalism or was one of its proponents. Although, like other economists of his time, he recognized that economic processes have their own laws, he by no means concluded from this that the state should have no authority whatsoever to guide the economy for the benefit of society as a whole.

A similar constellation arises with the accusation that the Enlightenment, with its economics of productive capital, theoretically initiated and justified the beginnings of the *Anthropocene*. This would amount to blaming the Enlightenment for the beginnings of the exploitation of natural resources and the destruction of the natural environment. But even in this case, it has been shown that early economic theory in France, with the school of the Physiocrats, chose the preservation of nature as its origin and goal. The name *Physiocracy*, which means "rule of nature," refers to the production of food in agriculture, which must adapt to natural conditions such as soil and climate.

Physiocracy—In his *Economic Table* (1758) François Quesnay explains, with the help of a schema in the form of a zigzag, the circulation of a national economy.[17] He declares as its foundation *agricultural production*, which for him is the only source of economic value. He sees the reason for this in the fact that agriculture produces the foodstuffs that ensure the subsistence of all people. This presupposes that the yields of agricultural labor feed more people than are employed in agriculture. For the land produces more than is needed to replace the means of production consumed by labor. It follows that the wealth generated by agriculture is not further increased in the rest of society, but only redistributed.

The agents of the *economic cycle* are not individuals, but social classes defined by their role in the production process. Thus, Quesnay distinguishes between "three classes" in a society.[18]—The "productive class" (classe

---

[16] Gabriel, M. 2020, pp. 295 f., 304 f.; see also Nida-Rümelin 2020, p. 58; Precht 2020, pp. 42 f.; Redecker 2020, pp. 75, 147.

[17] Quesnay 1976, vol. I, p. 90; cf. Francine Markovitz and Johannes Rohbeck in: Rohbeck, Holzhey 2008, pp. 799 f., 808–812.

[18] Quesnay 1976, vol. I, pp. 79 f., 88.—See also Quesnay's articles in the *Encyclopédie*: "Tenant Farmer" (fermiers), Encyclopédie 1972, pp. 564–571; "Grain" (grains), pp. 646–650; "Tax" (impôt), pp. 690–694.—Diderot's article "Man (Politics)" is likewise physiocratic: "There is no true wealth except man and the earth. Man is worthless without the earth and the earth is worthless without man." Ibid., p. 676.

productive) is the one that cultivates the land and produces the necessary foodstuffs for a society. This includes the tenant farmers of large estates and the wage laborers they employ.—The "class of proprietors" (propriétaires) comprises the owners of the land, who are supported by the tenants. Since these revenues presuppose the reproduction of the producers, the landowners can only receive that "surplus" which results from the difference between expenditures and yields. The corresponding category "net product" (produit net) makes it possible to determine the surplus or the increase of a national economy.—Quesnay refers to all other citizens who work as artisans, factory workers, manufacturers, or merchants as the "sterile class" (classe stérile). With the term "sterile," the claim is confirmed that only tenant farmers and agricultural laborers create economic value, from which trade and industry benefit.

The already mentioned key concept of *reproduction* has a double meaning in this context. On the *one hand*, it expresses the relationship to the natural conditions of life. Physiocracy means rule *of* nature, *not over* nature. And with the central category "productive," it is explicitly emphasized that not only foodstuffs are produced, but that this must be done *re*productively— today we would call this sustainably—. When Quesnay lists in detail the yields of the land, grain prices, and the resulting profits, he places particular emphasis on the warning that the land must not be overexploited.[19] In this respect, the political economy of the French Enlightenment has an ecological dimension. Not least, the Anthropocene begins with a theoretical reflection on the relationship of homo oeconomicus to cultivated nature.

On the *other hand, reproduction* means the maintenance of those people who work in agriculture. Thus, Quesnay repeatedly emphasizes that they can only be productive if they are able to *re*produce their own labor power and their means of production. He even desires a growing population, which presupposes a certain standard of living that should be promoted by state measures.[20] This plea is explicitly directed against the landowners, whom Quesnay instructs to demand only as much rent as allows for the reproduction of the tenant farmers and agricultural laborers. Although the tenant farmers already appear as capitalist entrepreneurs, he groups them together with the agricultural laborers into a common "class," thereby upgrading the

---

[19] Quesnay 1976, vol. I, pp. 80, 222 f.; likewise Rousseau 1978, p. 85, note d.; cf. Robertson 1841, p. 82; see Chap. 5.

[20] Quesnay 1976, vol. I, pp. 79 f., 87.—Let us recall the influence of the Physiocrats on the debate about the role of women, who were assigned a special task in the population problem. See the relevant section in Chap. 4.

latter. The conflict thus takes place between "idle rentiers" and industrious farmers. The later class struggle between wage labor and capital is not yet at issue. In this I see the social-political side of Physiocracy.

Of course, this physiocratic economic theory remains limited, because only agricultural production is regarded as the origin of economic prosperity, while artisanal and industrial labor are devalued. However, this view was revised very soon—and not first by Adam Smith, but already by Anne Robert Jacques Turgot, who is usually still counted among the Physiocrats.

In Turgot's *Reflections on the Formation and Distribution of Wealth* (1766) there are many statements that attest to his proximity to the physiocratic theory, especially to Quesnay: The land functions as the sole source of wealth, and the tenants and agricultural laborers as the only members of society who feed the other classes.[21] Yet Turgot then departs from his model and develops his own theory of the formation and distribution of capital. After summarizing the various methods of cultivation in agriculture and highlighting the capitalist leasehold system as the most advantageous method, he arrives at a general concept of capital. Accordingly, profit-generating capital exists not only in agriculture; rather, capital can also generate value and profits in other sectors.

Now, Turgot is one of the few Enlightenment economists who explicitly justifies the negative effects of bourgeois society. He is well aware that the development of science, technology, and the economy increases "inequality" among people and excludes the masses from progress. But he considers such a division necessary in the future as well, in order to guarantee the personal interest in improving one's own situation. He does not regard social inequality as a moral evil, but even as an advantage for social development. In a letter to Françoise de Graffigny he rejects her social criticism: "Inequality creates and increases wealth among virtuous and capable peoples. It is not a bad thing; it is a blessing for humanity."[22] This is the classic liberal position.

Political Economy.—As already Turgot so too does Adam Smith justify the inequality of wealth in a nation's economy. However, he considers a special legitimation necessary. His main work on the *Wealth of Nations* (1776) begins with a historical comparison between the beginnings and the present stage of civilization. His argument is that "a laborer, even from the lowest

---

[21] Turgot 1981, pp. 99–103; for what follows, pp. 134 f.; idem 1990, p. 175.

[22] *Lettre à Madame de Graffigny*, in: Turgot 1919, vol. I, p. 243.—This refers to the novel *Letters from a Peruvian Woman* (1747), in which Graffigny praises the "communal agricultural labor" among the Incas. Graffigny 1999, pp. 86 f.; cf. Steinbrügge 2020, p. 237.—See Chap. 2; for the aspect of colonial history, see ch. 9.

and poorest class, if only he is moderate and industrious, can consume a greater share of necessities and comforts than any savage is able to procure for himself."[23] In short: a simple worker today is better off than many a prince was in the past. Underlying this is the conviction that the increase in "general prosperity" ultimately benefits *all* members of society, down to the poorest day laborer. According to this argument, social inequality is justified to the extent that even the less advantaged benefit from it.

Overall, Smith holds the view that ultimately the state must ensure the well-being of a country's people through appropriate framework conditions. For example, he supports the import ban on printed calico to protect the domestic cotton industry; likewise, the then Poor Law, so that the reserve of labor could live in humane conditions.

Just as Turgot, Smith also turns away from the physiocratic doctrine that social wealth is generated solely in agriculture. But in contrast, he advocates much more decisively and systematically the principle that every form of human labor, that is, labor as such, is productive: "The annual labor of every nation is the fund which originally supplies it with all the necessaries and conveniences of life which it annually consumes."[24] Underlying this is the new conviction that it is above all labor in crafts and industry to which the people of a country owe their prosperity. Therefore, Smith argues that it is above all *this* productive sector of the economy that should be promoted by means of state legislation. He does not overlook the fact that the industrial production he favors, in turn, depends on the increasing productivity of agriculture, so that artisans and factory workers can be adequately fed.[25]

Smith sees the decisive factor in the *productivity of labor*, which is increased above all by *division of labor*. Here, a distinction must be noted, which he does not quite make explicit. In the first chapter of his work, it is the *division of labor within a manufactory* from which a "perfection of productive forces" results, as he illustrates with the example of a pin factory.[26] He warns of the negative effects of monotonous factory work on the bodies and minds of workers. In the second chapter, Smith addresses the *division of labor in society*, which is originally mediated by the exchange of various goods and then by money. What is important here is the conviction that

---

[23] Smith 1923, vol. I, p. 2; cf. p. 14.—The argument corresponds to the *Theory of Justice* of John Rawls 1975, pp. 28 f.

[24] Smith 1923, vol. I, p. 1.

[25] Ibid., vol. I, pp. 220 f.; vol. II, pp. 1 f.—Likewise Turgot 1990, p. 175; Montesquieu 1951, vol. II, pp. 132 f.

[26] Smith 1923, vol. I, pp. 5–16; on the negative consequences, p. 15.

the price of a commodity is determined by external circulation, its value by the labor expended in it.[27] Human labor is ultimately objectified in capital, from which wages, profit, and ground rent arise.

To demonstrate that there was also an elaborated political economy in *Italy*, I would like to touch on two authors whom we have already encountered in the context of anthropology, moral philosophy, and political philosophy. Pietro Verri criticizes in his *Reflexions on Political Economy* (1771) the French physiocrats and bases human labor both in agriculture and in crafts.[28]—Even more clearly, Cesare Beccaria in his posthumously published *Elements of Political Economy* develops a theory of productive labor and a corresponding theory of value. In this, he is considered the Adam Smith of Italy.[29] Here, once again, the high degree of interconnectedness in the European Enlightenment is confirmed.

Social policy.—In contrast to Quesnay and Smith, the Enlightenment is dominated by the social-political position of more or less far-reaching reforms, which were intended at least to mitigate the already visible hardships of the capitalist mode of production at that time. Thus, Helvétius criticizes the unequal distribution of social wealth and advocates increasing the number of property owners through state measures.[30] Above all, he demands that all inhabitants of a nation, especially the rich, be obliged to work. For human labor is by no means an evil, but rather contributes to the happiness of people. Another variant is found in Montesquieu, who laments the use of machines in factories because they simplify labor and reduce the number of workers.[31] In this way, both authors anticipate the social question of the 19th century in advance.

Similarly farsighted is Condorcet, who makes the mathematically supported prediction that the possibility of population growth is limited by the available food supply. This limit leads him to the insight of a "permanent cause of periodically recurring misery."[32] In doing so, he anticipates the so-called population law of the later economist Thomas Robert Malthus,

---

[27] Ibid., pp. 17–22, 35–38, 129, 192.—Karl Marx follows him in this: MEW, vol. 23, pp. 52 f.

[28] Verri 1966, pp. 52 f.; Rother 2005, p. 71; idem in: Rohbeck, Rother 2011, pp. 281, 290 f.

[29] Beccaria 1990, vol. III, pp. 99–102; Rother in: Rohbeck, Rother 2011, pp. 303, 310 f.

[30] Helvétius 1976, pp. 296–308, 364; likewise d'Holbach 1960, p. 572.

[31] Montesquieu 1951, vol. II, p. 134.—Diderot, on the other hand, praises the advantages of machine production using the example of a stocking-knitting machine: Article "Strumpf" (bas), Encyclopédie 1972, pp. 127–132.

[32] Condorcet 1976, p. 208, cf. p. 199.—Thomas Robert Malthus: *An Essay on the Principle of Population* (1820).

which states: When wages fall, workers have fewer offspring; the resulting shortage of labor causes wages to rise, which in turn leads to an oversupply that causes wages to fall again. While Malthus sees in this an unalterable "law," Condorcet is alarmed by such an inhumane prospect. He therefore demands that social wealth be distributed fairly among all strata of the population, so that social inequality is reduced and public education further expanded. To this end, he designs his own educational program,[33] whereby the prognosis leads to political action. Here, the difference between the socially engaged Enlightenment of the 18th century and the cynical apology of capitalism in the 19th century becomes strikingly apparent.

The most radical social critique comes from Rousseau. After all, he is the author of the article "Economy" (économie) in the French Encyclopédie, which appeared as early as 1755.[34] In truth, however, he does not deal with economic theory in it, but with traditional political science. This may be due to the early date of its composition, but it is probably also intentional, since he wants to replace bourgeois society with a powerful state. The critique of the new capitalist conditions, however, is found in his simultaneously published *Discourse on the Origin of Inequality among Men*.

On closer inspection, Rousseau points to two origins of social inequality. He locates the first origin in the beginnings of human communities, in which physical and mental differences between individuals were perceived. The second cause he sees in the emergence of private property and the division of labor between town and country, that is, in the beginnings of industrialization.[35] This turning point is much more significant for Rousseau, because it establishes the capitalist form of property and, in the form of wage labor, the appropriation of others' labor. As a way out, he proposes an agrarian society in which each member possesses only as much land as he can cultivate with his own hands manage.

Two lesser-known Frenchmen go a decisive step further. Étienne-Gabriel Morelly demands in his *Code of Nature* (1755) the general abolition of private property: "Every citizen shall have his plot of land as close together and as well measured as possible, not as property, but only sufficient for the maintenance of its inhabitants."[36] The precise distinction between possession and property is intended to allow only common property, of which people

---

[33] *Sur l'instruction publique*, in: Condorcet 1968, vol. VII, pp. 167–448.
[34] Encyclopédie 1972, pp. 224–384.
[35] Rousseau 1978, pp. 205, 213, 223; see also Rohbeck, Steinbrügge 2015, pp. 12 f.
[36] Morelly 1964, p. 184; this draft is explicitly directed against Montesquieu, pp. 121 f., 181.

make individual use.—A similar draft was presented by Gabriel Bonnot Mably at the end of the century. In it, he demands social equality, which alone is able to guarantee the happiness of people.[37]

This overview has revealed a diversity of topics and positions. Thematically, this concerns first the relationship of working humans to nature and thus the ecological aspect. Next come considerations about the social consequences of nascent capitalism. These range from a liberal justification of social inequality, through various reform proposals, to radical social critique, which is further differentiated into petty-bourgeois and agrarian-communist positions. All these facets will occupy us again at the end of this chapter, when we address the crisis of contemporary capitalism. But first, another crucial point must be addressed: the peculiar logic of economic processes and the associated experience of contingency.

Contingency of Social Systems

The foundation of political economy in the second half of the 18th century initially has an anthropological character. It is human beings who, driven by their needs, satisfy these needs through their labor and thereby create social wealth. But then a completely different mode of thought creeps into economic-theoretical discourse: objects such as commodities, money, and capital are attributed a dynamic of their own, which is precisely not intended by the acting individuals. Suddenly, it is said that the actors involved should adapt to the economic regularities that have only just been discovered. Today, this phenomenon is called *contingency*. It is important to distinguish between chance and contingency. While chance concerns individual events, contingency refers to the structures of social systems.[38]

Metaphorics.—In this respect, the name *Physiocracy* mutates into a metaphor for the naturalness of the economy. In his *Tableau*, Quesnay employs the biological model of the circulatory system. After all, he was a practicing physician who studied the controversial practice of bloodletting and thus the circulation of blood. He transfers the model of circulation from the natural body to the "body" of a national economy. While blood circulates in animal

---

[37] Mably 1975, pp. 213–218; cf. Israel 2009, p. 92; Reinalter 2016, p. 12.

[38] Arnd Hoffmann: *Zufall und Kontingenz in der Geschichtstheorie*. Frankfurt a. M. 2005, pp. 48–56; cf. Rohbeck 2020, pp. 184–188.

and human organisms, in a national economy goods, money, and capital circulate in a cycle.³⁹

The legitimating intention of this analogy consists in presenting the economic system as a sphere that requires no external intervention. Quesnay even claims that state interventions impair the functioning of the economy. He seeks to convince the government that it must recognize the "natural order." In this way, he advocates the *freedom of trade and economic freedom* for private individuals. Likewise, he argues for the free trade of grain with foreign countries in order to revive agriculture in France. However, this does not prevent him from his commitment to tenants and agricultural laborers, whose economic well-being he wants to see promoted by political measures.

While Quesnay bases his approach on a biological model, Hume in his essay "Of Commerce" (1741) draws on the mechanistic physics of Newton with the law of gravitation, speaking of a "moral attraction."⁴⁰ While in his *Treatise* he saw himself as the "Newton of anthropology," he also claims this not entirely modest title in his economic writings. In doing so, he criticizes mercantilist economic policy and advocates "free trade" with other countries, while supporting state promotion of manufactures domestically. At the same time, he asserts the scientific status of the new discipline of political economy.

In his *Wealth of Nations*, Adam Smith also speaks of the "natural course of things," which consists of three regulatory cycles: the regulation of commodity prices, wages, and capital. He likewise alludes to Newton's theory of gravitation when he lets the price of a commodity depend on supply and demand: "Thus the natural price is, as it were, the central price, toward which the prices of all commodities gravitate."⁴¹ In this context, those passages are particularly revealing in which Smith attempts to explain by which human *motives* the division of labor and exchange of goods came about at all:

> "This division of labor, from which so many advantages are derived, is not originally the effect of human wisdom, which foresees and intends that general opulence to which it gives rise. It is the necessary, though very slow and gradual, consequence of a certain propensity in human nature which has in view

---

³⁹ Quesnay 1976, vol. I, pp. 83 f.; for the following, pp. 294 f.
⁴⁰ Hume 1963, p. 321.—On the topic of "balance of trade," he employs the hydrodynamic model of communicating vessels. Ibid., p. 319.
⁴¹ Smith 1923, Book I, pp. 69, f., 74, 80–82; Book III, pp. 146, 192.

no such extensive utility—the propensity to truck, barter, and exchange one thing for another."[42]

Here Smith makes explicit the conviction underlying his economic analysis, namely that the fundamental structure of the economic system was precisely *not intended* by the individuals involved. But at the same time, he does not locate the cause of this kind of contingency in the economic sphere, but rather in human nature, to which he attributes a natural propensity to exchange. The transition from anthropology to economics thus succeeds only half-heartedly, because the driving force of economic development is, after all, anthropologized once again.

The famous metaphor of the "invisible hand" nvisible hand), which Smith uses in the *Wealth of Nations* at only a single point, is equally controversial. When an individual capitalist intensifies his own production, he simultaneously promotes the common good. For he "intends only his own gain, and he is in this, as in many other cases, led by an invisible hand to promote an end which was no part of his intention."[43] The half-heartedness in this case consists in the fact that the unintended effect of economic activity is illustrated by a pseudo-religious or teleological image.

A similar inconsistency is found in Kant. At first, he describes civil society as "unsocial sociability," which very aptly expresses the contradictory mediation of modern society through the market.[44] But then he adopts both of Smith's topoi by locating the origin of socialization in a corresponding "propensity" (Hang) of human beings. Beyond that, he invokes a higher "intention of nature" (Naturabsicht) to justify further development. Again, it can be observed how the insight into the contingency of economic systems is once more refracted in anthropological and metaphysical terms.

Conclusion.—In attempting to summarize the results of Enlightenment political economy, I arrive at *ambivalent consequences.*

First of all, it must be acknowledged that, since the middle of the century, the authors have discovered the *contingency* of social systems at all. While in seventeenth-century political philosophy the state was supposed to arise from a conscious act, now the civil society moves to the center, which develops both economically and morally as if by itself. The place of planning reason has been taken by the naturalness of economic and social processes. The

---

[42] Ibid., Book I, p. 17.
[43] Ibid., Book IV, p. 235.
[44] *Idea for a Universal History*: Kant 1965, vol. XI, pp. 37, 39.

old rationalism has thus been shaken not only by the new anthropology, but also as a result of social philosophy and economic theory. This includes the insight into the natural and social preconditions that must be preserved by means of reproduction. In this, as I have said, I see the specific modernity of the European Enlightenment.

Furthermore, this paradigm shift has significant effects on the Enlightenment's *conception of humanity* that should not be underestimated. As we saw in the fourth chapter, its proponents originally proclaimed the age of anthropology and chose human nature as the starting point for all reflection. But in the context of political economy, the autonomy of the individual recedes into the background. If it is proven that people can no longer steer their society as they could in the realm of politics, then human agency is severely curtailed. Thus, a paradoxical situation has arisen: while anthropology still counts as the leading science, the image of the human being suffers certain losses. With Freud, I would like to speak here of an *economic wound* to the human being. Just as in the psyche, there is also something unconscious in society that seems to elude our control.

Finally, from today's perspective, the question arises as to how one should practically deal with this kind of contingency. Even economists such as Quesnay and Smith, despite their emphatic credo for the "freedom" of the market, called for state intervention in the national economy for the benefit of the entire population. This distinguishes them from later liberal ideologies, even if the measures proposed at the time seem inadequate from today's perspective. This problem has become all the more urgent in the 21st century, as it is necessary to overcome the neoliberalism of recent years and to reclaim politics. As we have seen, almost all contemporary diagnoses lament the loss of political control over late modern capitalism. The task, therefore, is to explicitly highlight and strengthen the first element of the political in the tradition of the political economy of the Enlightenment.

Social and Ecological Upheavals

After the recent failure of neoliberalism, I consider it sensible in the 21st century to draw on the aforementioned theories of the Enlightenment. For it has become clear that there were already very different positions on capitalism in the 18th century. The spectrum ranged from the justification of social inequality to a moderately liberal reform course, and even to its abolition in the forms of petty-bourgeois society and agrarian communism. The authors did recognize the forces of economic processes, but did not advocate a pure market economy. They were aware that the new social formation also produced cultural side effects. What is important is the early fundamental idea that capitalist production is compelled to reproduce its social and natural conditions.

Transformations.—However, between the Enlightenment and the present lies the failure of socialism in the 20th century, making the alternative to capitalism more difficult. If not a planned economy, then only a more or less radical restructuring of the capitalist system remains. The corresponding proposals, as in the 18th century, include moderate reforms, profound transformations, or even demands to overcome capitalism. In the end, as I attempt to demonstrate, the concrete courses of action come surprisingly close to one another. In conclusion, I permit myself the heretical question of whether the proclamation of "post-industrial" capitalism and the farewell to human labor may have been somewhat premature.

Markus Gabriel shares the general view that neoliberalism has not fulfilled the expectations placed upon it. He distances himself from an unrestrained capitalism that leads to considerable economic inequalities. From this he infers the "limits of economism" and the necessity of a "reordering of the social market economy."[45] As a solution, he considers a "behavioral economics" through which economic and moral action are to be brought into harmony.[46] Ultimately, Gabriel interprets the crisis of the capitalist system as a moral crisis of orientation and believes that the system can be cured by "moral progress."

With the title *The Great Transformation* Uwe Schneidewind announces a much more decisive change of system. Yet in practice, he too is concerned with the "further development of a modern capitalism."[47] Thus, he advocates an institutionally organized reform program in "small steps of change." Of interest is the differentiated description of the actors involved in social change.[48] Schneidewind names first "civil society," which he declares to be the "pace-setter of the Great Transformation." This includes environmental organizations, churches, trade unions, and social movements. The second

---

[45] Gabriel, M. 2020, pp. 245–249.—Markus Gabriel opposes the critique of capitalism by "left-wing identity politics," which rises up indiscriminately against the "rich" and "elites." I consider this criticism polemical, as it ignores the rest of "left-wing" criticism of capitalism. Ibid., pp. 248 f., 294.

[46] Ibid., pp. 297, 299 f., 303; see also Nida-Rümelin 2020, p. 58; Precht 2020, pp. 42 f.; Redecker 2020, pp. 75, 147; Göpel 2020, pp. 67, 165–167.

[47] Schneidewind 2018, pp. 9, 21, 93.

[48] On politics: ibid., pp. 328–360; on entrepreneurship: pp. 361–428; much shorter on science: pp. 429–451.

group of actors are politicians, who set the content and develop political processes from it. From this, new forms of regulation are to emerge, from economics to investment control. Third, Schneidewind places great hopes in "sustainable entrepreneurship," which he believes can contribute to the "self-transformation of the economic system."

The concept of transformation refers to Karl Polanyi, who already in 1944 published his much-discussed book *The Great Transformation*. However, he holds a quite different view, namely that the market system has destroyed the "natural substance of society."[49] In earlier epochs, according to Polanyi, human economic activity was "embedded" in social relations, as the political economy of Adam Smith attests. In this tradition, he proposes a re-embedding of the economic within society.

Subsequently, Wolfgang Streeck developed the model of the "Keynes-Polanyi state."[50] In doing so, he follows the recent shift from neoliberalism to Keynesianism by advocating the primacy of politics over the economy. At the same time, he adopts Polanyi's program, countering the adaptation of society to capitalism with the adaptation of capitalism to society, which is to be transformed into a humane "knowledge society."

A radical critique of capitalism comes from Immanuel Wallerstein, who predicts—and arguably desires—the *collapse of the capitalist system*.[51] In three or four decades, it will fail due to the saturation of global markets. The struggle for an economic system capable of replacing capitalism has long since begun.

Slavoj Žižek also strikes this note, taking the Corona crisis as an opportunity to reflect on a new society.[52] He explicitly proposes to replace capitalism with *communism*. However, by this he means neither "old-style communism" nor an "obscure dream image"; instead, he wants to "reinvent communism." The economy is to be restructured so that it is no longer dependent on the market mechanism.

The irony of this parade of extreme positions—from the apology of capitalism to the revival of communism—lies in the fact that the concrete reform proposals show little significant difference.

---

[49] Polanyi 1978, pp. 20, 74, 89; on the following pp. 157 f., 173, 180; also Schneidewind 2018, pp. 10, 13, 65, 70; cf. Fraser, Jaeggi 2020, pp. 205 f.; Streeck 2021, pp. 437–439.

[50] Streeck 2021, pp. 437–443; cf. 202–2012; on the knowledge society pp. 439 f.; idem 2013, pp. 151–164.—As stated, Streeck considers this model to be feasible only in small nation-states.

[51] Wallerstein 2013, pp. 9 f., 32; idem 2019, p. 23; cf. Rapic 2020, p. 9 f.

[52] Žižek 2020, p. 39.

There is consensus on measures intended to overcome or at least mitigate *social inequality* both within individual countries and on a global scale. It begins with the demand for a changed *tax policy*. Domestically, there is a call for progressive taxation of the very wealthy; externally, tax havens are to be closed and a global capital tax introduced.[53] The program of social justice also includes state intervention in *wage policy*, by setting minimum wages and ensuring a general increase in real wages, not least also for the equalization of wages between women and men.[54] In the course of the Corona crisis, the collapsing healthcare system has also come into focus, and in some countries, its commercialization is to be reversed.[55]

A major focus is placed on the *ecological crisis*, which reveals the limits of the economic system.[56] In general, the ideal is that of a "sustainable capitalism," which must slow down or even halt its previous economic growth. First, the exploitation of natural resources must be stopped, especially that of fossil energy sources, the combustion of which produces harmful greenhouse gases. To achieve the two-degree target, CO_2 emissions in Germany must be reduced from the current nine tons per capita to a maximum of two tons. These and other demands amount to not only reducing production, but also changing citizens' patterns of consumption. There is talk of new models of prosperity that consume less while providing the same quality of life. This tendency has gained further momentum due to the energy shortages resulting from the sanctions against Russia.

Post-industrial capitalism?—Another commonality, now targeting the nature of capitalism itself, is that the aforementioned authors take digitalization as an occasion to proclaim a "post-industrial" or "digital capitalism."[57]

As is well known, this renaming has a longer history. As early as the 1960s, Daniel Bell spoke of a "post-industrial society," by which he meant the shift from industrial production to the sectors of services and knowledge generation. This diagnosis was accompanied philosophically by

---

[53] Gabriel, M. 2020, p. 248; Göpel 2020, pp. 174, 177; Streeck 2013, p. 237; idem 2021, p. 325; Žižek 2020, pp. 44 f.; cf. Piketty 2014, pp. 493, 505, 4015.

[54] Polanyi 1978, p. 332; Schneidewind 2018, pp. 380 f.; Streeck 2013, p. 237; Gabriel, M. 2020, p. 256; Žižek 2020, p. 45.

[55] Schneidewind 2018, p. 243; Gabriel, M. 2020, pp. 282, 294; Streeck 2021, pp. 316–322; Žižek 2020, p. 41.

[56] Above all Schneidewind 2018, pp. 23–166, especially p. 161; likewise Gabriel, M. 2020, pp. 146, 294; Göpel 2020, pp. 71, 150; Žižek 2020, p. 65; Streeck 2021, p. 320; cf. Birnbacher 2016, p. 10.

[57] Reckwitz in: Reckwitz, Rosa 2021, pp. 108 f.; Schneidewind 2018, p. 101; Precht 2020, p. 65; similarly Rapic 2020, p. 10; Gabriel, M. 2020, p. 18; Redecker 2020, p. 76; Streeck 2021, p. 85; Žižek 2020, p. 44; Nassehi 2021, p. 162.

Jürgen Habermas, who claimed an "obsolescence of the production paradigm."[58] Apparently, the intention was to leave behind the old modernity and thus a particular Enlightenment, which essentially included the onset of industrialization.

Today, it seems as if the new terminology is intended to suppress the current problems of industrial capitalism. It even appears as if there is an effort to transcend everything material along with industry and ascend into the intellectual programming heaven of symbolic signs. Yet I would caution whether this wholesale farewell to material production has not been somewhat one-sided. I would like to elaborate on this conviction in conclusion.

First of all, the observations regarding the post-industrial modernity are *geographically and socially limited*, as they are restricted to the traditional and wealthy industrialized countries. In fact, the proportion of people employed in manufacturing in Germany halved between 1970 and 2000; since then, it has remained fairly constant at about a quarter of all employed persons. In the USA, it has also remained steady at just under twenty percent since the beginning of the 21st century. However, in view of these figures, one must not overlook the fact that a large part of production has relocated abroad. For example, in Asia, industrialization is still in full swing, where more than ten times as many steel products, textiles, and computers are produced as in all of Europe, while this process in Africa has only just begun. It is therefore high time to abandon the narrow national perspective and to consider the problem of industrial society on a global scale.

Moreover, I consider it *superficial* to look only at the statistics of the employed and from this infer the fundamental significance of industrial production for a society. If it is true that modern societies are essentially driven by technological advances, then today's transition to late capitalism is owed to industrial development. If one focuses on digitalization, it must be pointed out that computers have to be manufactured industrially. Especially in times when there are bottlenecks in chip production, the dependence on production is painfully experienced.

Contrary to some notions that artificial intelligence operates only in the virtual realm, it is equally important—though often underestimated—that this would not be possible at all without *material object-systems*. It can be demonstrated concretely how leaps in software development have each been

---

[58] Daniel Bell: *The Coming of Post-Industrial Society*. Frankfurt a. M. 1985, pp. 130, 181; Jean Baudrillard: *Symbolic Exchange and Death*. Munich 1982, p. 18; Habermas 1985, pp. 95–103; Beck 1986, p. 15.—For a detailed discussion of this complex, see Rohbeck 2000, pp. 213–237.

initiated by technical innovations in hardware. In this way, human thinking is increasingly shifting to symbol-processing machines. These are industrial products that are becoming material carriers of intellectual competences and operations. It is not that production is being replaced by knowledge; rather, the production of knowledge is being industrialized. We are on the threshold of the industrialization of thinking. In this, I see the most radical continuation of the current third industrial revolution.

Finally, the relevance of industry becomes apparent in the *ecological crisis*. Through the global threat, what was repressed in the supposed knowledge society resurfaces. For the strain on the natural environment relentlessly reminds us that the devices we use are made from processed natural materials, consume electricity, and must be disposed of. It should not be forgotten that the rest of industry still consumes natural resources and damages the environment. The flip side is that even the ecological transformation is only possible through the industrial production of wind turbines, solar cells, and electric cars. And if all this is proceeding far too slowly, it requires the accelerated promotion of such an industry. That is why I consider talk of the "end of industrial society" to be even reckless. For it suggests as if we had long since overcome its negative side effects and no longer needed to concern ourselves with industry at all.

End of the work society?—A similar problem arises with the "work society," which has also been said to have come to an "end." "What lies ahead of us," wrote Hannah Arendt as early as 1958, "is the prospect of a work society in which work has run out." Jürgen Habermas complements this paradox with the diagnosis that work has "exhausted its utopian energies."[59] Apart from Marxism, this probably also refers to the Enlightenment, which hoped that human labor would bring emancipation from feudal constraints and general social prosperity. Even though I agree with Habermas that the utopia of the work ethic has now faded, such disillusionment by no means justifies the conclusion that work has only a marginal significance in the social life of late modernity.

In the case of the concept of work, the situation is even clearer, because gainful employment also includes all services. In the present day, it is also the case that, after phases of unemployment, there is even a shortage of labor, which has increased the value of work. Moreover, (not only) feminists demand that housework, care for relatives, and the upbringing of children

---

[59] Hannah Arendt: *The Human Condition*. Munich 1967, p. 12.; Jürgen Habermas: *The New Obscurity*. Frankfurt 1985, p. 145; cf. Böhme 2021, pp. 35–40; Harari 2018, pp. 49–78.

should also be recognized and remunerated as work, which would further expand the scope of paid work. Not least during the pandemic, people have missed being present at their workplace and have come to appreciate it in retrospect.

It is gainful employment that enables people to participate in *public and social life*.[60] Through economically purposeful work, people can free themselves from personal dependencies. In it, qualifications are acquired, fulfilling achievements accomplished, and social recognition gained. Where else do people gain so much information and have the opportunity for now global communication? Only through gainful employment can most people achieve a more or less modest standard of living. This general work, which has a correspondingly general benefit, gives the individual a social existence. Conversely, unemployment means exclusion from social life. As a rule, this means poverty, loneliness, self-doubt, and a sense of meaninglessness. No private sphere can replace the key function of public work.

For these reasons, I find talk of the "end" of industrial and work society unconvincing. Instead of a premature conclusion, what is needed is a social and ecological *transformation of industrial society*. And this industrial restructuring now explicitly refers to world society, which is already partially industrialized and, to another not insignificant extent, is still in the midst of the process of industrialization or has only just begun it. Especially in the latter case, there is a chance to avoid mistakes made earlier and to embark on a different form of industrialization from the outset. In the following, I will address this historical dimension of globalization.

---

[60] Negt 2001, p. 425; Herzog 2019, pp. 9 f.; Redecker 2020, pp. 69 f., 217–219; Nassehi 2021, p. 156.

9

World History and Globalization

Around the middle of the 18th century, yet another scholarly discipline was developed: the philosophy of history. The new term "philosophie de l'histoire," which originated with Voltaire,[1] was associated with the aim of systematically investigating and presenting history. Whereas philosophical reflections had previously been scattered throughout historiographical works, for the first time texts were also published that provided an overview of history as a whole or addressed general themes. While Friedrich Meinecke in *Die Entstehung des Historismus* had still claimed that the Enlightenment era lacked a "sense of history," at the latest since Wilhelm Dilthey and Ernst Cassirer the historical consciousness of the Enlightenment has been recognized. [2]

In its classical form, the philosophy of history of the Enlightenment lays claim to a *universal history* or *world history*. This is reflected in numerous titles that already express the universal scope: from Turgot's *Discourses on Universal History* (1751), Iselin's *History of Humanity* (1764) to Schlözer's *Outline of His Universal History* (1771).[3] It claims universality in both spatial and temporal dimensions.

---

[1] First published under a pseudonym: *La Philosophie de l'histoire, par feu l'abbé Bazin*, [Amsterdam] 1765; later as an introduction to the *Essai sur les mœurs*: Voltaire 1963, vol. I.

[2] Meinecke: Munich, Berlin 1932, p. 10; Wilhelm Dilthey: *Das achtzehnte Jahrhundert und die geschichtliche Welt*. In: idem, Gesammelte Schriften, vol. 3, Leipzig 1927, p. 235; Cassirer 1932, pp. 244–265; cf. Koselleck 1979, p. 39; Kittsteiner 1998, p. 12.

[3] Turgot 1990, pp. 168–220; Iselin 2014, vol. IV; Schlözer 1990.—See also Gatterer: *Handbook of Universal History* (1765); Kant 1965, vol. XI, pp. 33–50: *Idea for a Universal History with a Cosmopolitan Purpose* (1784); Herder 1984, vol. III: *Ideas for the Philosophy of the History of Mankind* (1784); Schiller 1970: *What Is, and to What End Do We Study, Universal History?* (1789); Forster 1991: *Guide to a Future History of Mankind* (1789); Carus 1809: *Ideas for the History of Mankind* (posthumous).

First, the concept of universal history encompasses all *spaces* of the entire globe. In the course of colonial discoveries and conquests, non-European countries and continents such as Persia, China, India and America also came into view. Despite the criticism of the Eurocentric standpoint—which is in part justified—it should not be overlooked that some Enlightenment thinkers, for the first time, sought to recognize the plurality of cultures, which were now concretely studied, compared, and appreciated. Moreover, even during the Enlightenment, critical voices against colonization and enslavement can be documented. Since by the end of the 18th century the exploration of the world had reached a geographically determined conclusion, it was this process of *expansion* and *limitation* at the same time that made the philosophy of history possible.

Next, universal history includes all *times* from the beginnings of humanity up to the then-present. Through the interest in early high cultures, such as Egypt and Babylonia, the beginning of human history was pushed back so far that it receded into uncertainty. While Bossuet had still followed the biblical chronology, in the 18th century the task arose of reconciling the chronologies of the Old Testament with the historical sources of Egyptian, Greek, and Roman antiquity, and even with those of the Orient and China. Through the secular ordering, history lost both beginning and end; it became a process open on both sides and thus "detemporalized."[4] In this way, historical thinking in general detached itself from the chronological schema and developed the novel idea of a distinct *historical time*,[5] oriented toward the cultural achievements created by human beings.

The temporal and spatial dimension of universal history has a theoretical consequence that should not be underestimated. From the comparison between peoples living in different regions and epochs arises the insight that different stages of civilization not only succeed one another in time in one place, but can also be found simultaneously in different places.[6] This is the important insight into the *simultaneity of the non-simultaneous* in history.

In our context, the discovery of *contingency* plays a special role, which has so far mainly been discussed in the eighth chapter on political economy. In Enlightenment philosophy of history, the experience of contingency culminated in the paradox that, although human beings make history through

---

[4] Odo Marquard: *Difficulties with the Philosophy of History*. Frankfurt a. M. 1973, pp. 364 f.
[5] Koselleck 1979, pp. 130–143.
[6] Turgot 1990, p. 198; cf. Koselleck 1979, p. 132; idem 2010, pp. 79 f.

their actions, they also do not make it. The self-empowerment of humanity already underwent a peculiar inflection at the dawn of modernity. For Bossuet, God was the guide of history. In the course of the Enlightenment, human beings took the place of God. At the same time, however, they had to realize that they were precisely not able to control the whole of history.[7] History was understood as a contingent process that is, as a whole, beyond human control.

The following attempt to update the philosophy of history, however, encounters certain difficulties. Since the advent of *historicism*, interest has shifted more and more from the content to the methods of the historical sciences. In the course of *analytic philosophy of history*, it culminated in the analysis of language and discourse, the semantics of temporal concepts, and the analysis of narrative structures. Complementary to this, studies on collective memory and cultures of remembrance emerged. In this way, substantive topics of the historical were set aside.

It seems that people no longer dare to ask the "big" questions about history. Such speculations are considered unscientific because they cannot be verified by empirical research. For these reasons, the philosophy of history has withdrawn from the analysis of historical content and concentrated on the reflection of historiographical methods. The problematic impression arises that all philosophical attempts to address "real" history are to be fended off under methodological pretexts. This development has led to a crisis that continues to the present day and has pushed this discipline to the margins of the philosophical canon.

In contrast, I am convinced that this restriction of the philosophy of history is by no means as compelling as the dominant literature suggests.[8] The very *separation* between a substantive philosophy of history and a philosophy of history reduced to methodology is not convincing. In detail, it can be shown that method and content cannot be separated, but rather refer to

---

[7] Koselleck 1979, p. 158; Kittsteiner 1998, p. 12.

[8] For example, Patrick Gardiner: *The Nature of Historical Explanation*. Oxford 1952; William Herbert Dray: *Laws and Explanation in History*. Oxford 1957; Edward Carr: *What is History?* Stuttgart 1963; Carl G. Hempel: *Aspects of Scientific Explanation*. London, New York 1965; Arthur C. Danto: *Analytical Philosophy of History*. Frankfurt a.M 1974; Karl Acham: *Analytical Philosophy of History*. Freiburg, Munich 1974; Frank Ankersmit: *Narrative Logic*. Groningen 1981; Paul Ricœur: *Time and Narrative*. Munich 1988; Hayden White: *Metahistory*. Frankfurt a. M. 1991; Chris Lorenz: *Construction of the Past*. Cologne 1997; Jörn Rüsen: *Historics*. Cologne 2013.—See also Hans Michael Baumgartner: "Philosophy of History after the End of the Philosophy of History." In: Herta Nagl Docekal (ed.): *The Meaning of the Historical*. Frankfurt a. M. 1966, pp. 151–164.

each other reciprocally.⁹ I am therefore concerned with the synthesis of *a methodologically reflected* and at the same time *substantive philosophy of history*. In doing so, I do not content myself with the usual aim of attaining a general orientation or meaning. Beyond that, I wish to show that the philosophy of history is capable of contributing to the solution of the pressing problems of the present.

In the following section, I turn against the current of so-called *Posthistoire*, according to which history has supposedly reached its "end." In this context, the recent trend to rehabilitate history and even to dare the "grand narrative" is favorable to my argument. The experience of catastrophes has now taken the place of a supposed end, an experience that no longer permits standstill but must be dealt with in the near and distant future. Furthermore, I engage with the current critique of *Postcolonialism* by rejecting sweeping accusations and attempting to draw as nuanced a picture as possible.

In the third section, I intend to connect the *theory of globalization* with a material philosophy of history. It is already obvious to consider the phenomenon of globalization from a historical perspective, since the Enlightenment philosophy of history as *world history* represented the first elaborate theory of globalization. This did not presuppose an abstract totality, but described and critically evaluated the concrete tendency toward worldwide cooperation and communication. To the extent that contemporary unleashed capitalism exacerbates social inequality, *global justice* becomes an ever more urgent task.

The Enlightenment can also serve as a reference point for an *ethics of the future*, which will be the subject of the fourth section. For the philosophy of history of the eighteenth century was from the outset oriented toward the future with the aim of drawing lessons from the past in order to improve the living conditions of human beings. Today, such *responsibility for future generations* first of all means averting certain catastrophes such as climate change, resource scarcity, global poverty, and increasing war. A possible "progress" could already consist in the avoidance of deterioration or even in its mitigation. In addition, there is the question of whether less developed peoples should be granted the right to catch-up development, which at the same time enables alternatives.

---

⁹ Here I can refer to Ernst Troeltsch, who was the first to distinguish between a *formal logic of history*, which refers to the historical method, and a *material philosophy of history*, which takes the contents of history as its subject: *Historicism and Its Problems*. In: Collected Writings, vol. 3. Tübingen 1922, reprint Aalen 1977, pp. 67 f.; see most recently Rohbeck 2020, pp. XI f., pp. 2–6.

Posthistoire and Postcolonialism

Critique of the philosophy of history is as old as the philosophy itself. Rousseau had already recognized in his *Second Discourse* that scientific and technological progress produces negative consequences such as social inequality, political despotism, and moral decline. Shortly thereafter, Herder in *This Too a Philosophy of History for the Formation of Humanity* (1774) opposed the idea that all peoples and epochs should be judged by a single standard, instead of recognizing the intrinsic value of each culture.[10] In *On the Advantage and Disadvantage of History* Nietzsche in turn criticized historicism, whose historical education is no longer able to provide orientation; history becomes ideology, history becomes a "carnival of masks." Subsequently, Foucault also declared history to be a "farce." In view of Hiroshima and Auschwitz, Horkheimer and Adorno in *Dialectic of Enlightenment* formulated a "critique of the philosophy of history," in which they reinterpreted progress as a process of decline.[11]

Posthistoire.—In the course of everyday experiences with modern civilization, other philosophers such as Arnold Gehlen diagnosed an *end of history*, which is meant to signify that technological progress has, in essence, become meaningless for human beings.[12] In industrial society, he diagnoses a stable situation that "arises when all the fundamental potentials inherent in it have been fully developed." However, this does not mean that no historical events are to be expected. The opposite is the case. "Please understand me correctly," Gehlen assures with regard to the stabilization he assumes, "here lie all the opportunities for progress, which must first and foremost be scientific and technological, and can only be so." It is not the development of modernity that is in question; rather, the problem arises as to how, in view of the dynamism of science and technology, the impression of stagnation can emerge.

---

[10] Rousseau 1978, pp. 191–265; Herder 1984, vol. 1, pp. 617 f.

[11] Friedrich Nietzsche: Complete Works. Ed. by Giorgio Colli and Mazzino Montinari. Munich, Berlin. 1988, vol. 5, p. 157; Michel Foucault: *Power/Knowledge: Selected Interviews and Other Writings*. Ed. and trans. by Walter Seitter. Frankfurt a. M. 1974, p. 104; Horkheimer, Adorno 1987, vol. 5, pp. 253–256.—From a utopian perspective, Adorno later develops an alternative concept of progress, which is to free itself from the spell of the domination of nature. Ibid., vol. 10.2, p. 17.

[12] *End of History? On the Situation of Human Beings in the Posthistoire*. In: Oskar Schwatz (ed.): *What Will Become of Humanity?* Graz, Vienna, Cologne 1974, p. 61; the following quotation p. 64.—He adopted the term post-histoire in 1953 from Paul de Man, or rather from his uncle Hendrik de Man.

This assessment is also found in Jean-François Lyotard, who famously proclaimed the *end of the grand narrative*.[13] On the surface, he assumes a loss of legitimation that discredits the Enlightenment-modern ideas such as freedom, emancipation and truth. But he sees the causes of this loss in technologization and economization, whose rapid advance he does not deny: "One can see in this decline of narratives an effect of the rise of techniques and technologies since the Second World War, which has shifted the emphasis more onto the means of action than onto their ends." This points to Max Horkheimer's *critique of instrumental reason,* according to which technical means become detached from the original ends of human beings, so that reason becomes blind to ends and loses its former legitimation.[14] Behind Lyotard's discourse-theoretical critique lies, in truth, a critique of technology and economics.

More than thirty years ago, Jean Baudrillard wrote a short treatise with the startling title *The Year 2000 Does Not Take Place*. Like Gehlen, he justifies this claim with the "petrification" of modernity in indifference and numbness. In contrast to Marx, he argues that capitalism has degenerated into "pure circulation." What Horkheimer and Lyotard called the "reversal" of ends and means, Baudrillard describes as a "mutation" of the law of value.[15] Whereas human labor in modern times was still "pervaded by a determination of ends" and constituted the referent for commodity exchange, the exchange system has meanwhile become autonomous through the real dynamics of capital. As a result, all referential ties to labor or use values have been dissolved. This condition thus means the "end of labor" and "production," the "end of modernity," and thereby also an "end of history."

In such theories, a *double loss of meaning* is suggested. First of all, the meaning rooted in the lifeworld of earlier cultures is lost. The rapidly spreading civilization of modernity overlays and displaces cultural traditions. But more important and far-reaching is the implicit conclusion that technological civilization itself is not capable of generating its own meaning for life. The transition to a specifically modern meaning, which could be grasped as a cultural consequence of the new technologies, is excluded. As with the division into *two cultures*, a gulf arises between a historical culture oriented

---

[13] Lyotard 1986, p. 54; the next quotation p. 112.
[14] Horkheimer, Adorno 1987, vol. 6, p. 136.
[15] Berlin 1990; idem: *Symbolic Exchange and Death*. Munich 1982, pp. 18, 25.—Likewise Vilém Flusser: *Afterhistory*. Ed. by Stefan Bollmann and Edith Flusser, Frankfurt a. M. 1997; Paul Virilio: *Frenetic Standstill,* Frankfurt a. M. 1997; cf. Grau 2022, pp. 66, 68, 70.

toward religious and national traditions on the one hand, and a technical civilization devoid of history and producing losses of history on the other. The *Posthistoire* culminates in the claim that this development is without culture and consequently without history.

This topos is found in a spectacular and at the same time popular form in Francis Fukuyama, who, during the fall of the Berlin Wall, likewise prophesied an "end of history." After state socialism had collapsed and Western capitalism had apparently "won," nothing truly new could happen in the world: "The end of history will be a very sad time,"[16] because only technical solutions for the satisfaction of consumer desires would remain. With an unjustified appeal to Hegel, Fukuyama characterized technological civilization as fundamentally uneventful and thus irrelevant to culture.

After the fall of the Wall, it could indeed seem as if history had come to a standstill. From a Western perspective, it appeared as if capitalism had triumphed and would no longer hold any surprises. For it should be recalled that the supposedly posthistorical period was, in essence, considered very successful. The eternal present of globalization appeared monotonous, but nevertheless resilient and comfortable. After the end of the Cold War, it was believed that global democracy and world peace had come a step closer. It was success that became the problem. Yet from an Eastern perspective, it was clear from the outset that violent upheavals and social deformations were to be expected.

In the meantime, this situation has changed completely. At the latest with the terrorist attack of September 11, 2001, there was once again a decisive event in history. Added to this were the Iraq war and the most recent military conflicts, the crisis of democracies, famines, flows of refugees, as well as the scarcity of natural resources and the environmental crisis. The *Posthistoire* is now being replaced by the looming *catastrophes*. In the cases of pandemic and the war in Ukraine, the catastrophic situation has already materialized.

This raises the question: What comes after the *post*, what constitutes the *post-post*? The banal answer is: After the "post-history," if it ever truly existed, only history itself can follow once again. Indeed, it has already returned in the wake of global experiences and threats. It has even gained new momentum, because addressing ecological, military, and social crises does not permit remaining in the status quo. Therefore, the demand for a radical *turn* within history is not so trivial.

---

[16] *The End of History?* In: The National Interest 16, 1989, pp. 3, 18; idem: *The End of History*. Munich 1989.

This new historical consciousness is reflected in recent attempts to once again venture a "grand" historical narrative.[17] In particular, the expectation of the future, so essential to the Enlightenment, requires updating—not, however, as hope for continual improvement, but as the avoidance of catastrophic deterioration. The task now is to master present and foreseeable future catastrophes and to pursue alternative paths of development. History is once again in demand, now as an opportunity for fundamental transformations.

Postcolonialism.—While the position of *posthistoire* has meanwhile become obsolete, postcolonialism presents a current critique of the philosophy of history. It does not claim an "end of history," but on the contrary, calls for a productive engagement with the colonial past from a future-oriented perspective. Ultimately, it is about the moral recognition and material compensation of past injustices in the present and future.

In particular, authors from countries outside Europe accuse European historiography and cultural studies of having justified the process of colonization, violent oppression, and enslavement. They criticize the focus on the history of Europe, whose culture is regarded as a universal standard used to discriminate against non-European cultures.[18] In this way, the supposed superiority of Western civilization is taken for granted in order to legitimize the subjugation of other peoples. Above all, the concept of race is said to be a construct to make the dominance of white Europeans and North Americans plausible. Ultimately, this form of Eurocentrism serves as an instrument for colonialism and imperialism.

In our context, however, the problem arises that the *Age of Enlightenment* is rarely addressed in postcolonial critique. And when the Enlightenment is thematized, it is usually through the repetition of well-known clichés. It is typically identified with an abstract rationalism and an egotistical individualism. Its anthropology is considered Eurocentric and racist. The concept of universal history is assumed to serve to justify the domination of Europe

---

[17] Yuval Noah Harari: *Sapiens: A Brief History of Humankind.* Munich 2013; systematically on this, Harari 2018, p. 37.

[18] The founding document for the establishment of *Postcolonial Studies* is Edward Said's book: *Orientalism.* New York 1978. Among others, it influenced Dipesh Chakrabarty's study *Postcolonial Thought* (2000). A radical critique of this can be found in Jean-François Bayart: *Les Études postcoloniales. Un carneval académique.* Paris 2010.—See Dhawan 2014, p. 9; Pečar, Tricore 2015, p. 91; Lilti 2019, pp. 42 f.; Roselli, Schlieper 2022, pp. 12 f.

over the world. Only rarely is it acknowledged that some Enlightenment thinkers already expressed criticism of colonization and enslavement.[19]

In view of such sweeping judgments, it is necessary to draw as nuanced a picture as possible of the position of the European Enlightenment toward colonial history. Several ambivalences come into play here. *On the one hand*, there are some Enlightenment thinkers who *devalue* foreign peoples by denying them the development of their own culture. Here, it is important to note the difference between discrimination based on external factors such as climate and soil, and the even more problematic logic of heredity. *On the other hand*, there are quite a few Enlightenment thinkers who strive for an *appreciation* of foreign cultures. This attempt is often accompanied by a condemnation of violent oppression. Yet this criticism, which is indeed typical of the Enlightenment, should not obscure the fact that slavery was by no means universally rejected. Only this ensemble of positions reveals the full ambivalence of the relationship between Enlightenment and colonialism. This now needs to be analyzed in detail.

Montesquieu stands as an example of the *devaluation* of non-European cultures, whose climate theory proves to be ambiguous in this context. While in *The Spirit of Law* he regards a temperate climate in continents such as Europe and Asia as favorable, he blames the downside of warmer regions for the lack of cultural development in the Orient and in Africa. "The heat of the climate can be so extraordinary that the body is completely enfeebled. Then the exhaustion is also communicated to the mind; there is no thirst for knowledge, no noble action, no generous feeling; inclinations remain passive, idleness is happiness."[20]

Raynal and Diderot also orient themselves by Montesquieu's climate theory in their *History of the Two Indies*. In a global comparison of cultures, they distinguish between the joy of life of the Indians, the gentleness of the inhabitants of South America, and the peacefulness of the Caribbean peoples. But they characterize Africans as "mentally sluggish and without their own virtue."[21]

This ressentiment is also found in Great Britain, where Hume in his essay *Of national characters* claims "the natural inferiority of the Negroes to the

---

[19] A sweeping critique of the Enlightenment is offered by Sala-Molins 2008; a more nuanced picture is provided by Carey 2009 and Muthu 2009; see d'Aprile 2016, p. 160; Lilti 2019, pp. 45, 49; see Chap. 1.
[20] Montesquieu 1951, vol. I, p. 314, cf. 311, 316; see Chap. 7.
[21] Raynal, Diderot 1988, pp. 203–206.

Whites" and denies Black people any "trace of a higher spirit."[22] In his *History of Civil Society* Ferguson qualifies this sweeping judgment by emphasizing the advantage of a temperate climate, but takes into account its contingent effects in order to distinguish among the people concerned between a "lack of skill" or a "lack of capacity."[23] In this way, he downplays the merely external factor of climate and declares the nature of human beings everywhere to be capable of development.

Particular attention has been drawn to Kant with his writings *On the Different Races of Human Beings* (1775) and *Determination of the Concept of a Human Race* (1785), which leads to the provocative question of whether he was a "racist."[24] At first, Kant follows the mainstream of the European Enlightenment by making climate responsible for the lack of development among Black people, stating that "hardly any other reason can be given why this race, too weak for hard labor, too indifferent for diligence, and incapable of any culture, for which there is ample example and encouragement nearby, still stands far below even the Negro, who occupies the lowest of all the other levels that we have called racial differences."[25]

But Kant goes clearly beyond the climate theory by introducing the concept of race and bringing the characterization of human beings close to a highly questionable theory of heredity. In his favor, it can be said that he limits the "races" he hypostatizes to different skin colors and maintains the idea of a common human species. Only in this way can the contradiction between his now untenable race theory and his other philosophy of universalist humanism be endured. Moreover, a single racist statement does not make one a racist. In the reception, the completely narrowed focus on Kant takes its toll here, because it obscures the European context, which contains many more and above all more positive facets, which are now to be discussed.

As shown, the theory of climate zones also allows for the *positive interpretation* that not only Europe, but also other distant countries can benefit from temperate conditions. Paradigmatic in this respect is *China*, whose highly developed civilization was already recognized by Montesquieu.[26]

---

[22] Hume 1963, p. 213.

[23] Ferguson 1986, p. 204, cf. 241.

[24] Kant 1965, vol. XI, pp. 11–30, 65–82.—See also the interdisciplinary discussion series of the Berlin-Brandenburg Academy of Sciences on the topic: *Kant—A Racist?* https://www.bbaw.de/mediathek/archiv-2020/kant-ein-rassist-interdisziplinaere-diskussionsreihe.

[25] *On the Use of Teleological Principles in Philosophy*, in: Kant 1968, vol. VIII, p. 176.

[26] Montesquieu 1951, vol. I, pp. 318 f.

Above all, Voltaire extensively praises the culture of the Chinese, to which he devotes the first two chapters of his *Essay on the Customs and the Spirit of Nations* (1756).[27] He is initially interested in Chinese historiography, which ties its epochs to astronomical observations and does without priesthood, miracles, and demigods. He admires the huge cities such as Beijing with their perfect provision for their inhabitants. In addition to agriculture, he describes the invention and production of silk, paper, porcelain, and glass. Even printing was known before Gutenberg. Overall, the image emerges of a high civilization that was already developed before civilization in Europe.

An original example is the culture of the *Incas in Peru*, which has aroused great interest through new travel reports. Pioneering were the *Letters of a Peruvian Woman* (1747), published by Françoise de Graffigny. While Turgot urges her to call the Incas "savages," she insists that they are an independent civilized people.[28] She concedes that it is at an earlier stage of human history, but emphasizes the harmonious order: "In this respect, the people were still at the beginning of a development, but they were already in the bloom of their happiness."[29] Thus, the Incas possessed writing, handicrafts, music, and poetry. In the style of Rousseau she emphasizes the communal agricultural work and the high morality. The protagonist of the novel, an Inca princess, is portrayed as intelligent and sensitive, mastering the knot script and then learning the alphabetic script. Even if Graffigny exaggerates the "writing" with knots, as if long love letters could be written with it, the attempt to appreciate the culture of the Incas as much as possible is nevertheless forgivable.

It is remarkable in this context that even in *Spain*, which was after all largely responsible for the colonization of Peru, a travel literature emerged during the 18th century in which the culture of the Incas was retrospectively recognized. Thus, José Gumilla in his *Historia natural, civil, y geográphica* (1741) compares this culture with the era of the ancient peoples of the Medes, Persians, Egyptians, Greeks, and Romans, thereby at least

---

[27] Voltaire 1963, vol. I, first part, 1st and 2nd chapters; see also chapter XVIII on China in the *Philosophy of History*, which was later presented as an introduction to the main work.—An eulogy of the political order in China can also be found in the economist François Quesnay: *Despotisme de la Chine*, Paris 1767.

[28] Graffigny 1999, p. 15; *Lettre à Madame de Graffigny*, in: Turgot 1919, vol. I, pp. 241–255; cf. Steinbrügge 2020, pp. 232–236.—See Chap. 5, where it is shown how Kant commented on the Lisbon earthquake with a laudatory comparison to Peru.

[29] Graffigny 1999, p. 17.—See again François Quesnay: *Analyse du gouvernement des Incas du Pérou*, Paris 1767.

establishing a common standard for cultural comparison.[30] While in Spain at that time there was still debate as to whether the indigenous peoples were even fully human, the long-overdue realization gradually took hold that they were not only human, but indeed cultivated beings.

It was precisely the particularly brutal role of Spain that gave rise to a widespread critique during the Enlightenment of colonization and enslavement. As early as Montesquieu in *The Spirit of Law* raises fundamental objections: "Slavery, moreover, is as contrary to civil law as it is to natural law."[31] In his *Essai*, Voltaire denounces slavery in Santo Domingo: "Slaves shorten their lives to satisfy our appetites." And in *Candide* he reproaches Europeans who consume sugar harvested by abused slaves: "Tears at the sight of the Negroes."[32] Raynal and Diderot describe in their *History of the Two Indies* in particular detail the "piracies" of the Portuguese in Asia, the "injustices and atrocities" of the Spanish in Central and South America, and the subjugation of the inhabitants of Africa by the Portuguese, Spanish, and Dutch. The epilogue states: "From this insatiable thirst for gold arose the most dishonorable, the most cruel of all trades, the slave trade."[33] Finally, Condorcet wrote his own treatise *Réflexions sur l'esclavage des Nègres* (1781), in which he condemns slavery as a "shameful crime" and calls for its abolition in stages.[34]

Even Kant, who changed his position in the 1790s, abandoned the racial hierarchy he had previously advocated and, in *Perpetual Peace* (1795), distanced himself from the "violence" and "oppression of the natives" as well as from the "most cruel and most contrived slavery." To justify this, he invokes his "idea of cosmopolitan right" as a "necessary supplement" to state and international law for public human rights.[35]

This topos of critique of slavery, however, does not change the paradoxical fact that some Enlightenment thinkers left themselves a back door to justify colonization and enslavement after all, provided it was not carried

---

[30] Helmut C. Jacobs in: Rohbeck, Rother 2016, pp. 286 f.
[31] Montesquieu 1951, vol. I, p. 332.—The entire 15th book is dedicated to the topic of slavery, pp. 329–351; see Turgot 1981, pp. 109 f.
[32] Quoted in Lilti 2019, p. 25; Voltaire 1948, vol. I, p. 223; see also Helvétius 1973, p. 25.
[33] Raynal, Diderot 1988, p. 302; see pp. 41, 160, 167, 186, 220, 230; likewise Volney 1977, p. 127.
[34] Condorcet 1968, vol. VII, pp. 63, 95; idem 1976, pp. 195 f.
[35] Kant 1965, vol. XI, pp. 214–216; see Pauline Kleingeld: *Kant's Second Thoughts on Race*, in: The Philosophical Quarterly 57, pp. 573–592.

out too cruelly and was regulated by principles. First, Raynal and Diderot refer to the theory of property of John Locke, according to which uncultivated land may be appropriated through human labor: "If the land is partly waste, partly occupied, then the waste part is mine. I can take possession of it through my industry."[36] Next, Montesquieu distances himself from the "abuses" of slavery and formulates new "regulations" for the relationship between master and slave. These include granting the slave sufficient food and clothing, caring for him in sickness and old age, and also freeing him under certain conditions.[37] John Millar introduces the economic calculation that well-treated slaves, like free wage laborers, ultimately yield greater benefit.[38] The illusory goal, therefore, consists in a "humane" form of slavery and a "gentle" colonization, which is supposed to consist merely in the expansion of world trade.

From a philosophical perspective, two problems and possible solutions arise here.

First, it is hardly understandable how certain representatives of the European Enlightenment, who were actually committed to the idea of human rights, excluded certain people from other continents. Although the climate theory appears relatively harmless, the truly fatal aspect is that it was partly perverted into a negative anthropology, in which external circumstances are transformed into supposedly natural characteristics. The current transformation consists in orienting oneself toward those authors who condemned slavery and valued foreign cultures.

The second problem of an allegedly socially compatible colonization can today be solved by transforming colonial dependencies into the fairest possible world trade. With some goodwill, one can already credit the Enlightenment thinkers with the intention of promoting the idea of a peaceful "spirit of commerce." In the present day, the imperative is to compensate for past damages and to participate in the economic development of poor countries. This points to the themes of global justice and responsibility for the future. In order to achieve this transformation, I will first draw on the philosophy of history of the Enlightenment.

---

[36] Raynal, Diderot 1988, p. 162; see Turgot 1981, p. 109.
[37] Montesquieu 1951, vol. I, pp. 340, 346, 348.
[38] Millar 1985, pp. 268 f.; see Condorcet 1976, p. 197.

Historical Contingency

If one asks about the subject of history, the answer is: Human beings "make" their history. Who else could do it? In any case, no other actors are in sight. Thus, there is consensus that the difference between nature and culture consists in the fact that nature is somehow given, and that culture—and thus also history—is produced by human beings. In the meantime, the boundary has shifted to such an extent that the realm of what has already been made and what is still technically feasible is expanding ever further, for better or for worse.

Philosophy of history.—That human beings shape their own history is one of the fundamental convictions of European Enlightenment. In particular, Voltaire understands his *Essay on the Customs and Spirit of Nations* as a counter-program to the earlier sacred history of Bossuet and deals exclusively with secular history, in which the human being is "master of his own fate."[39] This secular approach also leads to new content. In place of the divine kingdoms, epochs appear in the process of civilization in the fields of science, technology, and economics. Ultimately, there is an effort to transfer the achievements attained so far to morality and politics. The study of history is intended to serve the purpose of drawing certain lessons from the past for action in the present, thus enabling people to make history better.

A secular character is also borne by the almost simultaneously composed *Outline for Two Discourses on Universal History* by Turgot.[40] Although he no longer opposes Bossuet, God as the explicit ruler over history no longer appears. Instead, it is only human beings who are spoken of, who are now declared to be the agents of history. And because universal history tends to refer to all human beings, Turgot declares the whole of humanity, or the "human species," to be the bearer of successive "progress". Yet by this he does not mean an imaginary subject of action, but rather the succession of generations who pass on their cultural achievements as an "inheritance."

Stage theory.—In contrast to Voltaire, Turgot develops a theory of progressive forms of society. Montesquieu had already distinguished between

---

[39] Jacques Bénigne Bossuet: *Discours sur l'histoire universelle*, in: Œuvres, texts established and annotated by Abbé Velat and Yvonne Champaillier (Paris 1961) Paris 2001, pp. 665–1027, here: pp. 666–668.— Voltaire 1963, vol. I, pp. 5, 42–44, 67; vol. II, p. 800 f. The term "master" comes from Volney 1977, p. 43; cf. Rohbeck 2010, pp. 59–62, 71–75.

[40] Turgot 1990, pp. 140–163, 168–220; on the following concepts of species and inheritance, pp. 140, 168.

hunters, herders, farmers, and industrial peoples, but it is only Turgot who brings these modes of subsistence into a developmental context.

"Families or small peoples who live far apart because they need a vast space for their sustenance: that characterizes the stage of the hunters. [...] Everywhere that (certain) animals appeared, it was not long before the pastoral life set in. [...] Herding the flocks is a burden that the hunters do not have, and the herds feed more people than are needed to tend them. [...] The pastoral peoples who have lived in fertile lands were probably the first to move on to the stage of farmers. [...] Moreover, the land there feeds more people than are needed for its cultivation. Consequently, there are idlers, cities, trade, all the useful and pleasant arts; hence there is progress in all areas."[41]

If one pays close attention to the way in which Turgot explains the transitions from one phase to the next, it is the *surplus* of food produced in each case that enables the next level, because it frees people for the next, more highly developed activity. Without the economic theory of the physiocrats, which was presented in the eighth chapter, the criterion for such a justification would not have been available. For it is only the analysis of economic cycles that makes it possible to analytically grasp a quantitative increase in value and thus to identify a "surplus" that can be interpreted as a condition for further progress. Therefore, progress consists of two movements: the cycle of reproduction and the simultaneous increase of wealth. Thus, expanded reproduction forms the basic model of this theory of history.

Teleology.—In this explanatory model, the original *goals of the individuals involved* play a subordinate role. Turgot assumes certain motives such as needs, affects, and interests. But with regard to the "progress of the human mind," these anthropological constants are not anticipatory or planning intentions, as if, for example, the farmers had consciously aimed at the subsequent industrialization. He does not even attempt to explain the historical process by reference to purposes of action. In stage theory, reasons are given that are explicitly *not intentional.*

"It seems to me as if I see a huge army," writes Turgot, "whose movements are directed by a genius. At the sight of military signals, at the raging noise of drums and trumpets, whole squadrons are set in motion, even the horses are

---

[41] Ibid., pp. 171–175; cf. 143; Montesquieu 1951, vol. I, pp. 310–328.—On stage theory see also Condorcet 1976, pp. 45–66; Smith 1923, Book I, pp. 220 f.; Ferguson 1986, pp. 337–366; Smith 1928, pp. 10–16; Iselin 2014, vol. IV, pp. 304 f.; Kant 1965, vol. XI, pp. 96 f.; for a critical view see already Herder 1984, vol. I, pp. 613, 619.

filled with an inexplicable fire; each part goes its way over all obstacles, without knowing how it will end; only the commander sees the effect of so many united marches. In a similar way, it is the passions that have multiplied ideas, expanded knowledge, and perfected minds—in the absence of reason."[42]

In such formulations, the *contingency in history* is expressed. Again, contingency is to be distinguished from chance, because it refers to the development of social structures. Thus, people can produce certain goods and thereby improve their living conditions, but they are not able to control the further course of history. They may indeed pursue their individual purposes, but they can never foresee the ultimate purpose of history. Unambiguously, individuals as rational, planning subjects of history are excluded. This is especially evident in Ferguson, who speaks of a "blindness" of human beings and explicitly of a lack of "plan."

But in contrast to Ferguson, Turgot invokes an imaginary "commander" or even a "genius" who is supposed to secure a certain direction and a progressive course for history. And what Turgot initially formulates in military metaphors later appears in Kant as "nature's intention" and finally in Hegel as the "cunning of reason" (Naturabsicht und List der Vernunft).[43] This problematic response is usually interpreted as a *teleology of history*.

Of course, it is important to make careful distinctions. This is by no means a naive belief in an allegedly higher authority that would direct history. Neither the representatives of the French Enlightenment nor those of German Idealism conceive of a real subject that could in any way determine or even influence the historical process. The "intention of nature" is, as Kant announces in the title, only an "idea," which he describes in the *Critique of the Power of Judgment* as a "regulative idea" (regulative Idee). It serves as a heuristic principle for detecting order in the confusing course of history. Therefore, the intention of nature is merely a *metaphor* and the teleology of history is only a *hypothetical construction*. People imagine history *as if* it were being guided toward a goal.

Against the widespread tendency to identify philosophy of history with teleology, I consider it important to state that this conceptual pattern is rather the exception in the European Enlightenment. Thus, prominent

---

[42] Turgot 1990, p. 176.
[43] Kant 1965, vol. XI, pp. 34, 36, 39, 45, 47; Hegel 1969, vol. 12, p. 49.—Most often, the reference to Hegel's teleology serves as a critique of philosophy of history as such, without considering the other variants of European Enlightenment thought.

figures such as Voltaire, Raynal, Ferguson, Millar, Schlözer and Herder are not teleologists at all. Iselin appeals at the end of his *History of Humanity* to those politically responsible to ensure future progress.[44]

Prognostics.—This is especially true for Condorcet, although with his *Sketch for a Historical Picture of the Progress of the Human Mind* he is among the greatest proponents of the idea of progress. He grounds his expectations for the future not in a teleological manner, but with the help of rational *prognostics*.[45] This consists in a "social mathematics," by means of which mathematical calculation is applied to the "political sciences" in order, for example, to calculate birth and death rates. Using this method, he attempts to derive from observable "facts" the most "general laws" possible, which would allow "on the basis of the experience of the past to predict the events of the future with great probability." One may recall his prognosis regarding the periodic increase and decrease of the working population.

A reference to the statistics or probability theory discovered at the end of the eighteenth century is also found in Kant. At the beginning of his *Idea* he writes: "Thus marriages, the resulting births, and deaths, since the free will of human beings has such a great influence on them, seem to be subject to no rule by which their number could be determined by calculation; and yet the annual tables of these in large countries prove that they occur just as much according to constant natural laws."[46] From this observation, Kant, in contrast to Condorcet, derives the aforementioned idea of a "nature's intention," to which individual people, who pursue their own intentions, are supposedly subject.

Dealing with Contingency.—History and contingency belong together. From everyday life we know that intention and execution rarely coincide. This experience applies all the more to history, in which many people always act simultaneously and over a long period of time. History is characterized by the fact that human foresight and actual events diverge over the course of time. Therefore, it is a topos of historiography as well as of the theory and philosophy of history that history is an essentially contingent process. Through the self-dynamics of social processes, the experience of contingency is intensified and socially shaped. In this, the phenomenon reveals a peculiar ambivalence.

---

[44] Iselin 2014, vol. IV, pp. 359 f.
[45] Condorcet 1976, p. 216; for what follows, pp. 193, 208; on the so-called law of population, see Chap. 8.
[46] Kant 1965, vol. XI, p. 33.

On the *one hand*, contingency can be understood as the *unavailability of history*. Accordingly, teleology is regarded as an inadequate attempt to cope with contingency in history.[47] Human beings produce certain effects with their actions, but are by no means the masters of their history as a whole. Thus, this type of theory culminates in the insight that people are not able to make their history deliberately. The philosophy of history is then left only to seal the powerlessness of human beings.

With Freud, one could describe this experience as a *philosophy-of-history wound* of humanity. Analogous to psychoanalysis, contingency produces a traumatic anxiety that is collectively repressed in the teleology of history. History appears as fate or as something that befalls us. As with the unconscious ego in psychoanalysis, there also seems to be an *unconscious* in history.[48] The anxiety leads to a hidden repression, which finds its pathological expression in the philosophy of history. This is the supposed psychopathology of modernity. Yet I consider the talk of unavailability to be reckless, because it creates the impression that history is a natural process to which people must passively submit.

On the *other hand*, contingency can be positively revalued as a *possibility* for practical freedom and transformative intervention.[49] With the scope for human action thus gained, the question of ethical responsibility arises. We are jointly responsible for the attributable present and subsequent actions. For the malleability of history is not a historical fact, but a moral imperative. The issue is not empirical proof of whether history is feasible or beyond our control, but rather a norm that orients action. In Kant's terms, it is a *regulative idea* that serves to keep alive the hope for a possible improvement of the world, so that people at least strive to improve their living conditions, or at least not to worsen them.

In this context, the phenomenon of historical contingency appears in a new light. The indisputable fact that history is not determined, but consists of contingent processes, must not serve as a justification for refraining from formative interventions. On the contrary, contingency should be understood as a task to recognize and realize the possibilities that exist. It goes without

---

[47] Koselleck 1979, p. 260; Kittsteiner 1998, p. 162; Rohbeck 2020, pp. 177–191, especially on Koselleck pp. 159–169.—On "unavailability" in general: Rosa 2021, pp. 48–70; idem in: Reckwitz, Rosa 2021, p. 247; cf. Grau 2022, p. 87.

[48] As already in Ernst Troeltsch, *Historicism and Its Problems*. Aalen 1977, pp. 46 f.; cf. Kittsteiner 1998, p. 162.

[49] See Paul Ricœur: *Memory—Forgetting—History*. In: Klaus E. Müller and Jörn Rüsen (eds.): *Historical Meaning-Making. Problems, Concepts of Time, Horizons of Perception, Strategies of Representation*. Reinbek near Hamburg 1977, pp. 446 f.

saying that such shaping cannot refer to *history as such*, but only to specific actions *within* history. The aim is to do what is possible within the given limits. Such scopes for human action can only be determined concretely, as will be shown below.

Global Justice

In current theories of globalization, *history* is rarely addressed. Even less is said about the philosophy of history, especially since it has already fallen into disrepute. Yet, if one examines the relevant accounts more closely, it is clear that almost all pertinent discourses operate more or less explicitly with patterns of interpretation drawn from the philosophy of history. There are conjectures about which general tendencies of globalization are discernible, and whether it is accompanied by a *progress* or a *decline* of human civilization. This shows that globalization—as the term itself suggests—is essentially understood as a historical process. Even the questions of since which epoch one can speak of globalization at all, what is *new* about the current state of already achieved globality, and what can be expected in the future, cannot be answered without reflecting on history.

Globalization.—Looking back at the *history of globalization*, it becomes apparent that global interdependencies in the fields of economy, military, environment, society, and culture already existed earlier. This is true even for the *Anthropocene*, which is characterized as an epochal threshold during the 18th century by humanity's profound intervention in the Earth system. In the course of the voyages of discovery and colonizations of the 16th to 18th centuries, the idea of humanity as a whole spread.[50] As cross-border relations emerged, the task arose to shape these relations in legal form and to design a global legal order. In the economic sphere, globalization took place above all from the mid-19th century until the First World War. At the same time, the globalization of communication began with the invention of the telegraph and telephone, which became evident in 1858 with the laying of a telegraph cable from Europe to America.

If one emphasizes the *innovative potentials of globalization*, it must be admitted that this process only began in the 20th century. While in the period between the two world wars and shortly thereafter the economic

---

[50] Höffe 1999, p. 58; Figueroa 2004, p. 12; Keohane, Nye 2005, p. 75; Antweiler 2011, p. 122; Osterhammel 2017, p. 24.

process of globalization even stagnated, as nation-states withdrew from global networks and, in the course of Keynesianism, focused on regulating national economies, the economic crisis at the beginning of the 1970s was followed by a noticeable expansion of global trade through the liberalization of exchange rates and the reduction of tariffs.[51] What was also new was the emergence of a global financial market, which developed relatively independently of the circulation of goods and led to corresponding crises. Most recently, global production has been added,[52] which goes beyond the international division of labor in that joint products are manufactured at widely separated locations. The current disruption of supply chains demonstrates the worldwide interconnectedness of manufacturing processes.

The capitalist dynamic was fueled by a simultaneously emerging *global network* that enables direct cooperation over multi-continental distances without barriers and controls.[53] This not only intensifies and accelerates communication, but also makes it more intensive and profound. This applies not only to news, but also to the density, speed, and intensity with which institutions interact with one another. Thus, transnational and supraterritorial organizations cooperate, forming a global political system that goes beyond a network of international relations. At this point, however, the common mistake must be avoided of isolating and absolutizing individual aspects or events such as the Internet. In contrast, it is sensible to understand globalization as a novel, complex historical epoch.

Deglobalization?—In the current situation, globalization seems to be faltering. The striking example is the *pandemic*, which has thrown the entire globe into fear and terror and forced containment measures. In particular, international travel has suffered severe losses. As noted in the seventh chapter, nationalisms are on the rise, hindering the expansion and deepening of the European Union. Added to this are negative effects of globalization such as mass migrations with the evil of global terrorism. The war in Ukraine, the subsequent economic sanctions against Russia, and the correspondingly reduced gas supplies have restricted parts of world trade. There is also the blockade of grain exports, which threatens a worldwide famine. As in the phases of the 20th century mentioned, one could even speak of a new period of *deglobalization*.

---

[51] Beck 1997, pp. 61 f.; Reder 2009, pp. 26 f.; see Chap. 8.

[52] Hardt, Negri 2003, pp. 300 f.; Scholte 2005, pp. 159 ff.—Thus, production is not replaced and destroyed by circulation, but is itself revolutionized once again; see above the critique by Baudrillard.

[53] Negt 2001, pp. 36, 87; Lübbe 2005, p. 122; Keohane, Nye 2005, p. 78; Giddens 2005, pp. 60–62; Cheneval 2005, p. 187.

However, this claim contains only half the truth. It is true that the affected European countries are drawing on national resources. In Germany, domestic coal and nuclear power plants are even being reactivated instead of massively accelerating the expansion of renewable energies. But these measures do not signify an "end" to globalization; rather, global markets are shifting. For at the same time, the German government, like the USA, is seeking solutions on the world market. Despite unacceptable political and legal conditions, new deals are being made with Arab states. On the other side, Russia is expanding its trade relations with China. In these cases, it becomes clear that globalization is not a linearly progressing process, but is always also marked by setbacks, stagnations, and shifts.

In order to grasp the continuity and discontinuity of globalization, the *theory of historical transformation* serves as a framework.[54] If the process of globalization is understood as transformation, it becomes possible to characterize the transitions from earlier phases to the present situation as a sequence of upheavals in which the past passes over into the present. The categories that allow for such a description are the concepts of *potential* and *threshold*. The new does not simply arise through the destruction of the previous order; rather, the old potentials, such as the traditional nation-states, are guiding for the creation of new orders. So-called threshold points are present, for example, when an epoch dominated by the nation-state leads into a period in which political orders multiply and differentiate. The categories of potential and threshold then also mean that old and new forms exist simultaneously and form *hybrid forms* or *assemblages*. In terms of philosophy of history, these are cases of non-simultaneity.

Ethics.—Not least, *ethics of globalization* also requires a reflection in terms of the philosophy of history. For it is clear that the climate catastrophe and global poverty, which are partly interconnected, have been caused by humans over the course of their history. The ethical consequence to be drawn from this is that the damages caused must be remedied by compensatory measures. The current debate about such attempts shows how central the handling of history is in this context. Those who categorically deny a moral duty of industrialized countries toward poor countries already consider the historical context irrelevant. But even those who see the rich countries as obligated to help justify these duties independently of history. A responsibility that includes compensation for the consequences of harmful

---

[54] Sassen 2008, p. 17; for what follows, pp. 30, 42; cf. Roldán, Brauer, Rohbeck 2018, p. III; Rohbeck 2020, pp. 192–215.

behavior, by contrast, can only be justified with reference to the course of history so far.

Setting aside extremely liberal and nationalist positions, there is consensus that people living in wealthy countries are obligated to alleviate the distress of those in poor countries. This explicitly applies to states on a global scale as well. It is possible to distinguish between certain degrees of such duties to help, by granting special obligations to family members or members of one's own nation, from which a graded concept of justice results.[55] But this does not mean that a more far-reaching duty toward people living in distant regions is not justified. This raises the deeper question of the reasons why people are obligated to help other people. Here opinions diverge.

On the one side stands the position of the so-called *duty to aid* of Peter Singer, which is based on the argument that human beings, as such, have a duty to help other human beings, insofar as they are able to do so. Previous cooperation or even historical connections between these people are explicitly not to play any role. Yet the abstract imperative to provide humanitarian aid is not able to solve the problem of the corresponding responsibility.

For if one looks a little more closely at Singer's argumentation, one finds a paradoxical stance toward history. A completely unhistorical justification consists in the claim that the suffering and death of human beings is fundamentally something bad, which should in every case be overcome, without establishing a practical-historical relationship between those helping and those seeking help.[56] Those obligated to help function only as capable witnesses who observe the suffering from afar. Since, ultimately, it is a matter of an anthropological principle and thus the unity of the human species that obligates to help, this is a case of abstract cosmopolitanism.

Another justification is that people are obligated to prevent or alleviate suffering, however it may have arisen, insofar as it is within their *power* to do so. In this discourse, the repressed *history* reappears. For the ability to help people living at a distance depends crucially on the developed technical means of communication and transport. These constitute the real conditions of possibility for the global duty to aid. And because these conditions change over the course of history, the position of the duty to aid acquires an unexpectedly historical dimension. In contrast to traditional ethics, which

---

[55] Walzer 1999, p. 38; Zurbuchen 2005, p. 139; Joób 2008, pp. 35 f.; Hahn 2009, p. 32; Reder 2009, p. 42; Tillmann 2012, p. 55.
[56] Singer 2007, pp. 39 f.; cf. Schaber 2007, p. 139.

remained limited to the narrow circle of family, region, or nation-state, a new ethics of the global duty to aid now emerges.

If one reverses this argument, one could also formulate: Because people can help, they *ought* to do so. If one assumes that the alleviation of suffering is generally desirable, this is not a naturalistic fallacy, but rather the insight that new technical instruments give rise to new moral goals or historically conditioned norms, which amounts to a *technically induced change of values*. In this position, the historical does not refer to the prehistory of the fate of those suffering, but to the historically developed disposition of those helping. The question arises whether the justification of pure duties to aid is sufficient, and whether more far-reaching duties can be justified.

With regard to the *helpers*, the difficulty lies in the subjects who are obligated to help. Here, the impression arises that it is primarily individuals who, without mutual agreement, decide to provide assistance. Moreover, there is a lack of social differentiation among the wealthy and an assignment to social systems. Against this, it can be objected that in global aid actions, collective actors play a far greater role. Even in the case of a call for donations, which individuals follow spontaneously, it is a matter of coordinated action. This applies all the more to states and transnational organizations, which act as social institutions.

With regard to the *needy*, this leads to the predicament that those in distress appear merely as victims. They remain passive and anonymous sufferers, to whom there is no particular relationship. They figure only as objects of a beneficence that thereby harbors the danger of being authoritarian and arbitrary. Above all, it is striking that certain duties are ascribed to the rich, but no rights to the poor. Thus, the duties are not matched by rights that could be asserted in the form of legitimate claims. There is, in general, a lack of prior interaction between givers and receivers. As a result, all criteria of distributive justice are absent. However, if one insists that the poor have *certain rights* that go beyond universal human rights, then obligations arise that go beyond mere duties of assistance.

On the other hand, there is the position of *consequential responsibility* of Thomas Pogge, who assumes that the plight of individuals in poor countries is to be regarded as a "consequence" of actions carried out by the inhabitants of rich or powerful countries.[57] Here, the historical aspect comes into play, for such consequential responsibility is based on a historical process that has led to great injustices in the past. It follows that global responsibility for

---

[57] Pogge 2003, pp. 243 f.

people and peoples who have been treated unjustly, in turn, requires historical or even philosophy-of-history reflection.

For these reasons, I would like to speak of a *historical responsibility*. For behind this argument lies the insight that world poverty is the result of a historical process that includes the history of colonialism. The enormous economic superiority of the West is rooted in a centuries-long shared history. Thus, the vast majority of property rights have come about in unacceptable ways through enslavement, genocide, and exploitation. From this follows the demand to claim further-reaching duties to compensate for the injustice suffered. Here, the legal principle of liability for wrongdoing applies: whoever has actively brought about a state of distress is responsible for remedying it. The bringing about of an evil generates a particularly high degree of responsibility.

Last but not least, the fallacy must be rejected that historical responsibility would render duties of assistance superfluous, as if the two types of duties were mutually exclusive. Of course, all rich countries are obliged to provide assistance, even if they do not feel guilty or do not accept the conception of consequential responsibility. This principle was realized in the worldwide aid for Ukraine. Yet the further-reaching argument is that those states that were involved in causing harm in the past are, in the present, particularly obliged to provide compensation.

Responsibility for Future Generations

The philosophy of history of the Enlightenment is oriented above all toward the *future*. It harbors the expectation that the progress achieved so far in the fields of science, technology, and the economy can continue and may have positive effects on society and politics. In this, experiences with the past and present are projected into the future, just as ideas about the future influence orientation in the present. This reciprocal relationship was theoretically captured by Koselleck with the conceptual pair *space of experience* and *horizon of expectation (Erfahrungsraum und Erwartungshorizont)*.[58]

But the *posthistory* also makes statements about the future of history, even if this is supposed to result in an "end of history." In radical reversal, this applies to the most recent reinterpretations of the impending

---

[58] Koselleck 1979, pp. 349, 356; idem 2003, p. 249.

ecological catastrophe as a harbinger of the "apocalypse."[59] The following objections can be raised against this view: First, I see in it a secularized form of Christian eschatology. Second, such a cycle represents a premodern conception of history. Third, the claim that the catastrophe can no longer be stopped or prevented is ultimately irresponsible, because it stands in the way of committed action.

If, by contrast, one proclaims the *moral responsibility for future generations*, it makes sense to draw on the philosophy of history and to expand it into an *ethics of the future*. For the ethics of the future, it follows from this program that it opens itself to considerations from the philosophy of history and incorporates certain insights into the structure and function of historical consciousness into its own foundation. For the philosophy of history, this means that, with the perspective of the future, it participates in answering current questions and allies itself with practical philosophy. I therefore call it *practical philosophy of history*.

Timeframes of responsibility.—My conception now consists in structuring the *scope* of such responsibility in terms of time and space. From the various spheres of action results a *temporal gradation of the future*. In this way, responsibility can certainly be limited in order to provide the relief that is often desired. At the same time, the timeframes must be decisively extended whenever the consequences of technological action and the dangers lurking therein compel corresponding behavior. This proposal rejects both a universalistic extension and an abstract delimitation of moral responsibility.[60]

For such a differentiation, the concept of the *deadline* (Frist) is suitable, which I take from the essay *Endzeit und Zeitende* by Günter Anders and at the same time modify.[61] After the end of the Cold War, there is no longer *the* deadline by which the *catastrophe* will occur or can be prevented; instead, *multiple deadlines* are now apparent. Numerous dates or deadly markers arise—*deadlines* in the truest sense of the word, which must not be

---

[59] Already John Leslie proclaims the "end of the world" and the "extinction of humanity" (Leslie 1998, p. 12). Eva Horn suggests coming to terms with the catastrophe and settling into everyday life until then (Horn 2014, p. 149). Tim Morton claims to have established that the catastrophe is not still impending, but has "already taken place" (Morton 2018, p. 46). Gregory Fuller speaks of the "cheerful hopelessness in the face of ecological catastrophe" (Fuller 2017, p. 23). Marina Garcés notes a "posthumous condition" that means the death of humanity (Garcés 2019, pp. 12, 31, 40 f.). Urs Büttner and Steffen Richter likewise claim that the "threshold" has already been crossed, in which humanity has initiated its own downfall (Büttner, Richter 2021, pp. 11 f.).

[60] See Jonas 1979, pp. 9, 89 ff., 245.—Cf. Parfit 1981, p. 113; Laslett 1992, pp. 24 f.; Veith 2006, pp. 127 f.; Birnbacher 2003, p. 82; Leist 2005, pp. 4 f.; Sturma 2006, pp. 221 f.

[61] Günther Anders: *Die atomare Bedrohung*, Munich 1986, pp. 170, 203; cf. Rohbeck 2013, pp. 78–88; ibid. 2020, pp. 216–239.

exceeded. After history was "un-timed" during the Enlightenment era, there are now temporal *limitations* within history.

Long deadlines are primarily induced by technological and ecological practices. Here, the "long duration" refers less to the precautionary actions themselves, which take place over a few decades, than to the consequences of these actions, which, due to technology, reach very far into the future. In this case, we are responsible for effects even if they lie in the distant future. Although we can hardly imagine the people affected and can only provide for them indirectly, we are obligated to this guarantee. Extremely long deadlines arise in the disposal of radioactive waste, which must be kept away from the biosphere for almost immeasurable periods of time.[62] In view of this duration, the three-hundredth or even the thousandth generation is relatively real and concrete.

Despite the enormous temporal distance, there is no doubt that people in the present are responsible for such long-term effects. This responsibility is not based solely on a universalist ethics, which attributes to all people of all future times an interest in health and thus a corresponding right that obligates us today to precautionary actions. Due to the long-term danger posed by nuclear technology, it is unavoidable. If this risk can be eliminated or reduced by present action, there is a concrete obligation that goes beyond a three-generation limit or medium range. In this area, a blanket limitation of responsibility would even be highly immoral.

The times of "short duration" in historiography refer to individual events, mostly in the realm of political decisions. The same applies to *short deadlines* in the future. Insofar as they concern social systems, they usually involve financial crises, in the face of which action must be taken relatively quickly: within a few months, weeks, days, or even hours. Similarly, Ukraine required military and humanitarian support at short notice, not least also for the number of refugees from there. The embargo against Russia resulted in energy shortages, which had to be overcome within a year. In such cases, the agents are responsible for their own and the next affected generation—that is, explicitly not for people living later. The abstract obligation beyond this temporal boundary has no practical relevance here.

For *medium-term deadlines*, it is similarly the case that they are determined by different fields of action, whose time horizons depend on the natural and social systems, each of which has its own specific historical times.

---

[62] Böhler 2009, pp. 44 ff.; Leggewie, Welzer 2009, p. 11.—In the context of the *Anthropocene*, one also speaks of "deep time" or a "deep future"; Horn, Berthaller 2019, p. 198.

Medium-term periods, for example, concern the field of natural resources. After the oil crises of 1973/74 and 1979/80 triggered a last great wave of discovery and development, the global oil production peak (about 35 years later) will be reached in the near future. If consumption remains constant, fossil energies (especially oil) will be depleted or at least unprofitable to use by 2050. The periods still available to avoid the negative effects of climate change, whose consequences extend up to several hundred years, are also medium-term.[63] In these areas, actions in the next one to two decades are unavoidable. But the corresponding deadlines extend beyond that, since we are precisely responsible for those generations that will be directly affected. In this area, moral responsibility must therefore be clearly extended beyond the boundary of the three currently living generations.

Reversibility.—This problem becomes particularly acute when the deadlines not only point to the future but also refer to the *past*. Here it can be observed that certain climate goals have both a *prospective* and a *retrospective* aspect, as they are oriented toward an earlier stage of industrialization. If a return to earlier conditions proves necessary, this is linked to the desire for *reversions*.

Thus, climate researchers demand that global greenhouse gas emissions should fall to at least half the 1990 level by the middle of the 21st century. Other examples, which are more realistic and have already shown some success, are the disposal of waste, the cleaning of polluted water and air, the reversal of expanding desert areas, the compensation for soil erosion, the reforestation of cleared forests, and the recovery of fish stocks in the world's oceans. The goal is the restabilization of natural systems, as with the climate, or the regeneration of ecosystems, as with resources, within certain periods of time. The standard for remediation is thus defined so that a previous state is to be restored.

This phenomenon corresponds to the principle of *reversibility*. If the principle of responsibility is to consist in maintaining the possibility of reparation also for the future, because it is threatened by increasingly irreversible damage, then the following results: The development of technological civilization must be shaped so that reversible movements remain possible in the future as well. This not only demands that certain developments be revised in the present in order to remedy damage that has occurred. Beyond that, this principle means creating in the future the conditions of possibility for

---

[63] Welzer 2008, p. 57; Leggewie, Welzer 2009, pp. 12, 27, 68 f., 167; Gesang 2011, pp. 15 f.; Birnbacher 2016, pp. 8 f., 11 f., 62.

such reversions. This condition of possibility is to be implanted in the historical process of the future.

Deadlines have not only a temporal but also a *spatial* dimension. Therefore, it is necessary to determine more precisely for which generations, in which places, which living conditions are to be created.[64] For it is indisputable that the predicted ecological or financial crises will have very different effects on particular peoples. This results in a *historical map of the future*, on which desirable, crisis-ridden, or threatening conditions are marked in certain regions. If the past is also taken into account, the marked situations can be understood as the result of different developments, whereby the less developed countries are in particular need of support.

Catching-up development.—At this point, it is worth considering whether less developed countries may claim the right to catch up on a development that has long since been completed by the old industrialized countries. Incidentally, this also applies to the former communist states in Eastern Europe, which, after their collapse, wish to follow the path of Western capitalism. Thus, the contested concept of *catching-up development* and the modified concept of *sustainable development* are up for discussion.[65] If these countries are granted a *right to development*, it follows that there is an imperative to balance different levels. If one seeks the foundation of such a right, one is referred to the philosophy of history. I will begin with an explanation of the temporal implications and then attempt a normative justification.

The model of catching-up development has a complex *temporal structure*. It consists of asynchronies that are to be synchronized. Poor countries expect for the future a condition that already belongs to the past in rich countries. One could speak here of a *future past*. In the field of ecology, these are even conditions that are regarded in some wealthy countries as historically outdated and in need of revision. The current conflicts between old and new capitalist countries strikingly express this paradox. At the same time, they highlight the necessity of reaching an understanding about novel developments in the future.

If one further seeks a *normative foundation* for the postulated right to development, the question arises: Is this justification content to apply recognized theories of justice, which have proven themselves in the present, to the near, medium, and distant future? Or are there specific *norms from the*

---

[64] The thesis of an "ecological globalization," which supposedly affects all of humanity equally, must be rejected. Lienkamp 2009, p. 340, speaks of a questionable "catastrophe egalitarianism."
[65] For an exemplary discussion of this concept: Paehlke 1989, p. 113; Bartelmus 1994, pp. 78 ff.; Böhler 2009, pp. 16 f.

philosophy of history that can be brought to bear here? If such norms can be identified, the claim to provide a philosophical and at the same time normative justification of history can be fulfilled.

The classical *philosophy of history* (Geschichtsphilosophie) was characterized by the fact that it was essentially oriented toward the future and thus action-oriented. Its task was not only to philosophically reflect on past events and processes; above all, it had the function of providing orientation for a *future-oriented practice*. Thus, the concept of *progress* was not limited to the description of developments, but also included the positive evaluation of civilizational achievements. This was linked to the hope for further progress as well as the moral imperative to contribute to the improvement of the expected living conditions.

However controversial the idea of progress may appear today, since it has partly contributed to undesirable developments, the concern to care for the well-being of future generations remains highly relevant, i.e., to strive for better living conditions in the future or at least to ensure that no deterioration occurs or that it is kept within limits. Here we are dealing with a *genuinely philosophy-of-history norm* that can also claim validity in the present. If the expectation of progress is limited to certain sectors and differentiated in terms of space and time, it is possible to avoid absolutizing the concept of progress and exaggerating it teleologically.[66] Such a *desire for improvement* in the global historical process constitutes the core of a philosophy-of-history justification of world-historical justice.

This desire contains the historical awareness that the *conditions of possibility for human action* expand in history and thus open up new horizons for modern civilization. Insofar as an interest in this may be assumed, it follows that there is a practical intention not to be satisfied with absolute and often minimal standards as soon as the prerequisites for an increase in the standard of living are given.[67] People, if they consider an improvement in their circumstances to be realistic, will express this desire and make corresponding demands. As inhabitants of less developed countries, they will especially demand this when, in looking at richer countries, they already recognize

---

[66] This is assumed by Koselleck 1975, vol. 2, p. 400; idem 1979, pp. 50, 130; for a critical view see Rohbeck 2020, pp. 164 f.; for the general problem of conceptual history, see the end of the introduction.

[67] When historical comparisons are drawn, the following positions can be distinguished: 1. at least as high, possibly even better: Pogge 2002, pp. 143 ff.; Tremmel 2012, p. 291.—2. equivalent: Heubach 2008, p. 44; Gesang 2011, pp. 48 f., 93 ff.—3. perhaps even worse: Sturma 2006, p. 230.—On so-called sufficiency: Meyer 2018, pp. 55–72, 115–135.

their real possibilities as concrete reality. Such an appeal is justified if it can be realized under contingent conditions and integrated into a coherent system that is considerate of nature and respects social justice.

Such a modified model of progress has a threefold significance. For the *poor countries*, progress initially means nothing more and nothing less than achieving a minimum standard of living conditions under which they can satisfy their basic needs.[68] The *industrialized countries* do not, in the first instance, have an unlimited claim to progress that comes at the expense of social justice and the environment. They are even obliged to forgo it as long as the necessary progress has not been realized in the developing and emerging countries. Finally, the plea for progress in less developed countries is not to be confused with a naive optimism, because *alternative developments* are intended. Precisely for the disadvantaged countries, the opportunity arises to pursue alternative paths of modernization.

---

[68] Whereas the "basic needs" approach is primarily aimed at material aspects, the concept of "capabilities" is directed at the sum of abilities to satisfy one's own needs and to lead a self-determined life: Sen 2010, pp. 231, 271; Nussbaum 2001, pp. 87 f.; cf. Meyer 2018, pp. 33–43.

10

Transformations

In order to describe the Enlightenment as a process that transcends epochs, I use the term of *transformation*. By this I mean the transfer and reshaping of certain scientific and philosophical theories of the Enlightenment into other contexts. What is transferred functions as a *potential* that is realized in new contexts and thereby changes to a greater or lesser extent. By conceiving Enlightenment science and philosophy as such a horizon of possibilities, I understand the Enlightenment neither as a timeless principle nor as a purely historical epoch. As mentioned in the introduction, I distinguish between three stages of transformation.

The *first* transformation took place *within the epoch of the Enlightenment*. Even if one initially conceives of the Enlightenment as a longer period that already begins in the seventeenth century, what is decisive in our context is that around the middle of the eighteenth century a fundamental change occurred. In this process, anthropology advanced to become the leading science, in which the human being was thematized as a corporeal and thus also as a gendered being. Entirely new is political economy, with which for the first time an independent social theory emerged. From the analysis of economic developments, a philosophy of history finally arose, which is based on the "progress" of techno-economic stages. The emergence of these scientific disciplines led to the groundbreaking insight into social and historical *contingencies*, which are experienced as *wounds* (second section). In this way, I summarize my guiding thesis that the Enlightenment differs from the preceding modern era in that it assumes the character of the *modern*.

This transition to a specifically *modern Enlightenment* forms the core of my approach to the historical epoch of the Enlightenment.

The *second* transformation consists in the *transfer of Enlightenment theories into the present* of the twenty-first century. There are various responses to this project, with which I will first engage (first section). *Conservative* authors accuse the Enlightenment of having abandoned established traditions such as religion without providing an adequate substitute for meaning. Proponents of *Critical Theory* identify the Enlightenment with a domination of nature that turns into social and political relations of domination. This criticism is also followed by the representatives of the so-called "*postmodernity*", with the diagnosis that the utopian hope for a better future has been exhausted for all time. In response to these accusations, there are current attempts to update the ideas of the Enlightenment. I would like to align myself with this tendency toward rehabilitation. Just as sweeping accusations are rejected, so too must an uncritical apology for the Enlightenment be avoided. It is therefore important to work out the *limits and potentials* (third section) in such a way that the *ambivalences* of Enlightenment thought come to the fore.

The *third* transformation aims to draw on the scientific and philosophical achievements of the Enlightenment to *solve current problems* (fourth section). Against the background of contemporary denial of facts, the epistemological realism of the Enlightenment is to be revived. In view of the ecological crisis, one can refer back to anthropology, which placed the human being in relation to his inner and outer nature. In the context of the current gender debate, it makes sense to draw on the egalitarian side of the Enlightenment conception of humanity. In view of postcolonial reappraisal, the critique of conquest and enslavement must be continued. While late capitalism produces enormous social dislocations, it is important to recall the broad spectrum of the Enlightenment, from liberal reform proposals to radical social critique. Since the still prevailing neoliberalism has led to devastating social and ecological damage, the urgent question arises of how to regain the political. With regard to the current wars, the utopias of peace of the Enlightenment acquire an unexpected relevance. In doing so, one should adopt the future perspective of the Enlightenment philosophy of history. Overall, the task is to transform the experiences of the Enlightenment with technical, social, economic, and historical contingencies into the management of social and ecological crises.

Positions on the Enlightenment

In order to prepare the transformation of the historical Enlightenment into the present, I will now present and comment in somewhat more detail on the various positions on the Enlightenment. The spectrum ranges from the counter-Enlighteners of the eighteenth century to the conservative critics as well as representatives of Critical Theory and postmodernity in the twentieth and twenty-first centuries. In addition, I address current attempts to renew the philosophy of the Enlightenment. However, I would point out that not a few of these authors are still so caught up in criticism of the Enlightenment that they arrive only at a limited picture of this type of thought. In contrast, it is my intention to take into account the entire thematic and critical field of the Enlightenment.

Enlightenment and raison d'état.—Here it is necessary to recall the often overlooked fact that the Enlightenment was controversial from the very beginning. The critique of the Enlightenment is as old as the Enlightenment itself. The epoch of the Enlightenment began as a critique of the tradition that preceded it, especially the dogmas of the Catholic Church and the rule of absolutism. But since 1750, the critique of the Enlightenment has been directed at itself.

Initially, it was the clerical apologists who established what is called the *counter-Enlightenment*. In doing so, they not only condemned atheistic tendencies, but also insisted on the indispensability of religion for the existence of a society. Thus, they shifted from traditionally theological objections to a social-philosophical line of argument. The irony of this attempt at legitimation consists in the fact that the representatives of the Enlightenment themselves invoked the social function of religion (3,2).[1] This criticism should therefore not be dismissed as anti-Enlightenment in general, because it makes use of genuinely Enlightenment arguments. In this sense, both Enlightenment and counter-Enlightenment belong to the overarching epoch of the Enlightenment.

A similar situation applies to *Rousseau*, who radically criticized modern civilization. The advances of science, technology, and the economy, he interpreted as a process of decline that, he argued, had led to social inequality, individual egoism, as well as corruption in morals and politics (7,2; 8,2). In doing so, he employed arguments from contemporary sciences: from political economy, anthropology, moral philosophy, and political theory. Even

---

[1] The numbers in the following parentheses refer to chapter and section of this book.

though he attracted criticism from other Enlightenment thinkers such as Voltaire, his influence on the Enlightenment is nonetheless to be acknowledged. In this case, there is even no doubt that Rousseau was a representative of the Enlightenment. For he was perceived as such not only by Catholic critics, but also celebrated by the protagonists of the French Revolution. In Italy and Spain, with his civil religion, he had the dubious reputation of being a quite "normal" Enlightener, who was to be opposed.

Rousseau also impressed *Kant*, since he regarded progress less as an empirical fact than as a regulative idea that obligates moral action. His particular merit lies in the fact that he addressed the epoch of the Enlightenment at its end and thus contributed to the *self-reflection of the Enlightenment*. The occasion was a discussion in the *Berlinische Monatsschrift*, in which, in 1784, the question was posed, "What is Enlightenment?" In the article of the same name, Kant gives his now-famous answer: "Enlightenment is the emergence of man from his self-incurred immaturity."[2] Yet less well known are those passages in which he distinguishes between a "public" and "private" use of reason. *Public* use is when it is practiced by scholars within the "reading public," that is, restricted to the community of scientists and writers. *Private* use of reason is by those who hold a civil office in society and the state and thus exercise an official function. Ultimately, this means that civil servants in the bourgeois public sphere may not appear as representatives of the Enlightenment and should moderate their statements.

At the end of his text, Kant refers to "Herr Mendelssohn", whose article on the same question was announced in the aforementioned journal, but which Kant had not yet been able to read. For several months, the conflict between freedom of belief and civic duty had already been debated there. Yet what for Kant is a pragmatic arrangement becomes a problem for Mendelssohn. For "enlightenment of man can come into conflict with civic enlightenment."[3] While Kant considers this division within a person a politically necessary measure, Mendelssohn regards this inner conflict as an imposition. Nevertheless, like Kant, he ultimately sides with reason of state. He advises the "virtue-loving Enlightener" to exercise "caution and prudence." He should take the commonwealth into consideration, i.e., rather tolerate a prejudice than damage the established religion and morality.

---

[2] Kant 1965, vol. XI, pp. 53–61, here p. 53; on the reception of Rousseau ibid., p. 44.—Cf. Müller 2002, p. 63; Borgstedt 2004, p. 1.—In the self-reflection of the Enlightenment, Daniel Fulda sees a particular strength of the German Enlightenment; Fulda 2022, p. 96.

[3] *On the Question: What Does It Mean to Enlighten?* In: Mendelssohn 2009, vol. II, p. 212.

Both Kant and Mendelssohn advise the internalization of state censorship or, respectively, self-censorship by the citizen. They seek to confine the Enlightenment to the narrow circle of the educated and to protect it from overly radical positions. When Kant finally poses the question of whether his own era could be considered an "enlightened age" or an "age of Enlightenment," he believes himself to be on the path toward a "true" Enlightenment,[4] which is to practice moderation. In this, I see a typical feature of the German Enlightenment.

With his book *The True Enlightenment*, Werner Schneiders directly connects to Kantian philosophy.[5] He opposes a "false or bad Enlightenment," which he characterizes as naive, one-sided, and destructive. By "true Enlightenment," he understands German philosophy, while he rejects the English and especially the French Enlightenment as a "theoretical prelude to revolution."[6] In doing so, he criticizes not only materialist and atheistic tendencies, but also, overall, certain subject areas and contents such as bourgeois society with its technical, economic, and political developments. For him, these count as merely "external conditions" that do not reach the true core of the Enlightenment. Because, according to this reading, substantive topics are excluded, only formal and abstract principles remain, such as maturity and emancipation, critique and self-critique, as well as independent thinking.[7] This results in an insubstantial Enlightenment, which is supposed to preserve religious and moral traditions. But this does justice neither to Kant nor to the rest of the European Enlightenment. If Kant alone is always invoked, the other innovations fall by the wayside.

Enlightenment in critique.—From there, it is only a small step to an explicitly *conservative critique*, which even turns against Kant and reproaches the Enlightenment for having broken with tried and tested traditions without being able to fill the alleged void.[8] The idea of emancipation is said to

---

[4] Kant 1965, vol. XI, p. 59.
[5] Schneiders 1974, p. 10; idem 1997, p. 130.—See also Schmidt, J. 1989, p. 10; Mittelstraß 1989, pp. 341 f.; Kopper 1996, pp. 7 f., 12; Holzhey 1997, p. 24; Reinhalter 1997, p. 12; idem 2006, p. 18; Porter 2000, p. 9; Müller 2002, pp. 63 f.; Schmidt, G. 2009, pp. 394 f.; Stockhorst 2013, p. 20; Haag, Wild 2019, p. 110; Frick 2020, p. 25.
[6] Schneiders 1974, pp. 11, 189, 209; cf. Kopper 1996, p. 27; Godel 2007, p. 384; Frick 2020, pp. 57, 72 f.; Nassehi 2021, pp. 332, 337.
[7] Schneiders 1974, pp. 7, 9, 191, 195, 214; cf. Schmidt, J. 1989, p. 25; Holzhey 1997, p. 29; Thoma 2018, p. 148; Frick 2020, pp. 33, 72 f.
[8] Kondylis 1981, p. 27; Lübbe 1986, p. 207; Bubner 1989, pp. 416 f.; Saul 1992, pp. 38 f.; Goulemot 2001, pp. 76–85; Albertan-Coppola, McKenna 2003, p. 15.—For a critical perspective, see d'Aprile, Siebers 2008, p. 211; Rohbeck 2010, pp. 32 f.; Lilti 2019, pp. 9 f.

have led only to an absolutized individualism and subjectivism. With the rebellion of the bourgeoisie against church and monarchy, only another social group is said to have seized power, which proved to be just as totalitarian and unjust. Overall, rationalization and secularization are regarded as misguided paths on which humanity overestimated itself. The original liberation from constraints is said to have degenerated into a dictatorship of reason. Ultimately, the Enlightenment is said to have created only surrogates of Christianity and thereby left a worldview vacuum into which, in the nineteenth and twentieth centuries, disastrous ideologies could penetrate.

Another variant of critique is offered by the *Dialectic of Enlightenment* by Max Horkheimer and Theodor W. Adorno, who claim that the seed of the self-destruction of reason is inherent in Enlightenment thought. This, they argue, has led to "instrumental reason," which loses sight of human purposes and humane goals.[9] In light of the experiences with National Socialism, after two world wars, Hiroshima, and Auschwitz, they believe they have found in identifying thought and the resulting domination of nature, present since the beginnings of Western culture, the deeper reason for the self-destruction of modern civilization. In this sense, they hold the Enlightenment responsible for the catastrophes of the twentieth century. As in Horkheimer's *Eclipse of Reason*, the metaphor of "Enlightenment" is reinterpreted as a process of darkening.

It is problematic to hold the Enlightenment responsible for all the negative flip sides of contemporary scientific and technological civilization. This is not only historically incorrect, but also fails to recognize the achievements of the Enlightenment. Moreover, it should be noted that Horkheimer and Adorno use a very broad, temporally and conceptually "unbounded" notion of Enlightenment, which encompasses the emergence and development of bourgeois society from ancient Greece to the present. The Enlightenment in the narrower sense appears only with Kant. At the same time, attention should be drawn to the paradox that, despite their critique of the Enlightenment, the authors seek to rescue Enlightenment thought,[10] so that the possibility of an "other" Enlightenment might remain open.

---

[9] Horkheimer, Adorno 1987; Horkheimer 1985.—See also Habermas 1985, p. 131; Wellmer 1985, p. 48; Strasser 1986, p. 7; Schmid-Noerr 1988, p. 8; Rüsen, Lämmert, Glotz 1988, pp. 21 f.; Schnädelbach 2004, pp. 66 f.; Schmidt, A. 2006, p. 121; Stiegler 2008, p. 129; Israel 2009, p. 15; Andries 2009, p. 2; Faber, Wehinger 2010, p. 15; Pečar, Tricore 2015, pp. 11 f.; Hampe 2018, p. 72; Garcés 2019, p. 11.

[10] Horkheimer, Adorno 1987, vol. 5, p. 18.

The third type of critique comes from what is known as the *postmodern*, whose representatives continue and radicalize some of the aforementioned reproaches. While the "Dialectic of Enlightenment" still contained the possibility of self-correction, postmodern critique categorically denies the Enlightenment such a capacity for reflection. With the Second World War, the ideals of the Enlightenment, such as rationality, emancipation, humanism, are said to have discredited themselves; the utopian hope for a better future is said to have been definitively exhausted. Added to this is the diagnosis that modern civilization, with its technologization and commercialization, leads to cultural loss and alienation. According to Michel Foucault, the Enlightenment is characterized by a tendency to level out the ruptures of history, the singular, and the contingent.[11] Jean-François Lyotard considers the "grand narratives" of Christianity and the Enlightenment to be delegitimized, because they suppress and marginalize the many "small" stories of the lifeworld. The result, he argues, is a meaningless hegemony of bourgeois, Eurocentric, and masculine culture. All this culminates in the conviction that modern reason is at an end and that the Enlightenment is irretrievably dead.

Self-Enlightenment.—In response to the criticism from the Frankfurt School and postmodernism, there have been recent and very recent attempts to rehabilitate and thereby update the Enlightenment. The model is the *philosophy of the Enlightenment* by Ernst Cassirer, who, shortly before the outbreak of war, rediscovered the Enlightenment because he hoped for a powerful reason from it. When a cultural reform movement emerged after the war, an international renaissance of Enlightenment studies began as early as the 1960s and 1970s.[12] At the end of the 1980s, the volume *The Future of the Enlightenment* became prominent in Germany, in which a case is made for a reappropriation of the Enlightenment in order to counter tendencies

---

[11] Foucault 1990, pp. 35 f.; Lyotard 1986, pp. 96 f.—See also Wellmer 1985, pp. 49–58; Binder 1985, vol. 1, pp. 7 f.; Rorty 2001, pp. 19 f.; Bartlett 2001, pp. 3 f.; Žižek 2001, pp. 7 f.; Diner 2017, pp. 11 f.; Thoma 2018, pp. 7 f., 52, 128.—For a critical view of postmodernism as well as of posthistoire: Garcés 2019, p. 31; for a subsequent justification of postmodernism, see Zorn 2022, p. 14.

[12] John Stephenson Spink: *French free-thought from Gassendi to Voltaire*, London 1960; Werner Krauss: *Perspectives and Problems. On the French and German Enlightenment and other essays*. Neuwied, Berlin 1965; Victor Klemperer: *History of French Literature in the 18th Century*. Berlin 1966; Peter Gay: *The Enlightenment: An Interpretation*. 2 vols., New York, London 1967–1969; Roland Mortier: *Clartés et ombres du siècle des Lumières*. Geneva 1969; Franco Venturi: *Utopia e riforma nell'Illuminismo*. Turin 1970; Michèle Duchet: *Anthropologie et histoire au siècle des Lumières*. Paris 1971; Sergio Moravia: *Observing Reason. Philosophy and Anthropology in the Enlightenment*. Munich 1973.—In Spain, the country's own tradition of Enlightenment was only researched after the Franco dictatorship; exemplary: Francisco Sánchez-Blanco 2002; José Luis Villacañas in: Rohbeck, Rother 2016, pp. 3–26.

critical of modernization.[13] In recent times, affirmative titles such as *The Second Enlightenment*, *The Third Enlightenment*, *New Radical Enlightenment*, *Ecological Enlightenment*, or *Enlightenment as an Open Process* have been added.[14]

But what does "new" Enlightenment mean here? Even in earlier attempts at rehabilitation, it was taken for granted that one could not simply continue the "old" Enlightenment. In order not to fall back into a naïve epigonism, the new concept of Enlightenment should also include *critique of the Enlightenment*. First, Jürgen Habermas, who wanted to hold on to the "project of modernity," demanded that "the Enlightenment must enlighten itself about itself." He issued the slogan "Enlightenment as a task" and thus coined the much-quoted motto of an "enlightenment about the Enlightenment" or "self-enlightenment."[15] However appealing such a program may seem, I see two problems with it.

First, the Enlightenment is treated as a homogeneous *block* that one tries to restore. In a Hegelianizing manner, the Enlightenment appears as an identical entity to which one now prescribes self-reflection. Even if one wants to give the Enlightenment a new chance, it appears as a totality that merely has to come to itself and to its "true" essence. In contrast, I refer to the state of research, which shows that Enlightenment culture is composed of diverse sources and lives from the openness of its development. Therefore, I replace the model of reflection with the analysis of concrete discourses. I take this perspective into account by giving a voice not only to Kant in Germany, but also to as many contemporary authors as possible from other countries, with their different subject areas and diverse positions.

The *second* problem I see is that the repeatedly postulated *self-enlightenment* is supposed to consist in excluding certain sciences along with their respective objects. These include, in particular, the fields of technology and economics, which are assigned to "instrumental reason" and are considered per se self-destructive. As if in a reflex to Critical Theory and postmodern critique, the "new" Enlightenment is also supposed to keep its distance from technical production and focus on communicative action.[16] In opposition

---

[13] Rüsen, Lämmert, Glotz 1988; see also Schnädelbach 1988; Mittelstraß 1989.

[14] Postman 2000; Todorow 2009; Hardtwig 2010; Büscher, Japp 2010; Pagden 2013; Reinalter 2016; Hampe 2018; Pinker 2018; Garcés 2019; Frick 2020; Rohbeck 2021.—Enlightenment as a valuable "heritage" in Lilti 2019; Diderot as the undogmatic "periphery" of the Enlightenment in Gumbrecht 2020.

[15] Habermas 1981, pp. 444–464; cf. Schnädelbach 1988, p. 15; Mittelstraß 1989, p. 341.

[16] Habermas 1981, p. 446; cf. Schnädelbach 1988, p. 20; Mittelstraß 1989, p. 345; Reinalter 1997, pp. 12, 21; idem 2006, pp. 14 f.; idem 2016, p. 104; Reitz 2012, pp. 101 f.; Berndt, Fulda 2012, pp. 241 f.; Garcés 2019, p. 52.

to the self-propelling nature of means, subjective purposiveness is invoked, which is supposed to guarantee the moral autonomy of human beings. In this way, the Enlightenment is split into a technical-economic-instrumental and a moral-political-normative part. Only the latter half is allowed to remain as Enlightenment.

Behind this lies the problem of a dualism that divides modernity into *two cultures*—a dualism that has its roots in the emergence of the humanities in the nineteenth century, was effective up to the critique of civilization in the twentieth century, and is now being projected back into the eighteenth century.[17] When, in our present, theories of culture are being conceived, however, attempts are made to overcome such a split. This means, concretely, that the fields of science and technology are also granted a specifically cultural dimension. I now claim that the epoch of the Enlightenment, if one wishes to avoid the aforementioned anachronism, is particularly suited to an integrative perspective. If, therefore, I attempt a transformation of the Enlightenment, I explicitly include modern civilization. In this, the discovery of the contingency of cognitive, technical, and social systems plays a special role. I will now systematically address this experience of contingency in order to work out its emancipatory potentials.

Contingency as Wound

Contingency a dialectic of Enlightenment—this could be the heading of this section on the *first transformation*, because instrumental reason plays a not insignificant role in it. As outlined, in *my* version of a self-reflection of Enlightenment, I expressly do not wish to leave out the domains of technology and economy. In doing so, I grant to the Enlighteners that they recognized a dynamic of its own in the process of civilization and thus, for the first time, revealed the *contingencies* of modern society. The "dialectic" consists in the fact that the capitalist system has unintended consequences, some of which lead to social and ecological deformations. Such reversals are "instrumental" because, in the broad sense, they are technical means whose effects overshoot the original intentions.

---

[17] Johannes Rohbeck and Jost Halfmann: *Two Cultures of Science—revisited*. Göttingen 2007.

Nevertheless, I do *not see instrumentalism* in this fact, which would necessarily have to turn into total domination and self-destruction. The Enlighteners of the eighteenth century were indeed aware of the complementary insight that the contingency they had uncovered could also contain something liberating. The self-dynamics of bourgeois society were experienced as independence from the absolutist state and as a gain in personal freedom. Moreover, it was quickly realized that the self-regulation of economic and social action is by no means to be misunderstood as determinism, but that partial state interventions are always possible. Finally, some authors interpreted the surplus potentials of science, technology, and economy as the opening up of ever-expanding horizons of action.

When I refer to these phenomena as *mortifications*, I wish to give them an additional social-psychological connotation. As is well known, Sigmund Freud identified three mortifications of humanity: the *cosmological mortification*, in which Copernicus denied humans the central position in the cosmos; the *biological mortification* by Darwin, who made humans emerge from natural evolution; and the *psychological mortification*, with which the unconscious in humans comes to light.[18] In our context, it should be added that the Enlightenment had already inflicted a whole series of mortifications on humanity beforehand. Hardly had modern humans achieved a previously unimagined autonomy than their self-empowerment in the Enlightenment suffered some sensitive setbacks.

One can speak of a *geological mortification* in the debate about the Lisbon earthquake of 1755. It was above all Voltaire who declared this natural disaster not as a "punishment from God" but as pure "chance" (5.3). This verdict was directed against the religious notion that divine "providence" had arranged the whole world for the benefit of humans. From the standpoint of Catholic religion, the earthquake indeed had to appear as a mortification of humans, who lost their protected special status. If one mistakenly identifies the Enlightenment with such a theodicy, the destruction of Lisbon may even appear as a shock to the Enlightenment. The opposite is true, however, because theodicy itself had lost its plausibility and with Rousseau and Kant was replaced by a secular and pragmatic discussion aimed at the future avoidance of such crises. For these reasons, this discourse is even to be regarded as the end of a mortification and thus as the beginning of modernity.

---

[18] Sigmund Freud: *The Resistances to Psychoanalysis*. In: Collected Works. Ed. by Anna Freud et al., London 1947 ff., vol. 12, pp. 1 f.—See in this context Wellmer1985, pp. 70 f.

If one generalizes these considerations, one arrives at the *religion-critical mortification* of the Enlightenment (3.2). This kind of mortification goes beyond the doubts about theodicy, which with Leibniz represents a unique phenomenon from the theology of the early eighteenth century. It also surpasses the Copernican turn, through which humans were banished from the center of the universe. The critique of religion in the later Enlightenment is not even limited to skepticism about the existence of God as a possible creator of humans. Beyond that, it criticizes the affective and linguistic foundations of religion as well as the historical and social function of Christianity. Truly original is the accusation that the properties ascribed to the divine being are "anthropomorphic," that is, merely images of our own human nature.

In this context, there is also the *natural-historical mortification*, which though related to Darwin's theory of evolution, was already initiated in the eighteenth century (4.2). Even if the Enlighteners still shrank from the consequence that humans descended from apes, they nevertheless placed them close to the animal kingdom. With the abandonment of the biblical time scheme, the history of humanity loses its eschatological significance and must content itself with being an episode in the universe. From today's perspective, it is remarkable that humans were characterized by d'Holbach and Kant as a contingent product and by Herder as a deficient being, which also relativizes their prominent position in the Anthropocene. In addition, Montesquieu's climate theory (7.3) held that the ways of life, moral concepts, and forms of government of humans are influenced by contingent natural conditions.

From this follows the *anthropological mortification*, through which humans appear as natural beings driven by bodily needs, which they are able to satisfy through natural means of subsistence (4.2). Again, the Enlighteners hesitate to reduce humans to their bodies and to deny them a soul separate from it. Although only a few authors such as d'Holbach and La Mettrie advocated such materialism, the body-soul dualism of the seventeenth century gives way to a skeptical position of Hume and Kant. Thus, the hypostatization of the human mind also comes to an end. From the idealist standpoint, this disappearance of the spiritual can be interpreted as a mortification.

In the context of anthropology, *emotional wounding* is also at issue (7.2). Although Descartes, Hobbes and Spinoza had already made the "affections" of human beings a topic, it was always with the stipulation that human reason must control the emotions. With Hume, this relationship is reversed, so that feelings such as "sympathy" or "benevolence" are to form the foundations of morality. This concerns both the individual as well as communication in society. Rousseau even goes so far as to hold reason responsible for egoism and to condemn it morally. This position is not far from Freud's *psychological wounding*, because moral feelings are often unconscious and spread intuitively.

At this point, *cognitive wounding* follows, which reverses the relation between feeling and understanding (6,2). Beyond Locke's empiricism, the subsequent sensualism is devoted to the internal relations between sense impressions. Sensations not only rule over understanding, but, so to speak, penetrate cognitive activity itself. This already begins with perception, within which comparisons and connections are established, so that I have spoken of a *sensual intelligence*. Accordingly, Hume, who declares reason to be the "slave" of the passions, bases causal explanations on an instinctive power of habit, which I have called *emotional intelligence*. In this perhaps lies the greatest wounding of a previously absolutized faith in reason.

This is connected to *linguistic wounding*, because it too relocates the intellectual achievement of human beings to instances that become effective outside of reason (6,3). As we have seen, the emergence of the philosophy of language by Condillac, Beccaria, Herder and others belongs to the greatest innovations of the European Enlightenment. Accordingly, linguistic signs do not merely serve to express sensory ideas or finished thoughts; beyond that, they serve to connect ideas with one another and thereby to form thoughts in the first place. Thanks to this autonomy of signs, sense impressions can develop into stages of thinking. In a similar way, Condillac and Goguet reconstruct the history of mathematics, which, by means of written signs, has arrived at insights that supposedly pure reason would not have been able to achieve.

A parallel arises here with *technological wounding*, because in the field of technology as well, tools perform an expanding function.[19] In particular, in the philosophy of history, Turgot demonstrates how tools and devices expand the radius of human action. In their use, new possibilities for action emerge that were not foreseeable during their production. Ferguson sharpens this thesis to the point that instruments are even capable of contributing to the development of new needs and goals. Because this reverses the traditional relation of ends and means, the human subject is wounded in

---

[19] See 4,2 and 9,2.—Here the theorem of the "heterogony of ends" by Wilhelm Wundt is relevant: *Outline of Psychology*. Leipzig 71.905, p. 405; cf. Rohbeck 1993, p. 10.

its original competence for setting ends. Nevertheless, the Enlighteners also understand this inversion as a creative expansion of horizons.

A special position is taken by *economic wounding*, which concerns the foundations of bourgeois society (8,2–3). At the center of the physiocracy of Quesnay and the economics of Adam Smith stand the economic cycles and the *contingency of social systems*. Although it is still human beings who satisfy their needs through specific kinds of work, the network of social division of labor unfolds its own dynamic, which influences human actions. Although the Enlighteners chose anthropology as the leading science, they grant human beings in political economy only a conditional autonomy. This paradox also includes the fact that Smith justifies the self-regulation of goods, money, and capital as a "natural order," but then tries to mitigate the corresponding wounding with the help of the pseudo-religious instance of an "invisible hand."

This is followed by *philosophy-of-history wounding*, which is probably expressed most explicitly (9,2). This is not surprising, since history has always been understood as a contingent process that eludes rational treatment. When Enlighteners such as Voltaire, Turgot and Ferguson establish a new science of history, they aim at the development of social formations, which they attempt to explain by means of economic theory. But it is precisely this attempt to systematize history that fails, insofar as they must deny the people involved the ability to plan history as a whole. This result has led to the insight into the *unavailability* of history. Yet even in this case, authors such as Turgot and Kant offer a remedy for the wounding they themselves have inflicted, by countering the experience of contingency with an ultimately inadequate teleology.

Summary.—If we generalize these wounds to the fields of language, science, technology, society, and history, a common pattern emerges. It is the *externalizations* or *objectifications* that contain specific surpluses and thereby exert a determining influence on human beings. The means employed in each case are not limited to the conventional function of realizing purposes, but conversely shape human willing, thinking, and acting. In the linguistic signs that functioned as instruments of knowledge, cognitive structures can be discerned that were not at all foreseeable by human reason. Technical instruments allow for new applications that were not intended at the time of their creation. Economic means such as money lead to results that are not entirely controlled by the acting individuals. In history, these means drive social developments that are experienced as contingent and elude human control.

In this context, the phenomenon of *wounding* has proven to be *ambiguous*. At first, one can interpret the experience of the aforementioned contingencies as a damage to the human being, who is thereby made "ill" in the sense that he loses his original autonomy. But as in psychoanalysis, the wound can also be understood as the beginning of a therapy, in that what was previously unconscious is brought to light and processed. In our case, the absolutization of the human mind proves to be an illusion, which is now disappointed and at the same time overcome. It then becomes apparent that certain religious, rationalist, and subject-philosophical conceptions can no longer do justice to modern society and lose their former plausibility almost automatically. The wounds mentioned do not at all lead to a loss of human power; rather, the protagonists involved emerge from them strengthened.

Limits and Potentials

I now come to the *second transformation*, which consists in transferring certain scientific theories and philosophical ideas of the Enlightenment as a kind of "inheritance" into the present.[20] If this is not to happen uncritically, the *limits and potentials* of the Enlightenment must be taken into account. It should be noted that the Enlighteners treated almost every topic in an ambivalent manner and that these topics were controversially discussed throughout Europe, as should have become clear in the preceding chapters. But at this point, my aim is a final assessment, in which I will draw new lines of connection across the previous structure.

Limits.—I see the greatest deficit of historical Enlightenment in the absence of an independent theory of the state, indeed in a certain lack of interest in political philosophy (7.0). The authors express sympathy for the *Two Treatises of Government* by John Locke, but fail to comprehensively receive and conceptually continue this foundational work. Montesquieu addresses in his *Spirit of Law* only briefly and rather peripherally the principle of the separation of powers, which he supplements with the judiciary and brings into the form valid today. Otherwise, he describes the natural and cultural preconditions of different forms of government. Only Rousseau presents in the *Social Contract* a systematic theory of the state, which

---

[20] Zali 2006; Lilti 2019.—Compatible with this is Pierre Bourdieu's concept of "cultural capital": *Distinction: A Social Critique of the Judgement of Taste*. Frankfurt a. M. 1997, pp. 115 ff., 136 f., 187 f.—On this see Rohbeck 2020, pp. 149, 151.

transforms the contract theory of Hobbes and Locke into a model of direct democracy that ultimately bears totalitarian traits and remains incapable of consensus to this day.

The other Enlighteners come to terms with the constitutional monarchy in England, French absolutism, or the German principalities by moderating their criticism and nurturing the illusion of an "enlightened" ruler. Participation of the people, let alone suffrage for all citizens including women, is rejected. In Italy and Spain, rebellion against clerical despotism is in any case far too risky. This lack of democratic theory and commitment is not offset by the novel social philosophy, however innovative it may have been. Although the philosophy of moral sentiments and bourgeois public sphere has a communicative and democratic character, it is not able to replace politics.

This applies all the more to *political economy*, in which, although no radical liberalism is represented, the function of the state in containing the negative consequences of the nascent industrialization is only sporadically addressed and not worked out consistently enough (8.2). Of course, the catastrophic consequences of capitalism that occurred later were not yet foreseeable at the time and therefore should not be held against the representatives of the Enlightenment today. In this respect, it is remarkable how farsightedly Condorcet predicts the pauperization of wage laborers. Above all, the radicalism of the social critique formulated by Rousseau in the *Discourse on Inequality* is impressive, which resonated throughout Europe, even as far as Königsberg. But economists such as Quesnay, Turgot and Smith take a contrary position and justify social injustices, even if they do not believe the reproduction of the working population to be endangered or even expect an improvement in their living conditions.

The positions on the relationship between the *sexes* (4.3) are similarly ambivalent. The fate of women depended not least on the economy, because in the second half of the eighteenth century, for economic reasons, an increase in the population was desired, which was endangered by the high mortality of mothers and children. This led to women being confined to child-rearing and, overall, to the family sphere, and being banished from the public sphere of society. When contemporary medicine then began to study the female body in order to increase the birth rate, it was only a small step to reduce women to empathetic qualities and, in return, to deny them higher intellectual abilities. Despite the demonstrable egalitarian tradition, I consider it too one-sided to attribute the label "feminist" to the Enlightenment as a whole.

The ethos of the Enlightenment also includes propagating the *equality of all human beings*, which also encompasses the inhabitants of distant continents. There are, likewise, a variety of approaches to this position in the eighteenth century (9,1). Yet at the same time, some authors discriminate against other peoples, especially Africans, as allegedly less industrious and gifted. Here, the reasons must once again be carefully distinguished: whether, for this prejudice, as in Montesquieu, the external climate is held responsible, or whether, as in the early Kant, a theory of "human race" is invoked. The stance on the colonization of foreign countries and the enslavement of indigenous peoples is also divided. On the one hand, there are sentimental laments about cruel slavery. On the other hand, land appropriation and exploitation are again justified. The paradoxical aim consists in a colonization that is brought close to the idea of fair world trade, and a form of slavery that is trivialized as a transitional stage to capitalist wage labor.

Potentials.—I consider the greatest achievement of the Enlightenment in the second half of the eighteenth century to be the *anthropology*, which represents the leading discipline of the era (4,2). It ranges from Hume's *Treatise of Human Nature*, Helvétius' *On Man*, to the *Anthropology* of the late Kant. With it, not only is the human being placed at the center of scientific and philosophical discourse, but all thematic fields such as epistemology, morality, politics, economics, and history are also brought together within it. Anthropology integrates everything that human beings think, feel, and do. Here lie the origins of the modern human sciences.

At the beginning stands the discovery of the *human being as a natural being*. Yet this innovation must not be confused with naturalism, for no Enlightenment thinker reduces the human being to his biological functions. Even the few representatives such as d'Holbach, who adopt a materialist position, grant human beings psychic reactions. And those who adhere to a mind separated from the body nevertheless overcome the old dualism of body and soul. What they share is the conviction that human beings are initially moved by bodily needs. Some Enlightenment thinkers do indeed derive humans from animals, but then emphasize their diverging cultural development through tool use and linguistically supported cognition (4,2; 6,3). At this juncture, natural history transitions into a theory of cultural history.

The unfolding of human nature ultimately includes the *emotions*, to which Hume and others attribute outstanding significance (7,2). The feelings of human beings, above all "sympathy," form the foundation of a moral philosophy that seeks to displace political theory and to renew it by investigating spontaneous interactions within a community. Only Kant replaced this morality of feeling with a rationalist ethics, which, however, is no longer to be oriented toward a God-given natural law, but toward the subjective judgment of individuals. In contrast to Kant, Hume even allows the emotions to intervene in the activity of the understanding, so that he counts among the discoverers of *emotional intelligence*. Against the background of the current vogue for emotions, the sentimental anthropology of the European Enlightenment is of contemporary interest.

If one finally considers the relationship of the *human being to external nature*, the *ecological* dimension of anthropology comes into play. Just as in the eighteenth century the social question could only be recognized in its initial outlines, so too were there only a few statements regarding problems with the natural environment. This concerns dependence on natural disasters, the influence of climate on human culture, and the protection of natural resources. Here, different Enlightenment discourses must be taken into account.

The *Lisbon earthquake* provided the *first* opportunity to engage with Enlightenment reflections on the relationship between culture and nature (5,3). Particularly insightful is Rousseau's argument that this is less a *natural* disaster than a disaster of human *culture*. Human beings bear their own share of the blame for this misfortune, because they built this city too densely and too high . Kant, too, concurs with this astute judgment by holding the inhabitants of Lisbon responsible for the disaster. Both authors draw the remarkable conclusion that people ought to adapt their building practices to the laws of nature. "Man must learn to submit to nature," Kant summarizes, "but he wants nature to submit to him." It is hard to formulate a sharper critique of a civilization gone off the rails.

The *second* discourse, which addresses the influences of nature on human ways of life, is the then widespread *climate theory* of Montesquieu (7,3). Even though he takes other factors into account to explain the change in customs and habits, he maintains in *The Spirit of Law* that climatic conditions shape the moral concepts and forms of government of peoples. This theory proves to be ambiguous in that it grants all peoples and cultures of the same latitudes the same natural starting conditions, and yet then provides the pretext for the aforementioned discriminations. Nevertheless, climate theory has remained relevant, since it accords environmental influences such great significance in the first place.

The reverse component consists in human beings themselves intervening to alter nature. This aspect is the subject of the *third* Enlightenment discourse on *agriculture* in the newly emerged physiocratic doctrine (8,2). Its insight remains valid to this day: that every form of production must always also ensure the *reproduction* of its natural preconditions. If *physiocratie* means "rule of nature," this refers both to the sustenance of the working population and to the conservation of the land to be cultivated. This problem also arises for forests, which, since the middle of the century, have been endangered by excessive clearing . While Diderot merely laments the shortage of wood, Rousseau already recognizes the damage to air and soil (5,3). In this way, Rousseau's *discourse* overshoots its original aim. While he initially sought to investigate the causes of social inequality and the resulting depravity of human nature, what emerged was, unintentionally, a critique of the treatment of natural living conditions. In this I see early approaches to an ecological consciousness that already makes itself felt during the Enlightenment era.

The endangerment of the natural environment is a problem with an especially long-term perspective. Thus, the *future* occupies a decisive position in the philosophy of history of the Enlightenment. Just as the past is interrogated regarding which options it holds in store for the future, so too do expectations of the future shape the depiction of past events. An explicit example of this is Condorcet, who adds a final "Tenth Epoch" to his *Sketch for a Historical Picture of the Progress of the Human Mind*, which is dedicated to "the future progress." Despite rather gloomy forecasts, he speaks of "hopes for progress" that are reserved for future generations, so that what "may seem to us today as unfounded hope must gradually become possible, indeed even easy."[21] Even though the concept of progress has meanwhile fallen into disrepute, today we have no choice but to hold fast, in the spirit of the Enlightenment, to the hope for a livable future.

Kant's *Idea for a Universal History with a Cosmopolitan Purpose* also contains this perspective toward the future, although he dispenses with the concept of progress and instead speaks of a "progression toward the better." He wishes to awaken "hopes for better times" and even makes it a moral "duty" for people to work toward better living conditions for future generations.[22] In his later work *Perpetual Peace*, Kant aligns himself with the utopias of Saint-Pierre, Rousseau and Voltaire. Unlike these models, he does not limit himself to Europe, but instead seeks a global order of peace that is intended to supplement existing state and international law (2.3). As is well known,

---

[21] Condorcet 1976, p. 36; see 9.2.

[22] This also includes the first part of the *Conflict of the Faculties*: *Renewed Question: Whether the Human Race is Constantly Progressing toward the Better*, Kant 1965, vol. XI, pp. 49, 167 f., 357.

Kant does not propose a "state of nations" or a "world republic," but rather a "federation of nations" in the sense of a federation of autonomous states, to be realized through a "treaty of peace." Yet this theory can again be related back to Europe, where the idea of a federation of autonomous states has long since become the political model for the European Union. In the current crisis, this utopia is gaining particular relevance.

Enlightenment Today

The *third transformation* finally concerns the upheavals of contemporary civilization in the 21st century, whether already accomplished or still to be achieved. The parallel to the epoch of the Enlightenment consists in the fact (see Introduction) that a profound social transformation also took place in the second half of the 18th century. At that time, it was the beginnings of industrialization, the economic, social, and cultural consequences of which could only be dimly anticipated by those involved. Today, we find ourselves in a similar situation, in which the effects on our living conditions are difficult to assess. Social and ecological catastrophes loom, the management of which requires fundamental changes in the economy, politics, and society. In view of this analogy, the question arises as to what contribution the cultural heritage of the Enlightenment can make in this context.

When transformations are spoken of today, the issue is, first of all, the place of the present within the historical process of *modernity*. As has been explained in detail, it is especially important to me to distinguish the epoch of the Enlightenment from the preceding early modern period and to ascribe to it specific features of the emerging modern age. With this, I intend to extend the modern Enlightenment, understood in this way, up to the present day, and at the same time to reject the slogan of an alleged postmodernity. But how, then, should the current phase of modernity be designated? There are various proposals for this as well.

Concept of modernity.—The somewhat older proposal comes from Ulrich Beck, who, in the transition from the "old" modernity, conceived of an "other" or "second" modernity, which for the first time became "reflexive" because it had left behind rudimentary industry.[23] More recently, Ingolfur Blühdorn follows the first and second modernity with a "third" modernity, by which he means a "postindustrial" and "digital" society. In a similar way,

---

[23] Beck 1986, pp. 14 f., 115 f., 174 f.; cf. Rohbeck 2000, pp. 240 f.

Andreas Reckwitz distinguishes between a "bourgeois modernity" in the second half of the 18th century, an "industrial modernity" from the 19th to the end of the 20th century, and the "postindustrial late modernity" of the early 21st century.[24] According to this reading, late modernity distinguishes itself from the criticized postmodernity in that it does *not follow* modernity, but rather represents a new sequence *within* modernity.

Yet I would remind the reader that early modernity was by no means merely "bourgeois," but had already begun with industrialization, which was closely and sometimes critically observed by many Enlightenment thinkers. Moreover, I consider the diagnosis of a "postindustrial" modernity to be geographically narrow and substantively superficial (8.4). Not least, the ecological crisis stems from an industry that consumes dwindling resources and damages the environment. This message is also conveyed by the concept of the Anthropocene, which rather emphasizes the continuity of modernity. For these reasons, I advocate a *transformation of industrial society*. Even in this summary, in which I once again experiment with thematically focused cross-connections between the disciplines, I am guided by the aforementioned potentials of the Enlightenment.

A central characteristic of Enlightenment in the second half of the 18th century has proven to be the experience of *contingency*, with which I associate the aforementioned *wounds* (10.2). From today's perspective, the problem arises of how to deal with such experiences of contingency in practical terms. When there is recent talk of "unavailability," it should be noted that this refers not only to the accidents of everyday life, but to the specifically modern phenomenon of systemic contingency in bourgeois society.[25] And if such a maxim is not to serve as a pretext for neoliberal restraint or postmodern feelings of powerlessness, it is crucial, in particular, to make economic systems "available" again—or, more modestly put: to explore and utilize the conditions of possibility for political intervention. It is thus a matter of nothing less than the limited re-availability of contingency. Enlightenment today means coping with contingency.

Transformations.—In this case, one can connect to the social-critical tradition of the Enlightenment. For not a few economists and philosophers of that era were not advocates of *laissez-faire*, but rather criticized economic inequality and advocated for social reforms (8.2). At the beginning of the

---

[24] Blühdorn 2013, p. 51; Reckwitz 2019, p. 25; likewise Reckwitz in: Reckwitz, Rosa 2021, pp. 100–108.—On posthistoire 9.1.

[25] Rosa 2021, pp. 48–70; ibid. in: Reckwitz, Rosa 2021, p. 247; cf. Grau 2022, p. 87; see 8.3.

21st century, this corresponds to demands for an *end to neoliberalism*, which is now regarded as dysfunctional and harmful. The appropriate recommendations range from moderate reforms and profound transformations to the overcoming of capitalism (8.4). Yet in the end, the concrete courses of action are surprisingly similar. An important domain of the state is seen in tax policy, which should lead domestically to progressive taxation of the very rich and externally to the closing of tax havens as well as the introduction of a global capital tax. It is even demanded that the state intervene in wage policy by enforcing minimum wages and equal pay for women and men. In view of the coronavirus crisis, the commercialization of health systems must also be reversed. Last but not least, the state must control the runaway social networks in order to curb inhuman hate speech.

The issue of social justice concerns in particular the *gender question*, to which the Enlightenment contributed something. The debate of that time remains relevant insofar as the alternative between *equality and difference* is still being discussed today (4.3–4). Here, the emphasis shifts from the anthropological character of women to the social dimension of gender roles. Thus, not least through the feminist movement, the general principle of *equality of the sexes* was fought for in the professional, legal, scientific, and political spheres. Yet the concrete position of women in society indicates that existing hierarchies, prestige attributions, and evaluations of labor are *by no means universal*, but rather shaped by male-patriarchal norms. Not least during the Covid-19 pandemic, the social significance of classically female care work has become apparent. Here it becomes clear how urgent the development and renegotiation of appropriate forms of coexistence between the sexes is.

If one crosses the borders of individual nation-states, the problem of *global justice* arises. Again, it must be admitted that the Enlighteners had an ambivalent relationship to colonialism, in that they condemned military conquests but at the same time defended a "peaceful" colonization (9.1). In our time, this results in the moral duty not only to support poor countries in former colonial territories, but also to compensate for the damage caused in the former colonies (9.3). Such *historical responsibility* again presupposes that the harms previously inflicted can actually be proven and that the impairments of the past are still effective in the present. Finally, it must be conceded that essential factors for global poverty are also to be found within today's developing countries. Yet one should be wary of using such objections as a pretext for failing to provide assistance.

The *ecological crisis* has now also assumed global proportions. It should be noted that the inhabitants of the earth are affected by environmental damage in very different ways and to varying degrees. Especially in the South, global warming has disastrous consequences such as heat and drought, which often lead to famines. As shown, there were already, during the Enlightenment, in the era of the emerging *Anthropocene*, first approaches to an ecological consciousness. Since the end of the last century, it has become much clearer that the capitalist economic system depends on conditions of nature that it has already largely destroyed (5.3; 8.1). What is required, therefore, is a *sustainable capitalism* that restricts the exploitation of natural resources and the burning of fossil fuels in industry and transport in order to reduce harmful greenhouse gases. The current bottlenecks should be used as an incentive to accelerate the expansion of renewable energies.

To clarify the temporal dimension of such measures, I have introduced the concept of the *time frame*, which makes it possible to stagger responsibility for future generations (9.4). *Medium-term time frames* refer to climate change, which will reach a tipping point in just a few decades, after which further developments will no longer be calculable and the consequences would be irreversible. In the medium term, the extraction of gas and oil, which will soon be depleted, must also be reduced, and the dumping of plastic waste must be stopped. *Long-term time frames* arise in the disposal of radioactive waste, which must be contained for almost unimaginable periods of time. This phenomenon points to the principle of *reversibility*, which consists in shaping technical and economic civilization in such a way that certain developments that prove harmful can be reversed.

In order to achieve such goals, it is necessary to end neoliberalism and to rehabilitate a capable *state*. And since authoritarian governments, as experience shows, have little interest in social and ecological justice, it is necessary to revive the threatened democracies and to strengthen existing democratic institutions (7.4; 8.4). Even though I have just attested to certain democratic deficits among the Enlighteners, I consider it possible to draw on certain theorems to address current difficulties. Foremost among these is the principle of *separation of powers*, which is more relevant than ever in order to defend representative democracy against populism (7.3). If, moreover, democratic practice is not to be exhausted in formal electoral procedures, a civil society foundation is desirable. Especially for this aspect, the *moral philosophy* of the Enlightenment offers concrete models, by grounding the state in an affectively and interactively mediated civic public sphere (7.2). Here I see a model for a vibrant democracy that is based on a *social consensus*, which at the same time forms the normative framework for dealing with a reflective dissent (7.4). This relationship can also be described as *cooperation*, in which individuals assert their interests and at the same time recognize other people. The concept of *recognition* means that the citizens of a country draw their consent to a democracy from a social process of communication, in which they always participate in deciding on its appropriateness and correct application, and in determining whether the jointly practiced norms can be approved.

Yet in view of ongoing globalization, it must be examined whether the *nation-states* are still able to fulfill their old and new tasks at all (9.3). One response to this situation consists in a *cosmopolitan* attitude, which is oriented toward Kant's project of peace (2.3). Behind this stands the philosophy of history of the European Enlightenment, which represents the first systematic theory of globalization (9.2). Before hastily proclaiming the phase of deglobalization, one should hold on to this world-historical perspective. For the fatal alternative consists in fragmentation into small states and new nationalisms. In our context, the somewhat smaller solution of the *European Union* is recommended, which can draw on the quite differentiated self-presentation of the European Enlightenment (2.4). Regardless of the indisputable cultural identity, today the crisis of Europe is at the forefront. Internally, this concerns the delayed democratization, the lack of a common environmental policy, as well as fiscal policy agreement. Externally, Europe is fighting for its political and military influence in the world.

The recent campaign by Russia against *Ukraine* has once again brought into sharp relief the disastrous revival of a completely outdated nationalism. In the 21st century, Putin is waging a war with the means of the 20th century for imperial aims of the 19th century. In view of this absurd situation, the *discourses on peace* from the 18th century gain a remarkable relevance (2.3–4). For the Enlighteners advocated with all their might for the peaceful resolution of international conflicts. And they pleaded not only for peace in Europe, but in the whole world. Above all, Kant showed that European peace is ultimately a global challenge. This has two consequences for the war in Ukraine. First, it follows that negotiations must begin as soon as possible in order to find a peaceful compromise. This war cannot be won by any side and, with its cruelties against soldiers and civilians as well as damage to the civil and natural environment, cannot be ethically justified. Second, such a peace can only be achieved in cooperation with the other world powers such as the USA, China, and the European Union.

With Europe is associated the process of *secularization*, which has been carried out more consistently here than in any other region of the world. The historical roots again lie in the era of the Enlightenment, which, instead of theological claims to truth, placed the *social function of religion* at the center. This is precisely what is at stake in current debates about religion

(3.4). While the separation between knowledge and faith, as well as tolerance toward religious convictions, should today be taken for granted, the attitude of the constitutional state toward religious communities varies. The spectrum ranges from the laicist state in France, the "limping separation" in Germany, to the cooperation model in Italy and Spain. The highly topical question is whether French laïcité has maneuvered itself into a dead end, in which religious institutions shield themselves from the public and radicalize, and whether a cooperation might not ultimately function better, because, for example, it can exert a professionalizing and thus also moderating influence on the training of Muslim religious teachers. However the answer turns out, it is an equally current state imperative not to allow the Catholic Church any lawless spaces in which fundamental human rights of laypeople, women, and minors are violated. Finally, in the spirit of the Enlightenment, I advocate that not only church representatives, but explicitly also non-denominational people, be given a seat and a voice in the public sphere, for example in broadcasting and ethics councils or comparable bodies.

In modern communities, ultimately, *democracy and science* are closely interconnected. Without agreement on a reality secured by scientific knowledge, no democracy is possible (6.4; 7.4). This has long been evident in the case of climate change, which can only be politically overcome on the basis of scientific expertise, as well as more recently in the case of the Covid-19 pandemic, whose overcoming would fail without the support of expert advisors. This cooperation is contradictory: on the one hand, a democratically legitimized government increasingly requires scientific authority; on the other hand, science as an institution is itself democratically constituted and oriented toward dispute. Nevertheless, this ambiguity must not lead to a fundamental relativization, as can be observed among climate change deniers and anti-vaxxers. This problem has been dramatically exacerbated by the postmodern-tinged claim of a supposedly post-truth era. The only remedy is *enlightenment*. According to the previous explanations, this applies to an epistemological realism that is connected with the functional analysis of language and emotion (6.4). Such enlightenment can help to confront certain conspiracy ideologies with the help of a critique of prejudices, which often rest on one-sided language patterns and hate-filled motives for action.

For a different Enlightenment.—After this final *tour d'horizon*, I have returned once again to the starting point of the "classical" Enlightenment, which lays claim to freedom, reason and truth. I still wish to align myself with this ideal. Yet recently, the problem has arisen that even the so-called lateral thinkers have wrongly invoked the formal principle of thinking for oneself. For these reasons, I have tried to show that, in the second half of the eighteenth century, novel contents were addressed that promised a form of emancipation compatible with society and ecology. With the contingent experiences associated with this, the wounding insight has emerged that human thought and action can lead to unintended results. In this, we undergo the painful experience that these so-called unintended side effects have long since become the main issue, because they pose a lasting threat to our lives and perhaps even our survival. From this follows the imperative to avoid harm to the natural and cultural environment and to reverse, as far as possible, the damage that has already occurred. Enlightenment thus means a rational engagement with technical, social, and economic contingencies. It does *not represent the Other of Enlightenment*, but rather a *different, specifically modern Enlightenment*, which will hopefully be able to contribute to solving current problems.

Literatur

Die Bibliographie enthält nur Werke, die für die Argumentation dieser Studie relevant sind. Einige weitere Titel, die eher zum Kontext gehören, finden sich mit vollständigen Literaturangaben in den Anmerkungen.

Texts of the Enlightenment

Alembert, Jean Le Rond d' (1989): Einleitung zur Enzyklopädie. Hg. von Günther Mensching. Frankfurt a. M.
Bacon, Francis (1971): Neues Organon der Wissenschaften. Hg. von Anton Theobald Brück. Darmstadt.
Bayle, Pierre (1687): Dictionaire historique et critique. Paris.
Beccaria, Cesare (ab 1990): Edizione nazionale delle opere di Cesare Beccaria. Hg. von Luigi Firpo und Gianni Francioni. Mailand.
Beccaria, Cesare (1966): Über Verbrechen und Strafen. Hg. und übers. von Wilhelm Alff. Frankfurt a. M.
Berkeley, George (1964): Eine Abhandlung über die Prinzipien der menschlichen Erkenntnis. Hg. von Alfred Klemmt. Hamburg.
Buffon, Georges Louis Leclerc Comte de (2008): Allgemeine Naturgeschichte. Frankfurt a. M.
Carus, Friedrich August (1809): Ideen zur Geschichte der Menschheit. In: Nachgelassene Werke, Bd. VI. Hg. von Ferdinand Hand. Leipzig.
Clarke, Samuel (1998): A demonstration of the being and attributes of God and other writings. Hg. von Ezio Vailati. Cambridge.
Condillac, Étienne Bonnot (1798): Œuvres complètes. Paris.
Condillac, Étienne Bonnot (1983): Abhandlung über die Empfindungen. Hg. von Lothar Kreimendahl. Hamburg.

Condillac, Étienne Bonnot (2006): Versuch über den Ursprung der menschlichen Erkenntnis. Hg. und übers. von Angelika Oppenheimer. Würzburg.
Condorcet, Marie-Jean-Antoine-Nicolas Caritat de (1968): Œuvres de Condorcet. Hg. von A. Condorcet O'Connor und M. F. Arago, 12 Bde., Paris 1847–1849. Neudruck Stuttgart-Bad Cannstatt.
Condorcet, Marie-Jean-Antoine-Nicolas Caritat de (1976): Entwurf einer historischen Darstellung der Fortschritte des menschlichen Geistes. Hg. von Wilhelm Alff. Frankfurt a. M.
Diderot, Denis/D'Alembert, Jean Le Rond (Hg.) (1751–1780): Encyclopédie ou Dictionnaire raisonné des sciences, des arts et des métiers. Paris.
Diderot, Denis/D'Alembert, Jean Le Rond (1972): Artikel der von Diderot und d'Alembert herausgegeben Enzyklopädie. Hg. von Manfred Naumann und übers. von Theodor Lücke. Frankfurt a. M.
Diderot, Denis (1961): Philosophische Schriften. Hg. und übers. von Theodor Lücke. Berlin.
Feijoo, Benito Martínez (1726–1739): Theatro Crítico Universal, o discursos varios, en todo género de materias, para desengaño de errores comunes. Madrid.
Ferguson, Adam (1986): Versuch über die Geschichte der bürgerlichen Gesellschaft. Hg. von Hans Medick. Frankfurt a. M.
Forster, Georg (1991): Leitfaden zu einer künftigen Geschichte der Menschheit. In: Akademie-Ausgabe. Bearb. von Sigfried Scheibe. Bd. VIII, S. 185–193.
Gatterer, Johann Christoph (1765): Handbuch der Universalhistorie nach ihrem gesamten Umfange von der Erschaffung der Welt bis zum Ursprunge der meisten heutigen Reiche und Staaten. Göttingen.
Goguet, Antoine-Yves (1758): De l'origine des lois, des arts, et des sciences; et de leurs progrès chez les anciens peuples, Bde. I–III. Paris.
Gouges, Olympe de (2018): Die Rechte der Frau. Hg. und übers. von Gisela Bock. München.
Graffigny, Françoise de (1999): Briefe einer Peruanerin. Hg. von Renate Kroll. Königstein im Taunus.
Helvétius, Claude-Adrien (1973): Vom Geist. Hg. von Werner Krauss. Berlin, Weimar.
Helvétius, Claude-Adrien (1976): Vom Menschen. Übers. von Theodor Lücke. Berlin.
Herder, Johann Gottfried (1984): Werke. Hg. von Wolfgang Pross. München, Wien.
Hobbes, Thomas (1966): Leviathan – oder Stoff, Form und Gewalt eines kirchlichen und bürgerlichen Staates. Hg. von Iring Fetscher. Frankfurt a. M.
Holbach, Paul Thiry d' (1960): System der Natur, oder von den Gesetzen der physischen und der moralischen Welt. Eingeleitet von Manfred Naumann. Berlin.
Holbach, Paul Thiry de (o. J.): Das entschleierte Christentum, oder Prüfung der Prinzipien und Wirkungen der christlichen Religion. In: Religionskritische Schriften. Eingeleitet von Manfred Naumann. Berlin.

Home, Henry (Lord Kames) (1968): Sketches of the History of Man. Hildesheim.
Hume, David (1962): Untersuchung über die Prinzipien der Moral. Hg. von Carl Winckler. Hamburg.
Hume, David (1963): Essays: moral, political and literary. Oxford.
Hume, David (1964): Eine Untersuchung über den menschlichen Verstand. Hg. von Raoul Richter. Hamburg.
Hume, David (1968): Dialoge über natürliche Religion. Hg. von Günter Gawlick. Hamburg.
Hume, David (1973): Ein Traktat über die menschliche Natur. Hg. von Reinhard Brandt. Hamburg.
Hume, David (1984): Die Naturgeschichte der Religion. Hg. von Lothar Kreimendahl. Hamburg.
Hutcheson, Francis (1986): Eine Untersuchung über den Ursprung unserer Ideen von Schönheit und Tugend. Über moralisch Gutes und Schlechtes. Hg. von Wolfgang Leidhold. Hamburg.
Iselin, Isaak (2014): Gesammelte Schriften. Hg. von Sundar Henny. Basel.
Jaucourt, Louis de (1755): Artikel „Espagne (Géographie historique)". In: Diderot, d'Alembert (Hg.): Encyclopédie, Bd. 5, S. 953.
Jaucourt, Louis de (1756): Artikel „Europe (Géographie)". In: Diderot, d'Alembert (Hg.): Encyclopédie, Bd. 6, S. 211 f.
Jovellanos, Gaspar Melchor de (1984–2011): Obras completas. Hg. von José Miguel Caso González. Oviedo.
Kant, Immanuel (1968): Akademieausgabe von Immanuel Kants Gesammelten Werken. Berlin.
Kant, Immanuel (1965): Werke in 12 Bänden. Hg. von Wilhelm Weischedel. Frankfurt a. M.
La Mettrie, Julien Offray (2015): L'Homme machine. Der Mensch eine Maschine. Aus dem Französischen übers. von Theodor Lücke. Mit einem Nachwort von Holm Tetens. Stuttgart.
Leibniz, Gottfried Wilhelm (1965): Kleine Schriften. Hg. und übers. von Hans Heinz Holz. Darmstadt.
Locke, John (1962): Über den menschlichen Verstand. 2 Bde, Hamburg.
Locke, John (1967): Zwei Abhandlungen über die Regierung. Hg. von Walter Euchner. Frankfurt a. M.
Mably, Gabriel Bonnot de (1975): Sur la théorie du pouvoir politique. Hg. von Peter Friedmann. Paris.
Mandeville, Bernard (1968): Die Bienenfabel. Hg. von Walter Euchner. Frankfurt a. M.
Mendelssohn, Moses (2009): Ausgewählte Werke. Hg. von Christoph Schulte, Andreas Kennecke und Grażyna Jurewicz. 2 Bde., Darmstadt.
Mercier, Louis Sébastian (1982): Das Jahr 2440, ein Traum aller Träume. Hg. von Herbert Jaumann. Frankfurt a. M.

Millar, John (1985): Vom Ursprung des Unterschieds in den Rangordnungen und Ständen der Gesellschaft. Mit einer Einleitung von William C. Lehmann. Frankfurt a. M.
Montesquieu, Charles-Louis de (1951): Vom Geist der Gesetze. Hg. von Ernst Forsthoff. 2 Bde., Tübingen.
Montesquieu, Charles de (1988): Perserbriefe. Hg. von Jürgen Stackelberg. Frankfurt a. M.
Morelly, Étienne-Gabriel (1964): Gesetzbuch der natürlichen Gesellschaft. Hg. von Werner Krauss. Berlin.
Newton, Isaac (1963): Mathematische Prinzipien der Naturlehre. Hg. von Jakob Philipp Wolfers. Darmstadt.
Pope, Alexander (1997): Vom Menschen. Essay on Man. Hg. von Wolfgang Breidert. Hamburg.
Poulain de la Barre, François (1673): De l'Égalité des deux sexes. Paris.
Quesnay, François (1976): Ökonomische Schriften. Hg. von Marguerite Kuczynski. 2 Bde., Berlin.
Raynal, Guillaume/Diderot, Denis (1988): Die Geschichte beider Indien. Hg. von Hans-Jürgen Lüsebrink. Nördlingen.
Reid, Thomas (1967): Philosophical Works. Hg. von William Hamilton (Edinburgh 1886), eingel. von Harry M. Bracken. Hildesheim.
Reimarus, Hermann Samuel (1985): Die vornehmsten Wahrheiten der natürlichen Religion. Hg. von Günter Gawlik. Göttingen.
Robertson, William (1841): The History of the Discovery and Settlement of America. In: The Works of William Robertson. Hg. von Dugald Stewart. Edinburgh, Bd. II, 1.
Rousseau, Jean-Jacques (1964): Extrait du projet de paix perpétuelle. Jugement sur le projet de paix. In: Œuvres complètes. Bd. III. Paris, S. 563–589; S. 591–600.
Rousseau, Jean-Jacques (1972): Artikel „Ökonomie". In: Diderot, d'Alembert (Hg.): Enzyklopädie. Frankfurt a. M., S. 334–384.
Rousseau, Jean-Jacques (1976): Émile oder Über die Erziehung. Stuttgart.
Rousseau, Jean-Jacques (1977): Vom Gesellschaftsvertrag. In: Politische Schriften. Hg. von Ludwig Schmidts. Paderborn. Bd. 1, S. 59–208.
Rousseau, Jean-Jacques (1978): Schriften zur Kulturkritik. Die zwei Diskurse von 1750 und 1755. Hg. von Kurt Weigand. Hamburg.
Saint-Pierre, Charles Irénée Castel de (1713): Projet pour rendre la paix perpétuelle en Europe. 2 Bde., Utrecht.
Schiller, Friedrich (1970): Was heißt und zu welchem Ende studiert man Universalgeschichte? In: Nationalausgabe. Hg. von Karl Heinz Hahn. Bd. 17, S. 359–376.
Schlözer, Ludwig August (1990): Vorstellung seiner Universal-Historie. Hg. von Horst Walter Blanke. Hagen.
Shaftesbury, Anthony Ashley Cooper (2012): Inquiry Concerning Virtue or Merit. London.

Smith, Adam (1923): Eine Untersuchung über Natur und Wesen des Volkswohlstandes. Hg. von Heinrich Waentig. Jena.
Smith, Adam (1928): Vorlesungen über Rechts-, Polizei, Steuer- und Heereswesen. Hg. von S. Blach. Halberstadt.
Smith, Adam (1977): Theorie der ethischen Gefühle. Hg. von Walter Eckstein. Hamburg.
Sulzer, Johann Georg (2014): Kurzer Begriff aller Wissenschaften. In: Gesammelte Schriften. Hg. von Hans Adler und Elisabeth Décultot. Bd. I, Basel.
Turgot, Anne Robert Jacques (1919–1923): Œuvres de Turgot et documents le concernant. Hg. von Gustave Schelle. Paris.
Turgot, Anne Robert Jacques (1981): Betrachtungen über die Bildung und Verteilung der Reichtümer. Hg. von Marguerite Kuczynski. Berlin.
Turgot, Anne Robert Jacques (1990): Über die Fortschritte des menschlichen Geistes. Hg. von Johannes Rohbeck und Lieselotte Steinbrügge. Frankfurt a. M.
Vattel, Emer de (1758): Les droits des gens. London.
Verri, Pietro (1966): Meditazioni sulla economia politica. Hg. von Gian-Rinaldo Carli. Roma.
Verri, Pietro (1972): Discorso sull'indole del piacere e del dolore. Hg. von Armando Plebe. Mailand.
Verri, Pietro (1996): Discorso sulla felicitá. Hg. von Armando Plebe. Mailand.
Vico, Giovanni Battista (1990): Prinzipien einer neuen Wissenschaft über die gemeinsame Natur der Völker. Übers. von Vittorio Hösle und Christoph Jermann, 2 Bde., Hamburg.
Volney, Constantin François de (1977): Ruinen oder Betrachtungen über die Revolutionen der Reiche. Hg. von Günther Mensching. Frankfurt a. M.
Voltaire (1963): Essai sur les mœurs et l'esprit des nations et sur les principaux faits de l'histoire depuis Charlemagne jusqu'à Louis XIII. Hg. von René Pomeau. Paris.
Voltaire (1994): Dictionaire philosophique. Hg. von Alain Pons. Paris.
Voltaire (1948): Sämtliche Romane und Erzählungen in zwei Bänden. Hg. von Victor Klemperer. Leipzig.
Wollstonecraft, Mary (1989): Eine Verteidigung der Rechte der Frau. Hg. von Joachim Müller und Edith Schotte. Leipzig.

Literature on the 18th Century

Adler, Hans/Godel, Rainer (Hg.) (2010): Formen des Nichtwissens der Aufklärung. München.
Albertan-Coppola, Sylviane/McKenna, Antony (Hg.) (2003): Christianisme et Lumières. Paris.
Alt, Peter-André (1996): Aufklärung. Stuttgart.
Andries, Lise (Hg.) (2009): La construction des savoirs. Lyon.

Andries, Lise/Bernier, Marc André (Hg.) (2019): L'avenir des Lumières. Paris.
Asal, Sonja (2007): Der politische Tod Gottes: von Rousseaus Konzept der Zivilreligion zur Entstehung der politischen Theologie. Dresden.
Bartlett, Robert C. (2001): The idea of Enlightenment: a post-mortem study. London.
Beaurepaire, Pierre-Yves (2019): Les Lumiéres et le monde. Paris.
Berndt, Frauke/Fulda, Daniel (Hg.) (2012): Die Sachen der Aufklärung. Hamburg.
Binder, Klaus (Hg.) (1985): Der Traum der Vernunft. Vom Elend der Aufklärung. Darmstadt.
Blumenberg, Hans (1966): Legitimität der Neuzeit. Frankfurt a. M.
Borgstedt, Angela (2004): Das Zeitalter der Aufklärung, Darmstadt.
Breidert, Wolfgang (Hg.) (1994): Die Erschütterung der vollkommenen Welt. Die Wirkung des Erdbebens von Lissabon im Spiegel europäischer Zeitgenossen. Darmstadt.
Bubner, Rüdiger (1989): Rousseau, Hegel und die Dialektik der Aufklärung. In: Jochen Schmidt (Hg.): Aufklärung und Gegenaufklärung. Darmstadt, S. 404-420.
Butterwick, Richard/Davies, Simon/Sánchez Espinosa, Gabriel (Hg.) (2008): Peripheries of the Enlightenment. Oxford.
Carey, Daniel (Hg.) (2009): Postcolonial Enlightenment. Oxford.
Cassirer, Ernst (1932): Die Philosophie der Aufklärung. Tübingen.
Cheneval, Francis (2002): Philosophie in weltbürgerlicher Bedeutung. Basel.
D'Aprile, Iwan-Michelangelo/Siebers, Winfried (2008): Das 18. Jahrhundert. Zeitalter der Aufklärung. Berlin.
D'Aprile, Iwan-Michelangolo (Hg.) (2016): Aufklärung global – globale Aufklärung. Wolffenbüttel.
Darnton, Robert (1996): George Washingtons falsche Zähne oder noch einmal: Was ist Aufklärung? München.
Delon, Michel (Hg.) (1997): Dictionnaire européen des Lumières. Paris.
Dhawan, Nikita (Hg.) (2014): Decolonizing enlightenment. Toronto.
Diner, Dan (2017): Aufklärungen. Wege in die Moderne. Stuttgart.
Duchet, Michèle (1971): Anthropologie et histoire au siècle des Lumières. Paris.
Faber, Richard/Wehinger, Brunhilde (Hg.) (2010): Aufklärung in Geschichte und Gegenwart. Würzburg.
Faye, Jean Pierre (1992): L'Europe une. Les philosophes e l'Europe. Paris.
Foucault, Michel (1990): Was ist Aufklärung? In: Eva Erdmann u. a. (Hg.): Ethos der Moderne. Foucaults Kritik der Aufklärung, Frankfurt a. M., S. 35–54.
Frick, Marie-Luise (2020): Mutig denken. Aufklärung als offener Prozess. Stuttgart.
Fulda, Daniel (2022): Die Erfindung der Aufklärung. In: Archiv für Begriffsgeschichte, Heft 64/1, S. 9–100.
Garcés, Marina (2019): Neue radikale Aufklärung. Wien, Berlin 2019
Geier, Manfred (2012): Aufklärung. Das europäische Projekt. Reinbek b. Hamburg.

Gerrard, Greame (2006): Counter-Enlightenment. From the Eighteenth Century to the Present. London, New York.
Godel, Rainer (2007): Vorurteil – Anthropologie – Literatur: der Vorurteilsdiskurs als Modus der Selbstaufklärung im 18. Jahrhundert. Tübingen.
Godineau, Dominique (1996): Die Frau der Aufklärung. In: Michel Vovelle (Hg.): Der Mensch der Aufklärung. Frankfurt a. M., S. 321–358.
Goulemot, Jean-Marie (2001): Adieu les philosophes. Que reste-t-il des Lumières? Paris.
Gumbrecht, Hans Ulrich (2020): „Prosa der Welt". Denis Diderot und die Peripherie der Aufklärung. Berlin.
Günther, Horst (2016): Das Erdbeben von Lissabon und die Erschütterungen des aufgeklärten Europa. Frankfurt a. M.
Haag, Johannes/Wild, Markus (2019): Philosophie der Neuzeit. Von Descartes bis Kant. München.
Hampe, Michael (2018): Die dritte Aufklärung. Berlin.
Hardtwig, Wolfgang (Hg.) (2010): Die Aufklärung und ihre Weltwirkung, Göttingen.
Hellwig, Marion (2014): „Alles ist gut". Zur Bedeutung einer Theodizee-Formel bei Pope, Voltaire und Hölderlin. In: Gerhard Lauer und Thorsten Unger (Hg.): Das Erdbeben von Lissabon und der Katastrophendiskus im 18. Jahrhundert. Göttingen, S. 216–229.
Himmelfarb, Gertrud (2004): The Roads to Modernity. The British, French, and American Enlightenments. New York.
Höffe, Otfried (1995): Völkerbund oder Weltrepublik? In: ders. (Hg.): Immanuel Kant. Zum ewigen Frieden. Berlin, S. 109–132.
Holzhey, Helmut (1997): Kant und die Aktualität der Aufklärung. In: Helmut Reinalter (Hg.): Die neue Aufklärung. Wien, S. 25–43.
Honegger, Claudia (1991): Die Ordnung der Geschlechter. Die Wissenschaften vom Menschen und das Weib 1750–1850. Frankfurt a. M.
Horkheimer, Max/Adorno, Theodor W. (1987): Dialektik der Aufklärung. In: Max Horkheimer: Gesammelte Schriften, Bd. 5, Frankfurt a. M.
Im Hof, Ulrich (1993): Das Europa der Aufklärung. München.
Israel, Jonathan (2009): A Revolution of the Mind: Radical Enlightenment and the Intellectual Origins of Modern Democracy. Princeton.
Habermas, Jürgen (1981): Die Moderne – ein unvollendetes Projekt. In: ders.: Kleine Politische Schriften. Frankfurt a. M., S. 444–464.
Jacob, Margaret C. (2006): The Radical Enlightenment. London.
Jüttner, Siegfried/Schlobach, Jochen (Hg.) (1992): Europäische Aufklärung(en): Einheit und nationale Vielfalt. Hamburg.
Jung, Theo (2012): Gegenaufklärung: Ein Begriff zwischen Aufklärung und Gegenwart. In: Dietmar J. Wetzel (Hg.): Perspektiven der Aufklärung. München. S. 87–100.

Karremann, Isabel/Stiening, Gideon (Hg.) (2020): Feministische Aufklärung in Europa. Hamburg.
Kersting, Christa (2010): Ambivalenzen der Aufklärung am Beispiel weiblicher Bildung. In: Richard Faber und Brunhilde Wehinger (Hg.) (2010): Aufklärung in Geschichte und Gegenwart. Würzburg, S. 101–121.
Kittsteiner, Heinz-Dieter (1998): Listen der Vernunft. Motive geschichtsphilosophischen Denkens. Frankfurt a. M.
Kondylis, Panajotis (1981): Die Aufklärung im Rahmen des neuzeitlichen Rationalismus. Stuttgart.
Kopper, Joachim (1996): Einführung in die Philosophie der Aufklärung. Darmstadt.
Koselleck, Reinhart (1967): Richtlinien für das Lexikon politisch-sozialer Begriffe der Neuzeit. In: Archiv für Begriffsgeschichte 11, S. 81–99.
Koselleck, Reinhart (1975): Artikel „Fortschritt" und „Geschichte". In: Otto Brunner, Werner Conze und Reinhart Koselleck (Hg.): Geschichtliche Grundbegriffe. Stuttgart, Bd. 2, S. 351–423 und 593–717.
Lauer, Gerhard/Unger, Thorsten (Hg.) (2014): Das Erdbeben von Lissabon und der Katastrophendiskurs im 18. Jahrhundert. Göttingen.
Lilti, Antoine (2019): L'Heritage des Lumières. Paris.
Marquard, Odo (2014): Die Krise des Optimismus und die Geburt der Geschichtsphilosophie. In: Gerhard Lauer und Thorsten Unger (Hg.): Das Erdbeben von Lissabon und der Katastrophendiskus im 18. Jahrhundert. Göttingen, S. 205–215.
Martus, Steffen (2015): Aufklärung. Das deutsche 18. Jahrhundert. Berlin.
Merker, Nicolao (1982): Die Aufklärung in Deutschland. München.
Mittelstraß, Jürgen (1970): Neuzeit und Aufklärung. Berlin.
Mittelstraß, Jürgen (1989): Kant und die Dialektik der Aufklärung. In: Jochen Schmidt (Hg.): Aufklärung und Gegenaufklärung. Darmstadt, S. 341–360.
Möller, Horst (1986): Vernunft und Kritik. Deutsche Aufklärung im 17. und 18. Jahrhundert. Frankfurt a. M.
Mortier, Roland (1978): Diversité des Lumières européennes. In: Bernhard Fabian und Wilhelm Schmidt-Biggemann (Hg.): Das achtzehnte Jahrhundert als Epoche. Nendeln, S. 39–51.
Müller, Winfried (2002): Die Aufklärung. München.
Mulsow, Martin (2006): Die unanständige Gelehrtenrepublik. Stuttgart.
Muthu, Sankar (2009): Enlightenment against Empire. Princeton.
Neuhouser, Frederick (2012): Pathologien der Selbstliebe. Freiheit und Anerkennung bei Rousseau. Berlin.
Oelmüller, Willi (1969): Die unbefriedigte Aufklärung. Frankfurt a. M.
Opitz, Claudia (2002): Aufklärung der Geschlechter. Münster.
Pagden, Antony (2013): The Enlightenment and Why it Still Matters. London.
Pečar, Andreas/Tricore, Damian (2015): Falsche Freunde. War die Aufklärung wirklich die Geburtsstunde der Moderne? Frankfurt a. M.

Pinker, Steven (2018): Enlightenment Now. New York.
Pomeau, René (1966): L'Europe des Lumières. Paris.
Porter, Roy (1991): Kleine Geschichte der Aufklärung. Berlin.
Porter, Roy (2000): The Creation of the Modern World. New York.
Porter, Roy/Teich, Mikulás (Hg.) (2000): The Enlightenment in National Context. Cambrigde.
Postman, Neil (2000): Die zweite Aufklärung. Frankfurt a. M.
Pütz, Peter (1991): Die deutsche Aufklärung. Darmstadt.
Reed, Terence James (2009): Mehr Licht in Deutschland. Eine kleine Geschichte der Aufklärung. München.
Reinalter, Helmut (Hg.) (1997): Die neue Aufklärung. Wien.
Reinalter, Helmut (Hg.) (2006): Aufklärungsprozesse seit dem 18. Jahrhundert. Würzburg.
Reitz, Tilmann (2012): Aufklärung als Letzthorizont? In: Dietmar J. Wetzel (Hg.): Perspektiven der Aufklärung. München. S. 101–112.
Rheinberger, Hans-Jörg/McLaughlin, Peter (2021): Ordnung und Organisation. Begriffsgeschichtliche Studien zu den Wissenschaften vom Leben im 18. und 19. Jahrhundert. Rangsdorf.
Ricken, Ulrich (1984): Sprache, Anthropologie, Philologie in der französischen Aufklärung. Berlin.
Rohbeck, Johannes (1978): Egoismus und Sympathie. David Humes Gesellschafts- und Erkenntnistheorie. Frankfurt a. M.
Rohbeck, Johannes (1987): Die Fortschrittstheorie der Aufklärung. Frankfurt a. M.
Rohbeck, Johannes (2010): Aufklärung und Geschichte. Berlin.
Rohbeck, Johannes (2021): Zur Aktualität der Aufklärung. In: Zeitschrift für Didaktik der Philosophie und Ethik, Heft 1, S. 4–19.
Rohbeck, Johannes/Holzhey, Helmut (Hg.) (2008): Grundriss der Geschichte der Philosophie. Die Philosophie des 18. Jahrhunderts. Bd. 2.1 und 2.2: Frankreich. Basel.
Rohbeck, Johannes/Rother, Wolfgang (Hg.) (2011/2015): Grundriss der Geschichte der Philosophie. Die Philosophie des 18. Jahrhunderts. Bd. 3: Italien 2011; Band 4: Spanien, Portugal, Lateinamerika 2015. Basel.
Rohbeck, Johannes/Steinbrügge, Lieselotte (Hg.) (2015): Jean-Jacques Rousseau: Die beiden Diskurse zur Zivilisationskritik. Berlin.
Rorty, Richard (2001): The Continuity Between the Enlightenment and ‚Postmodernism'. In: Keith Michael Bake und Peter Hanns Reill (Hg.): What's left of Enlightenment? Stanford, S. 19–36.
Roselli, Antonio/Schlieper, Hendrick (2022): Transatlantische Aufklärung. Erfahrungen von Identität und Alterität im 18. Jahrhundert. Paderborn.
Rother, Wolfgang (2005): La maggiore felicità possibile. Untersuchungen zur Philosophie der Aufklärung in Nord- und Mittelitalien. Basel.
Rüsen, Jörn/Lämmert, Eberhard/Glotz, Peter (Hg.) (1988): Die Zukunft der Aufklärung. Frankfurt a. M.

Sala-Molins, Louis (2008): Les Misères des Lumières. Paris.
Sánchez-Blanco, Francisco (2002): El absolutismo y las Luces en el reinado de Carlos III. Madrid.
Saul, John Ralston (1992): Voltaire's Bastards. The Dictatorship of Reason in the West. New York.
Schmidt, Georg (2009): Wandel durch Vernunft. Deutschland 1715–1806. München.
Schmidt, Jochen (Hg.) (1989): Aufklärung und Gegenaufklärung. Darmstadt.
Schmitt-Maaß, Christoph/Stiening, Gideon/Vollhardt, Friedrich (Hg.) (2022): Katholische Aufklärung? Hamburg.
Schnädelbach, Herbert (1988): Was ist Aufklärung? In: Gunzelin Schmid Noerr (Hg.): Metamorphosen der Aufklärung. Tübingen, S. 15–19.
Schneiders, Werner (1974): Die wahre Aufklärung. Zum Selbstverständnis der deutschen Aufklärung. Freiburg.
Schneiders, Werner (1997): Das Zeitalter der Aufklärung. München.
Schröder, Winfried u. a. (1979): Französische Aufklärung. Leipzig.
Schröder, Winfried (1998): Ursprünge der Atheismus. Stuttgart-Bad Cannstatt.
Steinbrügge, Lieselotte (1987): Das moralische Geschlecht. Theorien und literarische Entwürfe über die Natur der Frau in der Aufklärung. Weinheim.
Steinbrügge, Lieselotte (2020): Françoise de Graffigny und Anne Robert Jacques Turgot im Streit um die Weibliche Aufklärung. In: Isabel Karremann und Gideon Stiening (Hg.): Feministische Aufklärung in Europa. Hamburg, S. 225–243.
Steinbrügge, Lieselotte (2020): Weltbilder geraten ins Wanken. Das Erdbeben von Lissabon und seine Konsequenzen für das aufklärerische Denken. In online: Metaphorik.de 31/2020, S. 117–130.
Steinkamp, Volker (2000): Der Europa-Begriff der norditalienischen Aufklärer. In: Helmut C. Jacobs und Gisela Schlüter Jacobs (Hg.): Beiträge zur Begriffsgeschichte der italienischen Aufklärung im europäischen Horizont. Frankfurt a. M., S. 119–131.
Stenger, Gerhard (2013): Diderot. Le combattant de la liberté. Paris.
Stockhorst, Stefanie (Hg.) (2013): Epoche und Projekt. Perspektiven der Aufklärungsforschung. Göttingen.
Stollberg-Rilinger, Barbara (2000): Europa im Jahrhundert der Aufklärung. Stuttgart.
Strasser, Peter (1986): Die verspielte Aufklärung. Frankfurt a. M.
Thoma, Heinz (Hg.) (2015): Handbuch Europäische Aufklärung. Begriffe, Konzepte, Wirkung. Stuttgart.
Thoma, Heinz (2018): Ende einer Epoche? Zur Geschichte und Kritik der Bürgerlichen Formation seit der Aufklärung. Halle.
Todorow, Tzvetan (2009): In Defence of the Enlightenment. London.
Trabant, Jürgen (2006): Europäisches Sprachdenken: von Platon bis Wittgenstein. München.

Vierhaus, Rudolf (1988): Aufklärung als Emanzipationsprozess. In: ders. (Hg.): Aufklärung als Prozess. Hamburg, S. 9–18.
Wagner, Astrid/Asmuth, Christoph/Roldán, Concha (2017): Harmonie, Toleranz, kulturelle Vielfalt. Aufklärerische Impulse von Leibniz bis zur Gegenwart. Würzburg.
Weinrich, Harald (1971): Literaturgeschichte eines Weltereignisses: Das Erdbeben von Lissabon. In: ders., Literatur für Leser. Stuttgart, S. 64–76.
Zali, Anne (Hg.) (2006): Lumières! Un héritage pour demain. Paris.

Literature on the Present

Adloff, Frank (2020): Zeit, Angst und (k)ein Ende der Hybris. In: Michael Volkmer/Karin Werner (Hg.): Die Corona-Gesellschaft. Bielefeld, S. 145–153.
Antweiler, Christoph (2011): Mensch und Weltkultur. Bielefeld.
Bartelmus, Peter (1994): Environment, Growth and Development. London.
Beck, Ulrich (1986): Risikogesellschaft. Frankfurt a. M.
Beck, Ulrich (1997): Was ist Globalisierung? Frankfurt a. M.
Birnbacher, Dieter (2003): Verantwortung für zukünftige Generation. In: Handbuch Generationengerechtigkeit. München, S. 81–103.
Birnbacher, Dieter (2016): Klimaethik. Nach uns die Sintflut? Stuttgart.
Boehm, Omri (2022): Radikaler Universalismus. Jenseits von Identität. Berlin.
Block, Kathrina (2020): Die Corona-Pandemie als Phänomen des Unverfügbaren. In: Michael Volkmer und Karin Werner (Hg.): Die Corona-Gesellschaft. Bielefeld, S. 155–163.
Blühdorn, Ingolfur (2013): Simulative Demokratie. Frankfurt a. M.
Bogner, Alexander (2021): Die Epistemisierung des Politischen. Stuttgart.
Böhler, Dietrich (2009): Zukunftsverantwortung in globaler Perspektive. Bad Homburg.
Böhme, Gernot und Rebecca (2021): Über das Unbehagen im Wohlstand. Berlin.
Büscher, Christian/Japp, Klaus-Peter (Hg.) (2010): Ökologische Aufklärung. Wiesbaden.
Butter, Michael (2018): „Nichts ist, wie es scheint". Über Verschwörungstheorien. Frankfurt a. M.
Büttner, Urs/Richter, Steffen (Hg.) (2021): Endzeiten. Apokalypse – Eschatologie – Risiko. Hannover.
Casanova, José (2016): Die Erschließung des Postsäkularen. In: Matthias Lutz-Bachmann (Hg.): Postsäkularismus. Frankfurt a. M., S. 9–40.
Chakrabarty, Dipesh (2010): Europa als Provinz. Frankfurt a. M.
Chakrabarty, Dipesh (2022): Das Klima der Geschichte im planetarischen Zeitalter. Berlin.
Cheneval, Francis (2003): Die Europäische Union und das Problem der demokratischen Repräsentation. Basel.

Literatur

Cheneval, Francis (2005): Zwischenstaatliche Integration als Vorbild neuer Weltordnung. In: Emil Angehrn und Bernard Baertschi (Hg.): Globale Gerechtigkeit und Weltordnung. Studia philosophica, Vol. 64, S. 179–201.

Cheneval, Francis (Hg.) (2006): Legitimationsgrundlagen der Europäischen Union. Münster.

Crouch, Colin (2008): Postdemokratie. Frankfurt a. M.

Davies, Jeremy (2016): The Birth of the Anthropocene. Oakland.

De Beauvoir, Simone (2000): Das andere Geschlecht. Hamburg.

Elis, Erle C. (2018): The Anthropocene. A very short introduction. Oxford.

Eyal, Gil (2019): The Crisis of Expertise. Cambridge.

Figueroa, Dimas (2004): Philosophie und Globalisierung, Würzburg.

Forst, Rainer (2003): Toleranz im Konflikt. Frankfurt a. M.

Fraser, Nancy (1994): Widerspenstige Praktiken. Macht, Diskurs, Geschlecht. Frankfurt a. M.

Fraser, Nancy/Jaeggi, Rahel (2020): Kapitalismus. Ein Gespräch über kritische Theorie. Berlin.

Freiburghaus, Dieter (2000): Wohin des Wegs? Ein Lesebuch über die Vergangenheit, Gegenwart und Zukunft der europäischen Integration. Bern.

Fricker, Miranda (2007): Epistemic injustice: Power and the ethics of knowing. Oxford.

Fuller, Gregory (2017): Das Ende. Von der heiteren Hoffnungslosigkeit im Angesicht der ökologischen Katastrophe. Hamburg.

Fuller, Steve (2018): Post-Truth. Knowledge as a Power Game. London.

Gabriel, Karl (2016): Langer Abschied von der Säkularisierungsthese – und was kommt danach? In: Matthias Lutz-Bachmann (Hg.): Postsäkularismus. Frankfurt a. M., S. 211–236.

Gabriel, Markus (Hg.) (2014): Der neue Realismus. Frankfurt a. M.

Gabriel, Markus (2018): Der Sinn des Denkens. Berlin.

Gabriel, Markus (2020): Moralischer Fortschritt in dunklen Zeiten. Berlin.

Gesang, Bernward (2011): Klimaethik. Frankfurt a. M.

Giddens, Anthony (2005): The Globalizing of Modernity. In: David Held und Anthony McGrew (Hg.): The Global Transformations Reader. Cambridge, S. 60–66.

Goodman, James (1998): Die Europäische Union. In: Ulrich Beck (Hg.): Politik der Globalisierung. Frankfurt a. M., S. 331–373.

Göpel, Maja (2020): Unsere Welt neu denken. Berlin.

Graf, Friedrich Wilhelm (2004): Die Wiederkehr der Götter. München.

Grau, Alexander (2022): Entfremdet – zwischen Realitätsverlust und Identitätsfall. Springe.

Grießer, Wilfried (2015): Europa als Kategorie. In: ders. (Hg.): Die Philosophie und Europa. Würzburg, S. 7–17.

Habermas, Jürgen (1985): Der philosophische Diskurs der Moderne. Frankfurt a. M.

Habermas, Jürgen (1988): Nachmetaphysisches Denken. Frankfurt a. M.
Habermas, Jürgen (2005): Zwischen Naturalismus und Religion. Frankfurt a. M.
Habermas, Jürgen (2008): Ach, Europa. Frankfurt a. M.
Hahn, Henning (2009): Globale Gerechtigkeit. Frankfurt a. M.
Hamilton, Clive (2017): Defiant Earth. The Fate of Humans in the Anthropocene. Cambridge.
Hamilton, David L. / Stroessner, Steven J. / Driscoll, Denise M. (1994): Social cognition and the study of stereotyping. In: P. G. Devine, D. L. Hamilton, T. M. Ostrom (Hg.): Social cognition and the impact on social psychology. San Diego, S. 291–321.
Harari, Yuval Noah (2018): 21 Lektionen für das 21. Jahrhundert. München.
Hardt, Michael/Negri, Antonio (2003): Empire. Die neue Weltordnung. Frankfurt a. M.
Heidenreich, Felix (2022): Demokratie als Zumutung. Für eine andere Bürgerlichkeit. Stuttgart.
Herzog, Lisa (2019): Die Rettung der Arbeit. Berlin.
Heubach, Andrea (2008): Generationengerechtigkeit – Herausforderung für die zeitgenössische Ethik. Göttingen.
Höffe, Otfried (1999): Demokratie im Zeitalter der Globalisierung. München.
Honneth, Axel (2000): Das Andere der Gerechtigkeit. Frankfurt a. M.
Honneth, Axel (2018): Anerkennung. Frankfurt a. M.
Horkheimer, Max (1985): Kritik der instrumentellen Vernunft. Frankfurt a. M.
Horn, Eva (2014): Zukunft als Katastrophe. Frankfurt a. M.
Horn, Eva/Bergthaller, Hannes (2019): Anthropozän zur Einführung. Hamburg.
Irigaray, Luce (1980): Speculum. Spiegel des anderen Geschlechts. Frankfurt a. M.
Jonas, Hans (1979): Das Prinzip Verantwortung. Frankfurt a. M.
Joób, Mark (2008): Globale Gerechtigkeit im Spiegel zeitgenössischer Theorien der Politischen Philosophie. Ödenburg.
Keil, Geert/Jaster, Romy (2021): Nachdenken über Corona. Stuttgart.
Keohane, Robert O. / Nye Jr., Joseph (2005): Globalization, What's New? What's Not? (And So What?). In: David Heldund und Anthony McGrew (Hg.): The Global Transformations Reader. Cambridge, S. 75–83.
Knoblauch, Hubert/Löw, Martina (2020): Dichotopie. Die Figuration von Räumen in Zeiten der Pandemie. In: Michael Volkmer und Karin Werner (Hg.): Die Corona-Gesellschaft. Bielefeld. S. 89–99.
Kocka, Jürgen (1984): Zurück zur Erzählung? Plädoyer für historische Argumentation. In: Geschichte und Gesellschaft 10, S. 395–408.
Kohler, Georg (2006): Demokratie und Großraum. In: Francis Cheneval (Hg.): Legitimationsgrundlagen der Europäischen Union. Münster, S. 29–46.
Kortmann, Bernd/Schulze, Günther (Hg.) (2020): Jenseits von Corona. Bielefeld.
Koselleck, Reinhart (1979): Vergangene Zukunft. Frankfurt a. M.
Koselleck, Reinhart (2003): Zeitschichten. Frankfurt a. M.

Kotzur, Markus (Hg.) (2018): Wenn Argumente scheitern. Aufklärung in Zeiten des Populismus. Paderborn.
Kreis, Georg (2006): Die EU: legitimiert aus dem Gang der Geschichte? In: Francis Cheneval (Hg.): Legitimationsgrundlagen der Europäischen Union. Münster, S. 61–76.
Kumkar, Nils V. (2022): Alternative Fakten. Berlin 2022.
Laslett, Peter (1992): Is There a Generational Contract? In: Peter Laslett und James S. Fishkin (Hg.): Justice between Age Groups and Generations. New Haven, London, S. 24–47.
Lavenex, Sandra (2006): Neue Ansätze des Regierens in der EU. In: Francis Cheneval (Hg.): Legitimationsgrundlagen der Europäischen Union. Münster, S. 95–114.
Leggewie, Klaus/Welzer, Harald (2009): Das Ende der Welt, wie wir sie kannten. Frankfurt a. M.
Leist, Anton (2005): Ökologische Gerechtigkeit. In: Julian Nida-Rümelin (Hg.): Angewandte Ethik. Stuttgart, S. 426–513.
Leslie, John (1998): The End of the World. London, New York.
Lienkamp, Andreas (2009): Klimawandel und Gerechtigkeit. Paderborn.
Lübbe, Hermann (1986): Religion nach der Aufklärung. Graz.
Lübbe, Hermann (2005): Die Zivilisationsökumene. München.
Luhmann, Niklas (1970): Soziologische Aufklärung 1. Opladen.
Luhmann, Niklas (1977): Funktion der Religion. Frankfurt a. M.
Lutz-Bachmann, Matthias (2016): Die postsäkulare Konstellation. In: ders. (Hg.): Postsäkularismus. Frankfurt a. M., S. 79–96.
Lyotard, Jean-François (1986): Das postmoderne Wissen. Wien.
Mau, Steffen (2021): Sortiermaschinen. Die Neuerfindung der Grenze im 21. Jahrhundert. München.
McIntyre, Lee (2018): Post-Truth. Cambridge.
Meyer, Kirstin (2018): Was schulden wir künftigen Generationen? Stuttgart.
Misselhorn, Catrin (2021): Künstliche Intelligenz und Empathie. Stuttgart.
Morton, Tim (2018): Ökologisch sein. Berlin.
Mukerji, Nikil/Mannino, Adriano (2020): Was in der Krise zählt. Stuttgart.
Münkler, Herfried und Marina (2020): Der Einbruch des Unvorhersehbaren. In: Bernd Kortmann und Günther Schulze (Hg.): Jenseits von Corona. Bielefeld, S. 101–108.
Nassehi, Arnim (2021): Unbehagen. Theorie der überforderten Gesellschaft. München.
Negt, Oskar (2001): Arbeit und menschliche Würde. Göttingen.
Negt, Oskar (2010): Der politische Mensch. Demokratie als Lebensform. Göttingen.
Neiman, Susan (2017): Widerstand der Vernunft. Salzburg.
Nichols, Tom (2017): The Death of Expertise. Oxford.

Nida-Rümelin, Julian (2020): Die gefährdete Rationalität der Demokratie, Hamburg.
Nussbaum, Martha Craven (2001): Women and human development. New York.
Osterhammel, Jürgen (2017): Die Flughöhe der Adler. Historische Essays zur globalen Gegenwart. München.
Osterhammel, Jürgen (2020): (Post-)Corona im Weltmaßstab. In: Bernd Kortmann und Günther Schulze (Hg.): Jenseits von Corona. Bielefeld, S. 255–262.
Ostheimer, Jochen (2020): Einfache und vertrackte Probleme. Strukturelle Unterschiede zwischen der Corona-Pandemie und der Klimakrise. In: Wolfgang Kröll u. a. (Hg.): Die Corona- Pandemie. Baden-Baden. S. 179–198.
Paehlke, Robert C. (1989): Environmentalism and the Future of Progressive Politics. London.
Parfit, Derek (1981): Future Generations: Further Problems. In: Philosophy & Public Affairs 11, 2, S. 113–172.
Piketty, Thomas (2014): Capital in the Twenty-First Century. Cambridge.
Pogge, Thomas W. (2002): World Poverty and Human Rights. Malden.
Pogge, Thomas (2003): ‚Armenhilfe' ins Ausland. In: Analyse & Kritik, 25, S. 220–247.
Polanyi, Karl (1978): The Great Transformation. Berlin.
Pollack, Detlef/Rosta, Gergely (2015): Religion in der Moderne. Frankfurt a. M.
Precht, Richard David (2020): Künstliche Intelligenz und der Sinn des Lebens. München.
Rapic, Smail (Hg.) (2020): Jenseits des Kapitalismus. Freiburg.
Rawls, John (1975): Eine Theorie der Gerechtigkeit. Frankfurt a. M.
Rawls, John (2003): Politischer Liberalismus. Frankfurt a. M.
Reckwitz, Andreas (2019): Das Ende der Illusionen. Berlin.
Reckwitz, Andreas (2020): Risikopolitik. In: Michael Volkmer/Karin Werner (Hg.): Die Corona-Gesellschaft. Bielefeld, S. 241–251.
Reckwitz, Andreas/Rosa, Hartmut (2021): Spätmoderne in der Krise. Berlin.
Redecker, Eva (2020): Revolution für das Leben. Frankfurt a. M.
Reder, Michael (2009): Philosophie und Globalisierung. Darmstadt.
Reinalter, Helmut (2016): Der aufgeklärte Mensch. Würzburg.
Renner, Tobias (2017): Postsäkulare Gesellschaft und Religion. Freiburg.
Rohbeck, Johannes (1993): Technologische Urteilskraft. Frankfurt a. M.
Rohbeck, Johannes (2000): Technik – Kultur – Geschichte. Frankfurt a. M.
Rohbeck, Johannes (2004): Geschichtsphilosophie zur Einführung. Hamburg.
Rohbeck, Johannes (2013): Zukunft der Geschichte. Berlin.
Rohbeck, Johannes (2020): Integrative Geschichtsphilosophie. Berlin.
Rohland, Eleonora (2020): Corona, Klima und weiße Suprematie. In: Michael Volkmer/Karin Werner (Hg.): Die Corona-Gesellschaft. Bielefeld. S. 45–53.
Roldán, Concha/Brauer, Daniel/Rohbeck, Johannes (Hg.) (2018): Philosophy of Globalization. Berlin.
Rorty, Richard/Vattimo, Gianni (2006): Die Zukunft der Religion. Frankfurt a. M.

Rosa, Hartmut (2021): Unverfügbarkeit. Wien.
Sassen, Saskia (2008): Das Paradox des Nationalen. Frankfurt a. M.
Schaber, Peter (2007): Globale Hilfspflichten. In: Barbara Bleich und Peter Schaber (Hg.): Weltarmut und Ethik. Paderborn, S. 139–151.
Scharpf, Fritz (1999): Regieren in Europa. Frankfurt a. M.
Schmid-Noerr, Gunzelin (Hg.) (1988): Metamorphosen der Aufklärung. Tübingen.
Schmidt, Alfred (2006): Übergang zur verwalteten Welt. Max Horkheimer und Theodor W. Adorno: Dialektik der Aufklärung. In: Helmut Reinalter (Hg.): Aufklärungsprozesse seit dem 18. Jahrhundert. Würzburg, S. 121–143.
Schnädelbach, Herbert (2004): Die Zukunft der Aufklärung. In: ders.: Vorträge und Abhandlungen. Frankfurt a. M., Bd. 4, S. 66–89.
Schneidewind, Uwe (2018): Die Große Transformation. Frankfurt a. M.
Scholte, Jan Aart (2005): Globalization. A Critical Introduction. New York.
Sen, Amartya (2010): Die Idee der Gerechtigkeit. München.
Shklar, Judith (1992): Über Ungerechtigkeit. Berlin.
Singer, Peter (2007): Hunger, Wohlstand und Moral. In: Barbara Bleich und Peter Schaber (Hg.): Weltarmut und Ethik. Paderborn, S. 37–51.
Steinbrügge, Lieselotte (2010): Egalität oder Differenz? Das andere Geschlecht im Licht feministischer Theoriebildung. In: Stephanie Bung und Romana Weiershausen (Hg.): Simone de Beauvoir. Göttingen, S. 200–210.
Stichweh, Rudolf (2020): Simplifikation des Sozialen. In: Michael Volkmer und Karin Werner (Hg.): Die Corona-Gesellschaft. Bielefeld, S. 198–208.
Stiegler, Bernard (2008): Die Logik der Sorge. Frankfurt a. M.
Streeck, Wolfgang (2013): Gekaufte Zeit: die vertagte Krise des demokratischen Kapitalismus. Berlin.
Streeck, Wolfgang (2021): Zwischen Globalismus und Demokratie. Berlin.
Striet, Magnus (2020): Nichts gewesen? Ein theologischer Versuch im Zeichen der Pandemie. In: Bernd Kortmann und Günther Schulze (Hg.): Jenseits von Corona. Bielefeld, S. 157–164.
Sturma, Dieter (2006): Die Gegenwart der Langzeitverantwortung. In: Claus Langbehn (Hg.): Recht, Gerechtigkeit und Freiheit. Paderborn, S. 221–238.
Taylor, Charles (2007): A Secular Age. Cambridge.
Tillmann, Jenny (2012): Was heißt historische Verantwortung? Bielefeld.
Tremmel, Jörg (2012): Eine Theorie der Generationengerechtigkeit. Münster.
Utzinger, André (2006): Mythen oder Institutionen? In: Francis Cheneval (Hg.): Legitimationsgrundlagen der Europäischen Union. Münster, S. 235–251.
Veith, Werner (2006): Intergenerationelle Gerechtigkeit. Stuttgart.
Verovšek, Peter (2020): Memory and the Future of Europe. Manchester.
Vielmetter, Georg (2021): Die Post-Corona-Welt. Frankfurt a. M.
Wallerstein, Immanuel (2013): Structural Crisis, or why Capitalism may no longer Capitalism rewarding. In: ders. u. a.: Does Capitlism have a Future? New York, S. 9–35.
Wallerstein, Immanuel (2019): Welt-System-Analyse. Wiesbaden.

Walzer, Michael (1999): Zur Erfahrung von Universalität. In: Karl-Josef Kuschel, Alessandro Pinzani, Martin Zillinger (Hg.): Ein Ethos für eine Welt? Frankfurt a. M., S. 38–47.
Wellmer, Albrecht (1985): Zur Dialektik von Moderne und Postmoderne. Frankfurt a. M.
Welzer, Harald (2008): Klimakriege. Frankfurt a. M.
Werth, Lioba/Mayer, Jennifer (2008): Sozialpsychologie. Berlin.
White, Hayden (1986): Auch Klio dichtet. Stuttgart.
White, Hayden (1990): Die Bedeutung der Form. Frankfurt a. M.
White, Hayden (1991): Metahistory. Frankfurt a. M.
Willke, Helmut (2016): Dezentrierte Demokratie. Berlin.
Wingens, Matthias (1998): Wissensgesellschaft und Industrialisierung der Wissenschaft. Wiesbaden.
Žižek, Slavoj (2001): Die Tücke des Subjekts. Frankfurt a. M.
Žižek, Slavoj (2020): Pandemie! Covid-19 erschüttert die Welt. Wien.
Zorn, Daniel-Pascal (2022): Die Krise des Absoluten – Was die Postmoderne hätte sein können. Stuttgart.
Zuboff, Shoshana (2018): Das Zeitalter des Überwachungskapitalismus. Frankfurt a. M.
Zurbuchen, Simone (2005): Globale Gerechtigkeit und das Problem der kulturellen Differenz. In: Emil Angehrn und Bernard Baertschi (Hgg.), Globale Gerechtigkeit und Weltordnung. Studia philosophica, Vol. 64, S. 121–141.

GPSR Compliance

The European Union's (EU) General Product Safety Regulation (GPSR) is a set of rules that requires consumer products to be safe and our obligations to ensure this.

If you have any concerns about our products, you can contact us on ProductSafety@springernature.com

In case Publisher is established outside the EU, the EU authorized representative is:

Springer Nature Customer Service Center GmbH
Europaplatz 3
69115 Heidelberg, Germany

Batch number: 08977762

Printed by Printforce, the Netherlands